OFFENDERS IN

Risk, responsivity and c

Kathryn Farrow, Gill Kelly and Bernadette Wilkinson

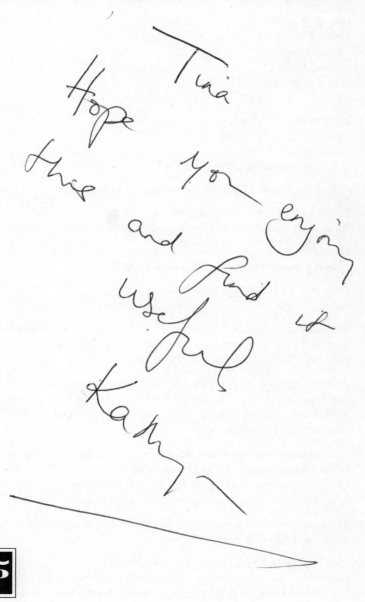

Tina
Hope you enjoy
this and find it
useful

Kathryn

First published in Great Britain in 2007 by

The Policy Press
University of Bristol
Fourth Floor
Beacon House
Queen's Road
Bristol BS8 1QU
UK

Tel +44 (0)117 331 4054
Fax +44 (0)117 331 4093
e-mail tpp-info@bristol.ac.uk
www.policypress.org.uk

© Kathryn Farrow, Gill Kelly and Bernadette Wilkinson 2007

British Library Cataloguing in Publication Data
A catalogue record for this book is available from the British Library.

Library of Congress Cataloging-in-Publication Data
A catalog record for this book has been requested.

ISBN 978 1 86134 786 2 paperback
ISBN 978 1 86134 787 9 hardcover

The right of Kathryn Farrow, Gill Kelly and Bernadette Wilkinson to be identified as authors of this work has been asserted by them in accordance with the 1988 Copyright, Designs and Patents Act.

The statements and opinions contained within this publication are solely those of the authors and not of The University of Bristol or The Policy Press. The University of Bristol and The Policy Press disclaim responsibility for any injury to persons or property resulting from any material published in this publication.

The Policy Press works to counter discrimination on grounds of gender, race, disability, age and sexuality.

Cover design by Qube Design Associates, Bristol.
Front cover: photograph kindly supplied by www.jupiterimages.com.
Printed and bound in Great Britain by Hobbs the Printers, Southampton.

Contents

List of figures

Acknowledgements

We are grateful to a number of people for offering expertise and constructive comments to different parts and earlier drafts of this book, namely: Denise Astley, Jeff Baker, Phil Dooley, Inderbir Kaur, Marj Rogers (National Probation Service – West Midlands); Paula Jones (National Probation Service – South Yorkshire); Bob Matthews and David Stephenson (University of Birmingham); Jan Clare (University of Central England); Sarah Jones and Grainna McMahon (University of Oxford); Stuart Wix (Reaside Clinic); Jenny Roberts, Chair Asha Women's Centre; Debra Nash, Ian Hill and Nikki Kendrick.

We appreciate the influential contribution made by friends, family members and colleagues, past and present, to the thinking behind this book and the encouragement that this was a project worth making time for.

Lastly, we have particularly valued the guidance and support provided by Jo Campling during the early stages of this project. Even when ill she continued to offer encouragement when she could and we have chosen to dedicate this book to her in recognition of the part she played and the contribution she has made to learning and development across disciplines and even across continents.

Introduction

Welcome to this book about face-to-face work with offenders. It connects research and theory with practice, and explores how the key concepts of risk, responsivity and diversity can be applied in practice. By presenting ideas in an accessible form, it seeks to create a new 'practice wisdom' for engaging effectively with offenders.

Developing effective practice

The development of the concept of effective practice has revolutionised how offenders are worked with. With this development has come the recognition of the need for consistency and accountability in the way that services are delivered and offenders are managed. At the same time there has been a significantly heightened concern about risk and security and an increased desire to rely on procedures which offer technical certainty and greater defensibility. The downside to this development has been the increasing tendency for practitioners to adopt blanket approaches which seek to fit offenders to programmes rather than match interventions to offenders. It is our view that working effectively with offenders requires practitioners to keep offenders in focus by paying careful attention to the detail and complexity of offenders' lives and not to make assumptions about how, or why, offending has occurred. This is in tune with one of the core principles of effective practice, that of targeting "energies, time and scarce resources on the right people and on those things that work" (Chapman and Hough, 1998: viii). We need to be building a body of knowledge which makes the connections between research, theory and practice and encourages practitioners to reflect on the detail of why some interventions have worked and others have not, and, as a result, refine their practice. This book does not claim to offer definitive knowledge or to be the only book you ever need to read about work with offenders. Inevitably, within the size and scope of this text, some important and specialist practice areas, for example, sexual offending and restorative justice, have not been included. Overall, this book strives to promote reflective and research- aware practice that is appropriate to a range of offenders.

Who is this book for?

This work is aimed to be informative for the student, trainee, practitioner and practice developer/manager, and all those involved, or interested in, making face-to-face work with offenders as effective as possible. It recognises that there are no easy or instant solutions to challenging offending behaviour but it will equip the reader with a practice text that brings together research, theory and the practitioner perspective to promote a sense of competence and confidence when working with a broad spectrum of offenders.

How the book is set out

The chapters differ in style and content; this is primarily a reflection of the state of knowledge in each subject area. Each chapter has been tailored to meet the current challenges to practitioners.

The organising principle for the chapters is that of diversity. It sets out to capture some of the diverse sources of knowledge and ways of thinking about offenders and offending while seeking throughout to link that diversity to understandings about risk and responsivity.

Part One sets the context for the rest of the work.

Chapter One introduces readers to face-to-face work with offenders. It includes a brief history of how and why agencies have worked with offenders in the way that they do and outlines more recent effective practice developments.

Chapter Two explores the key concepts of risk, responsivity and diversity, and provides the meaning and significance of these concepts for practice.

Services for offenders tend to be designed for the majority, who are adult, White and male. Part Two covers work with specific offender groups that fall outside the majority.

Chapter Three encompasses research and criminological analysis about women's offending particularly in terms of understanding attitudes towards women in society as a whole. It also promotes approaches to work with women which are responsive to them and their situations, whilst avoiding a narrow focus on 'welfare' issues.

Chapter Four brings together ideas about working with young people who offend (aged 10 to 21), presenting developmental approaches to understanding offending behaviour that are particularly associated with a youth-informed perspective but also have relevance to work with many adult offenders.

Chapter Five concentrates on 'race' and culture and encourages the reader to think about identity and the impact this has on responsivity. It provides practical approaches to help practitioners work across a range of differences in ways that address risk.

Part Three examines the complexities of working with offenders who have other significant problems.

Chapter Six focuses on mentally disordered offenders, who form a significant group within the offender population. It offers information to help practitioners be confident in their knowledge base and techniques for working across professional boundaries. It also provides practical guidance for dealing with the issue of suicide and self harm.

Chapter Seven helps practitioners clarify the complex relationship between substance use and offending behaviour and on the implications for responsivity.

Chapter Eight deals with links between poor basic skills, social exclusion, restricted life opportunities and the risk of becoming entrenched in an offending lifestyle.

Patterns of offending behaviour illustrate different aspects of risk. Part Four takes two contrasting types of offending behaviour to exemplify those differences.

Chapter Nine draws on a significant body of research and theory to provide practical approaches to working with violent offending to ensure that interventions are appropriately targeted and that risk of harm to others is properly considered.

Chapter Ten brings together research and theory into property crime, particularly burglary and theft, and explores how practitioners can engage with lower risk/higher volume offenders who form a significant percentage of the offender population.

Part Five is about conclusions, encouraging a reflective and evaluative approach to practice and to individual professional development.

Chapter Eleven examines the process and potential of evaluation for the benefit of the practitioner and the offender.

Chapter Twelve briefly sums up the book as a whole and sets the reader a number of challenges for the future.

Please use this book as a resource; there are lots of ideas in different places. Use it in whatever way suits your learning style or situation, either by dipping into chapters according to your interest or by reading it as a whole. We hope you will find it thought-provoking and practically useful.

Part One
Context

ONE

The changing face of practice

There has been an evolution of face-to-face work with offenders over the past century, as understandings of practice have altered and become more complex and as the world within which that practice occurs has developed. Philosophical, theoretical and organisational contexts have changed (see Chui and Nellis, 2003) but, throughout all of those changes, the responsibility to work with individual offenders, who are often flawed human beings, leading chaotic lives, has remained a constant.

This chapter primarily focuses on the development of practice with adult offenders, but the authors acknowledge that equally far-reaching changes have taken place in how society views and responds to offending by young people (see Burnett and Roberts, 2004; Muncie, 2004; Goldson and Muncie, 2006). There has been a growth of the number and range of professionals and organisations involved in work with offenders both adults and young people. As the delivery of practice has become more diverse, so too have understandings of crime and those who commit it (see Gelsthorpe, 2003). Society itself has become more culturally diverse, with implications for the shape of services. The relative simplicity of the original police court missionary's role has given way to more complex and complicated responses to crime; responses which require policy, coordination and management. See McWilliams (1983, 1985, 1986, 1987) for a detailed overview of key developments in conceptual and political understandings of crime and offenders and the consequent characteristics of probation service interventions (also Robinson and Raynor, 2006).

The new millennium was followed by a plethora of publications which review contemporary practice (see Burnett and Roberts, 2004; Mair, 2004; McNeill et al, 2004), explore competing views of justice (see Worrall and Hoy, 2005; Farrant, 2006; Robinson and Raynor, 2006) or stimulate reflection upon the experience of practitioners in this climate of change with reference to the place of traditional skills (Leach, 2003; Atkinson, 2004; Farrow, 2004).

While there may be a sense of some continuity with the past, there are also, of course, some significant differences of emphasis that have stimulated changes in the way services to offenders and the courts are organised and delivered (see Worrall and Hoy, 2005; Gorman et al, 2006).

The main thrust of this book is to explore the practice implications of research and theoretical approaches with specific offenders and offence groups and cannot offer a comprehensive résumé of the criminal justice developments which have been so authoritatively written about elsewhere (see McGuire et al, 2002; Chui and Nellis, 2003; McNeill et al, 2004). This chapter briefly touches on some of the developments that have taken place over the last century in face-to-face practice with offenders. It is inevitably selective and may be seen as idiosyncratic in terms of the developmental influences selected for inclusion. The chapter emphasises the changing nature of the worker–offender relationship and its continued importance as an alliance in the process of managing change. It also seeks to be a reminder that learning from the past is important and will continue to be for practice to develop.

A brief reminder of early history

McWilliams identified three phases of development. The first phase was from 1876, when the first police court missionary was appointed, through to the 1930s, a period distinguished by its early emphasis upon the redemption of individuals through faith, where the practitioner was an enthusiastic Christian amateur.

The second phase covering the years between 1930 and the early 1970s saw the decline of the missionary calling with practitioners increasingly influenced by what were perceived to be scientific understandings of human thinking and behaviour which informed professional knowledge and skills. During the 1960s/1970s those working with offenders enjoyed a high level of professional autonomy through the development of an individualised casework approach. Burnett and Roberts (2004: 193) describe face-to-face work during this period as "a lucky draw" for probationers since:

> ... practice was highly individualised according to home-grown philosophies and idiosyncratic working styles of officers, and when 'personal integrity' and genuine concern for individuals were valued ... at least as much as ... theoretical knowledge and professional training.

The caseload was largely low risk as contact with prisoners was limited and it was only in the 1967 Criminal Justice Act that parole was introduced. The impact of the 1967 Act upon face-to-face work was significant. As Mott (1992) points out, practitioners had to learn how to work with "dangerous criminals": whilst they had always taken into account the "estimated needs of the client ... now there were other considerations, not least of which were security and sometimes, protection" (Mott, 1992: 76-7).

Significant principles

For practitioners operating within the current criminal justice system and coping with a rapid pace of change it is possible to identify principles of value from those early beginnings that need to continue to inform practice:

- While the religious framework has long gone it is helpful to hold onto the need for practitioners, if not to have a vocation, then, to have belief in the potential for change and their ability to help bring that change about.
- The centrality of human relationships to the process of change, and specifically face-to-face engagement with offenders, as crucial elements of practice.
- While professional autonomy is much reduced there is still a need for practitioners who can make, and act upon, their own professional judgements.

More recent history

McWilliams' third phase, the 1970s through to the late 1980s, was a period which was influenced, in part, by some scepticism about the effectiveness of interventions, particularly the impact of casework, and saw an expansion of the breadth of work being undertaken by the Probation Service.

Since the 1970s it is possible to identify influences and key debates that have impacted on criminal justice interventions through to the late 1980s. The story of Martinson (1974) and his 'nothing works' research has been widely told (Whitehead, 1990; Raynor, 2002). This undermined confidence in professional practice leaving individuals and organisations without the security of long-held values, methods and roles. There were also growing debates about the place of custody and alternatives to custodial penalties, balancing proportionate punishment (just deserts) with interventions designed to rehabilitate (see Worrall and Hoy, 2005).

This sense of professional drift coincided with political change in the arrival of the Conservative government in 1979 and its focus on value for money, efficiency and effectiveness. For the first time, central government moved to define a framework of accountability for practitioners that was linked to planned and evaluated service delivery and cash-limited budgets (Jarvis, 1996). These developments influenced legislation in a series of Criminal Justice Acts in the 1990s (Home Office, 1989, 1991, 1994a, 1998a) which reflected some of the philosophical tensions (see Worrall and Hoy, 2005, for a useful discussion about this period).

Several writers have argued that, as approaches to crime have become increasingly politicised, this has led to a more and more centralised approach and the elevation of government policy (see Nellis, 1999; McCulloch, 2004; Winstone and Pakes, 2005). From the 1970s onwards there has also been an expansion of the breadth of work being undertaken by criminal justice agencies and an increased reliance upon the development of policies required to give overall direction and coordination to a range of different roles and interventions. With policy came the elevation of the managerial role necessary to oversee its implementation and coordinate the activities of individual practitioners.

The introduction of National Standards in 1992 meant that face-to-face work with offenders was no longer to be "secretive and something of a mystery to the wider public" (Winstone and Pakes, 2005: 18). For some practitioners this was a welcome development as practice could now be more easily evaluated and shared. It could be standardised to ensure a greater degree of transparency and fairness, and practitioners were encouraged to engage critically in discussion about each other's work. Against this background, the interest of practitioners shifted towards the content of their work with offenders and away from the dynamics of the worker–offender relationship.

The introduction of community service in the mid-1970s, in the 1972 Criminal Justice Act, brought an expansion of the workforce to include professionally unqualified staff who often had a range of other more practical skills. This initiative proved to be a marketing success, representing as it did discipline, accountability to the community and a popular alternative to custody. It also added to the crisis in confidence in the traditional casework relationship, as practitioners saw other, more narrowly defined, interventions, with clearer rationales, grow in status and confidence.

'What Works' and the development of effective practice

In the late 1980s came the promotion of 'What Works'. This was largely practitioner-led, in partnership with a small group of influential researchers and chief officers who were keen to challenge the 'nothing works' consensus of the time (Raynor, 2002). Practitioners were keen to rediscover which aspects of their work were effective and to recapture the sense of belief in their ability to bring about real change. For those attending 'What Works' conferences in the early 1990s, these were heady days. The conferences promoted discussion and debate about practice and attracted, in the earlier years, more practitioners than service managers.

One of the messages from research stressed the importance of enthusiastic, committed and well-trained staff and also management support. However, herein lay a tension. Managerialism and the elevation of policy had become key features of the Probation Service in the 1990s. The service did take on the 'What Works' principles (see Chapman and Hough, 1998; Underdown, 1998; Chui, 2003; Harper and Chitty, 2004) but focused upon the technical aspects (methods and programmes), at the expense of other elements. There was an implicit association between one-to-one interventions and ineffective eclectic practice (Burnett and Roberts, 2004) and hence those relationships were given less attention, as was the importance of generating and sustaining practitioner enthusiasm (Kemshall et al, 2004). Arguably, the focus on programmes based upon 'What Works' principles has tended to overemphasise individual pathology as a cause of crime, paying insufficient attention to the context, both social and political, within which offending is occurring with implications for the ability of practice to be related to the diversity of needs of a wide range of offenders (Shaw and Hannah-Moffat, 2004). During the 1990s the 'What Works' agenda gained momentum attracting national and governmental attention such that effective practice became both a strategic as well as an operational imperative (Underdown, 1998). Risk, need and responsivity became the key operating concepts that practitioners had to adopt to guide work with offenders (see Chapman and Hough, 1998; Chui, 2003).

Risk

The 'What Works' developments were also part of an increased focus on the risk of reoffending and what is effective in bringing about its reduction. This ran alongside a parallel development, a growing focus on risk, its assessment and management. Kemshall (1998a: 1) suggests:

> Risk has become the dominant *raison d'etre* of the Service, supplanting ideologies of need, welfare or indeed rehabilitation as key organising principles of service provision (Kemshall et al, 1997). Risk is now the central focus of practitioner activity and a key area of scrutiny.

This attention to risk is not confined to criminal justice agencies but is part of a change in emphasis within society more generally, linked to a decline in trust for the expert and a greater requirement for accountability in decision making (Kemshall, 1997).

The principle of risk along with that of public protection has emerged as the cornerstone of work with offenders (see Kemshall, 2003). With increased accountability came increased scrutiny and a greater requirement to work with other organisations and with more complex and demanding offenders. With the crisis in confidence about 'traditional' work with offenders, the increased complexity of the task and greater awareness of public accountability, the role of practitioners was bound to change. The emphasis on face-to-face work now had to shift to the type of interventions that would follow upon assessments and to the element of control, both of the offender, and what they might do in the future.

Organisational changes and case management

One practical consequence of this dilution of reliance upon the worker–offender relationship was the beginning of the move towards the notion of the practitioner as case manager. In this role the practitioner would be assessing the needs of the individual but then increasingly liaising with, and coordinating the interventions of, others. The main focus of the one-to-one relationship between the generic practitioner and offender in the 21st century is now perceived by many to be case management, especially within the National Offender Management Service (NOMS) with practitioners renamed as offender managers. However, views as to what case management consists of range from what Holt (2000) has described as "a minimal approach ... [involving] ... simple brokerage and administrative tasks" to a more comprehensive model which encompasses assessment and reassessment, planning, referral, advocacy, casework, support, monitoring, crisis intervention, coordination and reinforcement.

This has also meant relationships between agencies have become more important, for example the development of Multi Agency Public Protection Arrangements (MAPPA), also the growing work involving health professionals alongside criminal justice practitioners in the provision of interventions for drug abusing offenders.

In this context, there have been radical developments in the organisation of both the Probation and Prison Services, culminating in the establishment of the NOMS. There have also been significant changes in the way that services to young offenders are organised and delivered, as encapsulated in the 1998 Crime and Disorder Act (see Muncie, 2004) with a multi-agency approach through the introduction of Youth Offending Teams (YOTs) in 2000. The variety and complexity of measures aimed at reducing individuals' offending behaviour has therefore changed the role of individual professionals. They have extended the type and number of people who undertake face-to-face work with adult and young offenders, across all of the agencies in the criminal justice system.

Conclusions and implications for face-to-face practice

The place and centrality of face-to-face work with offenders (implying as it does interventions founded upon a direct, influential relationship between worker and offender) has altered, as the conceptual and technical context in which it takes place has changed. Arguably, the relationship between worker and offender has been seen latterly as less instrumental in promoting change and the emphasis has shifted (unhelpfully, from some perspectives) towards technical skill and management of people through a process (Burnett and Roberts, 2004). However, as Farrall (2002) notes, one-to-one work remains highly significant, with very few offenders completing supervision either as an adult, or as a young person, without receiving one-to-one supervision.

Many writers suggest that the relationship between worker and offender needs fresh attention (see Trotter, 1999; McMurran, 2002b; McNeill et al, 2004; Cherry, 2005); as McNeill et al (2004: 6) comment, "practice skills in general and relationship skills in particular are at least as critical in reducing reoffending as programme content".

The focus of work with offenders is also the subject of debate with exploration of the strengths and limitations of what is sometimes referred to as the risk–needs model (McGuire, 2004) of offender rehabilitation. Farrall (2002) stresses that the role of social and personal factors in supporting desistance from offending deserves greater attention (see Rex, 1999; Blackburn, 2004; Maruna and Immarigeon, 2004; Ward and Brown, 2004).

There is now a sense that face-to-face work is once again at the heart of debates about effective practice. The balance may need to shift back towards the worker–offender relationship within a wider understanding of motivation and change to ensure offender engagement. Careful attention to the principles of risk, responsivity and diversity supports the potential to provide relevant and effective interventions for offenders and the next chapter on key concepts will consider these concepts in more depth.

TWO

Key concepts

Risk, responsivity and diversity, the key concepts covered in this book, can help practitioners from a variety of contexts whose task it is to contribute to the reduction of offending behaviour. The hope is that such a reduction will be in the best interests of victims, of society and of the offenders themselves. In fact, this simple idea contains within it layers of complexity, in considering how to achieve this end, while balancing sometimes competing demands and responsibilities.

In a discussion of the goals of rehabilitation for mentally disordered offenders, Blackburn (2004) differentiates between reintegration, where the service provider is as much the agent of the offender as of society, and a narrower interpretation, in which the goals of intervention are to prevent offending and to protect the public. In this interpretation offender-centred goals are simply a means to those ends. Ward and Brown (2004: 244) in explaining the 'good lives model' suggest that "management of risk is a necessary but not sufficient condition for the rehabilitation of offenders" and go on to state the importance of equipping them "with the tools to live more fulfilling lives". Arguably, those working with offenders have to make risk management and rehabilitation work together. Practitioners can be helped to do this by focusing on risk and responsivity and drawing on the knowledge base and skills that support these terms.

Risk focuses attention on public protection and the reduction of offending. It also seems reasonable to assume, however, that avoiding offending and consequent involvement with the criminal justice system will, of itself, be of benefit to many offenders. Responsivity draws attention to how interventions are delivered, in order to increase their effectiveness (Andrews, 2001). The aim of a responsive service is to engage the offender in working towards change and this necessitates a focus on them as an individual. There is much appeal in Blackburn's (2004: 302) premise, therefore, that the goals of intervention should (where possible) be "offender focused as well as offence focused", providing this does not detract from protection of the public.

Both an accurate assessment of risk and a proper consideration of responsivity require practitioners to work with the detail of an individual offender's life. This requirement leads to the final focus of this book, that of diversity.

For each offender the diversity of potential influences upon their behaviour and the interactions between them must be considered and understood. Face-to-face contact between practitioner and offender is one crucial source of that understanding, provided the practitioner is able to make best use of those opportunities. They will be more able to do so, if they tune into the diversity of influences affecting individuals, including the influences that may shape their own professional judgements (Kemshall et al, 2006).

This book therefore draws on these three key concepts to help practitioners engaged in face-to-face work with offenders to improve their ability to reduce the risk of reoffending, while actively engaging the offenders concerned. Practitioners have a responsibility to continue to add to their knowledge base, accessing relevant research and literature, and this book can act as a starting point for further reading. They should also listen to the offenders with whom they work (Pycroft, 2006) and reflect on and evaluate their own practice. This is considered further in Chapter Eleven.

In this chapter the concepts of risk, responsivity and diversity will be explored in turn and a start made in considering their repercussions for practice. These implications are then explored in more depth in subsequent chapters.

Risk

The language that is used to describe the world is not neutral. A choice of terms can shift our perceptions and understandings. Language can, if used imprecisely, lead to miscommunication between individuals and organisations. Some of the complexities of language use are discussed again in Chapter Five. In this introduction some of the meanings associated with the term 'risk' will be considered. Risk can refer to:

- The risk of reoffending – how likely an offender is to reoffend and within what timescale?
- The risk of harm to others – will the offender commit an offence that is likely to inflict serious harm to others?
- The risk of harm to the offender – will they be harmed by their own actions or by the actions or omissions of others (YJB, 2005)?

Practitioners in different settings may be concerned with particular forms of those risks, or with other risks not fully captured above.

In the context of prisons, for example, staff are likely to be concerned about risks to security, including the risk of escape. They have a responsibility to be alert to the harm an individual may pose to other inmates or staff, as well as to the risk of self-harm or suicide during incarceration (Kemshall et al, 2006). Prison staff may therefore use the word 'risk' differently to the definitions above and this can have an impact on practice. For example, an offender may be compliant with prison rules, thereby lessening their risk to the smooth and safe running of the establishment. If risk is understood in this way, prison staff may underestimate the extent to which attitudes and behaviours likely to make the offender a risk to others on release are still in existence; making a difference to the assessments they make. This might have serious repercussions, for example, in the parole process.

While of relevance to anyone engaged in face-to-face work with offenders, this book is primarily concerned with the risk of reoffending and of harm to others, posed by offenders in the community. Again language should be clarified:

- *Risk of reoffending* is most often estimated in research using the proxy measure of *reconviction*. While many more offences are committed than the numbers that result in arrest and conviction, reconviction is assumed to have a reasonable relationship with actual reoffending and, in particular, reductions in convictions are deemed to be a reasonable test of a reduction in underlying offending behaviour. This is not without difficulties, including differential rates of conviction for different offences (see Lloyd et al, 1994). Both terms may be used but readers need to be aware of the sometimes complex relationship between them.
- Guidance relating to the use of the OASys risk assessment tool defines serious harm as "a risk which is life threatening and/or traumatic and from which recovery, whether physical or psychological, can be expected to be difficult or impossible" (Home Office, 2006: Ch 8). This is the definition of risk of harm used throughout this book.

The third type of risk described earlier, risk to the offenders themselves, is considered in less detail in this chapter. It is referred to in several chapters that consider a range of vulnerabilities amongst offenders and, in more depth, in a consideration of suicide and self-harm, in Chapter Six.

Different risks have relationships to each other, whilst also needing to be kept conceptually separate. The 'What Works' developments, briefly referred to in Chapter One, drew attention to the 'risk principle'

(Andrews and Bonta 1994; Chapman and Hough, 1998). This asserts that the intensity of service provision should match the level of risk of the offender, with the most intensive services being reserved for the highest risk offenders. Risk in this sense implies likelihood of reoffending, judged by taking into account risk factors; that is, those variables associated with populations of offenders which have been found to be most predictive of offending behaviour. Risk factors for offending that have the potential to change, or *dynamic risk factors*, include, for example, pro-criminal attitudes, lack of employment and substance misuse. Such factors, termed 'criminogenic needs', are targets for interventions, as changes in them are linked to reductions in reoffending (Andrews et al, 1990). This use of the term 'needs' can however be confusing. McGuire (2004) questions whether the term 'criminogenic need' was appropriate in the first place, as it is not how the word 'need' is commonly understood, or used in thinking about human motivation. Again, there is a question of language, its precision and helpfulness. In this book use of the term 'criminogenic need' is largely avoided, instead referring to dynamic risk factors, reinforcing the link between the assessment of risk and subsequent interventions. Offender needs in their more general sense remain important, however, and are returned to later in the context of a discussion of responsivity (Andrews et al, 1990).

There has also been the development of an emphasis, in criminal justice, on *public protection* (Kemshall, 1998a). All offending behaviour is harmful because, to some degree, it damages other individuals and society. Public protection therefore includes a consideration of the likelihood of reoffending, particularly by prolific offenders (Merrington, 2006). Public protection, however, emphasises the risk of harm to others posed by some offending behaviour, using the definition given earlier.

As concepts, and in their practical application, both risk of reoffending and risk of harm assume that risk, in terms of probability, is to some extent predictable (Kemshall, 1996; Kemshall et al, 2005). Again, it is important to be clear about language. The term 'risk' is appropriate because there can be no certainty about how an individual will behave in the future. Risk is used here in a negative sense – the risk of something undesirable happening. Positive risk-taking is also necessary and the term 'risk' may be used in that sense by other professionals, for example, in health and social care (see Titterton, 2005). In criminal justice a decision to allow an offender to remain within the community is taking a positive risk, that this will best allow them to change their behaviour. The balance between reducing risk and taking risks is an issue decision makers in criminal justice have to work with. They also have to balance the rights of the offender with the need for public protection (Moore, 1996).

A consideration of the risk both of reoffending and of harm asks how likely it is that an individual offender will commit further offences. A focus on harm has, in addition, a more specific concern with what impact that behaviour will have, in terms of the degree of harm to others that is likely to result. Assessments of risk require practitioners to gather information about risk factors, in order to make judgements about likelihood and impact. This should then inform the design of the plans aimed at managing those identified risks. For both kinds of risk two sorts of information inform those judgements, derived from *actuarial and clinical assessments* (Kemshall, 2001).

In actuarial assessment statistical calculations are used to predict the likelihood that an offender will be reconvicted, based on the reconviction rates for large populations of offenders with similar characteristics, in like situations. Actuarial information does not provide a detailed individual assessment and some of the most significant actuarial information is static, including age, gender and criminal history. This information is very important in terms of risk classification, as it can provide the most accurate predictions of likelihood of reconviction; however, it gives less help in planning interventions. Static risk factors, as the term implies, cannot be changed and information based on groups does not provide a complete assessment of an individual.

Actuarial information gives indicators; for example, someone's criminal history offers clues to potential patterns of behaviour and thought. What is also needed for a full understanding of an offender is information about dynamic risk factors (Andrews and Bonta, 2003; Kemshall et al, 2006). These dynamic risk factors are also statistically based, in that they have been found to be associated with the likelihood of offending; however, they encourage a more individualised assessment, using clinical skills in information gathering, to establish the specific influences for each individual offender in context. It is the dynamic risk factors that best guide the risk management plan, by suggesting interventions most likely to reduce risk in the future (Kemshall, 1996, 1997, 1998a).

Increasingly, a variety of *risk assessment tools* are used to support practitioners in making judgements about reoffending and about harm. Some are actuarial in nature, for example the Offender Group Reconviction Score (OGRS) currently in use in England and Wales. Other tools involve structured professional judgement, requiring the assessor to evaluate the risk factors being assessed and sometimes allocating a score based on that evaluation. Examples include OASys used with adults, Asset used with young people, and LSI-R (RMA, 2006). These 'third generation' risk tools (Merrington, 2004) combine structured clinical assessment with actuarial judgements, so that each can inform the other. Harris (2006) supports the potential development of a fourth generation of tools, "outcomes are tied not just to predicted risk but the offender's needs, strengths and responsivity factors". Assessors need to consider those elements as part of a holistic assessment and to inform the plan of intervention.

The quality of completion of risk assessment tools cannot be taken for granted and will depend on the skills of the compiler in eliciting information from the offender and others and their ability to understand its significance. Small details of offending behaviour and of the offender's history and current circumstances may be of great importance. For example, evidence discussed in Chapter Seven on substance misuse suggests that for many offenders offences of dishonesty precede their use of substances, but change in nature as their dependency increases (Allen, 2005). An assessor who is aware of this will look for patterns in the offending record and structure their interview with the offender to examine changing motivations. If the earlier onset of dishonesty is linked to pro-offending attitudes still in existence, then both those attitudes and the addiction itself may be risk factors for offending and both may need to be prioritised in a risk management plan (Lipton et al, 2002). This attention to detail becomes even more crucial in assessing risk of serious harm. For example, understanding the different motivations for violent offending, explored in Chapter Nine, should lead an assessor to seek and be alert to signs of instrumental or sadistic motivations (Rutter et al, 1998). Such signs may increase likelihood, or potential impact (HMIP, 2006c).

Research suggests that a reduction of risk can be brought about by changes in dynamic risk factors (Andrews et al, 1990). While any offending is undesirable, the impact of serious violent and sexual offending on its victims is much greater. Any individual instance of reoffending is therefore of more significance. Risk of serious harm carries with it an increased emphasis on the *external management of risk*, through the monitoring, surveillance and control of behaviour (Kemshall, 2001; Kemshall et al, 2006). This emphasis has led to significant developments in interagency sharing of information and intelligence, particularly to facilitate external control, for example via MAPPA (Kemshall et al, 2005). This book does not explore the procedural aspects of risk management, but addresses the knowledge base that can, alongside other sources of guidance (Kemshall et al, 2006), help practitioners assess the individual in context.

Levels of risk are also relevant for the allocation and management of resources. Criminal justice agencies increasingly adopt the risk principle, and a focus on public protection, to guide *resource allocation*, aiming for resources to follow risk (YJB, 2005). Greater resources will be directed towards those offenders judged to pose a risk of serious harm and those offenders whose likelihood of reoffending is high. This is not an unproblematic process however, particularly in considering risk of serious harm. An analysis (HMIP, 2006c) of serious further incidents committed by offenders under supervision shows that the 7% of offenders designated as posing the highest risk of harm commit 20% of serious further incidents thus supporting an approach that concentrates resources on this group. However, the same information indicates that 80% of serious further incidents are committed by the remainder of offenders, designated as posing a low to medium risk of harm. Practitioners therefore need to have sufficient knowledge and skills to be alert to risk factors for harmful behaviour in all offenders and to changing levels of risk.

Collecting and evaluating information and the provision of risk management plans linked to identified risk factors are among the elements considered essential for *defensible decision making*; a decision that will withstand 'hindsight scrutiny' should the case 'go wrong' and negative outcomes occur (Carson, 1996; Kemshall, 1998a, 1998b). This concept is covered in more depth in Chapter Nine in relation to violent offenders. Practitioners who have a good understanding of the potential range of influences on offending behaviour will be better able to seek the right information and to understand its significance for assessment and for risk management. A note of caution should be struck, however. Risk assessment and management take place within an organisational context and practitioners must also have regard to policy, for example, they should always make careful use of the risk assessment tools required by their organisation (Kemshall et al, 2006).

A focus on risk therefore frames the focus and intensity of interventions. Those interventions also need to be *multi-modal* (Lipton et al, 2002). Intervention plans that cover a range of dynamic risk factors are more likely to be successful as they will include cognitive behavioural programmes addressing factors such as attitude change and the acquisition of new skills. Interventions should also consider other dynamic risk factors such as substance misuse. Raynor (2004) suggests that resettlement plans for offenders on release from custody should provide opportunities and resources for development, alongside interventions targeting changes in thinking. Each will reinforce the impact of the other, an absence of either may undermine the efficacy of the other. Approaches to intervention planning that integrate different elements are more likely to make sense to offenders themselves and contribute to their own 'self-talk', supporting desistance from offending (Maruna, 2001; Blanchette and Brown, 2006).

The success of interventions will then depend on how they are implemented and delivered (Burnett and Roberts, 2004; Harper and Chitty, 2004; Hollin et al, 2004; Kemshall et al, 2004). The implications for individuals delivering face-to-face interventions are now considered further, in relation to the second of the key concepts, that of responsivity.

Responsivity

"The most effective styles and modes of treatment service are those matched with the needs, circumstances and learning styles of high risk individuals" (Andrews, 1995: 43). Responsivity has sought to specify the characteristics of interventions that are more likely to work with most offenders and has included cognitive behavioural methods and pro-social modelling, suggesting that practitioners should deliver structured interventions in a warm and empathic way, while adopting a firm but fair approach (Blanchette and Brown, 2006).

The understanding of responsivity has developed over time. More recent writing by Andrews (2001) and Andrews and Bonta (2003) has included a broader range of issues within the concept of responsivity. They continue to stress the importance of structured and active approaches, in contrast to verbally based therapies that are focused on helping individuals increase their insight into the causes of their problems. They also now include principles such as authority and anti-criminal modelling. McGuire (2002b) cites Andrews' inclusion of specific responsivity factors taking account of variations in age, level of maturity, cultural background and other factors. Blanchette and Brown (2006) identify responsivity factors within the offender such as personality, emotional and mental heath, cognitive and intellectual abilities, motivation and strengths which will need to be taken into consideration in how interventions are planned and delivered. They also make clear that responsivity includes attention to practitioner skills, with an emphasis on their ability to make good relationships with offenders.

Despite these developments there have been criticisms of the risk and responsivity approach and its focus on cognitive behavioural interventions. Commentators have questioned the precise applications of those principles in practice, particularly in nationally led programmes (Burnett and Roberts, 2004; Harper and Chitty, 2004; Hollin et al, 2004; Kemshall et al, 2004). There are tensions between consistency in targeting the highest risk offenders and a service that responds to individuals, as individuals (Burnett and Roberts, 2004), as well as between an emphasis on enforcement and an approach that individualises service provision (McGuire and Raynor, 2006).

There have been a number of challenges to the relevance of cognitive behavioural approaches for all offenders, particularly for minority ethnic offenders and women (Kendall, 2004; Shaw and Hannah-Moffat, 2004). There are indications however that programmes can be of benefit (Dowden and Andrews, 1999) and that there can be a positive response from minority ethnic participants (Calverley et al, 2004). Attention is being drawn, by the developing research base, to the specific responsivity considerations that may need to be developed for particular offender groups, for example paying attention to victimisation issues in programmes for women offenders (Blanchette and Brown, 2006). There remains an acknowledged need for much more research into the needs of particular offender groups (Utting and Vennard, 2000; Blanchette and Brown, 2006) and encouragement within this book for practitioners to evaluate their own practice.

Others have argued that an overemphasis upon risk produces a negative orientation, by focusing on deficits in offenders that have to be corrected (Ward and Brown, 2004). Such an orientation is a potential obstacle to constructive engagement and needs to be balanced with an awareness of positive factors (Rutter et al, 1998).

Paying specific attention to positive factors, as part of the assessment process, will alert the practitioner to existing strengths that can be drawn on to support desistance from offending. Ward and Brown (2004: 246), in their 'good lives model', stress the importance of a strengths-based approach to work with offenders helping them develop "primary human goods". Farrall's (2002) findings suggest the importance of taking into account not just the removal of risk factors, but the development of human and social capital to support desistance (see Chapter Eight, also Raynor, 2004).

Ward and Brown (2004) emphasise the importance of offender readiness for treatments and the impact of the therapist themselves. This emphasis is reinforced by others who suggest that the state of readiness to change of the offender should be taken into account in the delivery of interventions. Again, this supports the importance of both factors within the offender (self-belief, positive goals) and in their environment (social supports) that may support motivation (McMurran, 2002b). This approach emphasises the skills of the practitioner in assessing offender readiness to change and building in external supports and rewards (McMurran, 2002b; see also Rex, 1999, 2002; Burnett and Roberts, 2004).

Blanchette and Brown (2006: 136) make the helpful point that "the vast majority of criticisms that have been levied against the responsivity principle can generally be remedied if the full breadth and intended spirit of the responsivity principle are considered". Practitioners engaging in face-to-face work with offenders must pay attention to the impact of their actions on the effectiveness of interventions (Trotter, 1999; Cherry, 2005).

McGuire (2004) acknowledges that whilst the 'good lives model' lacks an empirical base, it does help to support the integration of different theory bases in working with offenders, integrating offender rehabilitation and human motivation. Practitioners also have to focus on risk while engaging motivation. The final of our key concepts, diversity, provides another way of working with the complexity of individual human beings.

Diversity

The variety of individuals involved in criminal justice can be obscured by overarching labels, particularly that of 'offender'. The influence of these 'labels' may be heightened in a climate where risk factors and risk assessment tools tempt assessors to seek definitive answers, rather than living with complexity (Baker, 2007). Tuklo Orenda Associates (1999: 19) talk about "the multi-dimensional nature of the individual". For example, an offender may have a mental disorder, but mental disorders are themselves diverse. In addition, that same offender will also have experiences associated with their gender and age; they may have a history of involvement in particular offending behaviours; they will also have differing abilities and an ethnic and cultural identity and some may have dual diagnoses with co-occurring mental disorders and substance misuse (see Chapters Five, Six and Seven).

The starting point for a practitioner engaging with an individual offender might be any one of the above elements. However, a broad knowledge base will be needed beyond that starting point for a proper assessment of risk and for the delivery of interventions most likely to engage the active participation of that offender.

Of course there are, in a sense, no limits to diversity. In this book the authors have chosen to focus on certain aspects which seem to be particularly significant for offending behaviour and the criminal justice system (see Bowling and Phillips, 2002; Blanchette and Brown, 2006). This focus on diversity encourages attention to the detail of an offender's life, to draw out information that will be significant for assessment and for interventions.

Understanding the significance of that detail will, however, be easier with some offenders than others and for some aspects of offenders' lives and circumstances. Some practice areas have been more comprehensively researched than others. For example, Blanchette and Brown (2006: 54) suggest that while there is a significant body of research supporting the risk principle, meta-analytic reviews "have either excluded female offender samples, or have failed to disaggregate the data by gender". Utting and Vennard (2000) cite the lack of research into effectiveness with young women and offenders from minority ethnic backgrounds.

Understanding diversity goes beyond simply gathering a range of information. Baker (2006), in a discussion of risk assessment, reinforces the value of information gathering, but stresses that practitioners need to analyse that information and use it to develop whole case hypotheses, or formulations (Persons and Silbersatz, 1998; Sheppard, 2000). Such whole case hypotheses help evaluate how risk factors interact with and influence each other and this will have implications for judgements about the level and type of risk posed by the individual and how best to respond to them (Raynor, 2004).

Practitioners need to be able to make such formulations, but with sufficient confidence that they are willing to review and if necessary alter them as new information emerges. This is something that can be difficult to achieve in practice. Towl (2005) discusses the effect of 'anchoring bias' in risk assessment, making practitioners less willing to change their minds once they have been made up. Baker (2006) suggests that current risk assessment tools may increase that tendency by giving the impression that there is 'one correct answer', so although the tool incorporates a review, the process may actually encourage practitioners to hold onto existing beliefs. This may be particularly so when under pressure of time and resources (Taylor and White, 2006).

Practitioners with an extensive knowledge base and the ability to use it may be more likely to have the professional confidence to be better able to change formulations in the light of new information.

It is important therefore that practitioners keep adding to their knowledge base and reflecting upon it, using a range of sources, in a breadth of subject areas. The belief systems of practitioners need to remain open to change, otherwise this can lead to bias in their decision making within the criminal justice system (see Bowling and Phillips, 2002). The influence of beliefs on the actions of practitioners is also significant in terms of the ways in which they respond to the demands of their jobs. Birgden (2004: 291) stresses the need for staff development to target "private perceptions, attitudes and feelings".

Understanding diversity helps to sharpen the focus on the individual offender and their situation. It also encourages an open-minded and questioning approach by practitioners and with it an appreciation of their ability to make a difference.

Conclusions and implications for practice

The final section of this chapter looks ahead to the practical implications for face-to-face practice of all three key concepts. Before doing so the reader may be helped by completing the following task.

Activities and reflection 2.1

Go back to each of the sections on risk, responsivity and diversity:

- Identify at least one idea or concept under each heading that is new to you or challenges your existing thinking.
- What effect might these new ideas have on how you currently work with offenders (or how you visualise doing so in the future)? Make a couple of notes under each heading in terms of implications for your practice.

Bonta and Andrews (2003: 217) suggest a good theory has to be both "empirically defensible" and have "practical utility". So how can the concepts of risk, responsivity and diversity be applied practically? The following checklist highlights some core principles that flow from the key concepts and suggests where particularly to look within this book for more detailed explorations.

Risk

Practitioners will need to:

- *Identify the dynamic risk factors for a particular offender and understand the interaction between those risk factors.* The model, Figure 4.1, explored in Chapter Four in relation to young offenders, offers a visual reminder of the range of dynamic risk factors (offender-focused) and their interactions considered as part of a risk assessment.

- *Understand how risk factors impact at the point of an offence taking place.* The framework for assessment or 'Journey to the Offence', Figure 3.1, outlined in Chapter Three in relation to women offenders, offers a model to support information gathering and a tool for analysis that is 'offence-focused'. It is returned to in Chapter Four in relation to young offenders and in Chapter Ten for work with property offenders. An alternative model, Figure 9.1 in Chapter Nine, offers a framework for analysing violent behaviour which particularly emphasises cognitive processes and defects in thinking and their impact on offending.
- *Recognise that risk reduction needs to include strategies to reduce reoffending and also to encourage the offender to desist and manage their own risks.* Discussion about the concept of a 'criminal career' and the development of desistance factors in relation to young people takes place in Chapter Four. In Chapter Nine self-risk management is emphasised.
- *Ensure that the assessment of the offender and their offending informs subsequent intervention plans.* Chapter Nine on violent offending and Chapter Three on working with women demonstrate how assessment feeds into appropriate interventions.

Responsivity

Practitioners need to be able to:

- *Set positively oriented and achievable goals.* The process of negotiating realistic goals with an offender in ways which generate commitment and motivation is explored in Chapter Seven in relation to working with substance misuse. Ensuring that these goals are subsequently reviewed within the framework of supervision is explored in Chapter Eleven as part of a discussion about evaluation and 'ending well'.
- *Understand that efforts to target dynamic risk factors may be undermined if other significant problems within the offender's life are not tackled at the same time.* Mental disorder is discussed in depth in Chapter Six, substance misuse in Chapter Seven and lack of basic skills in Chapter Eight.
- *Recognise that they themselves are potential 'agents of change' for the offender.* Holt (2002) has provided a set of principles – the four 'C's – which underpin effective case management. These principles

are explored in more detail in relation to high volume/lower risk property offenders in Chapter Ten.

Diversity

Practitioners need to:

- *Be aware of the potential impact of their own beliefs and attitudes upon relationships with other people.* They will be helped by understanding more about their own identity, including the influences of culture, ethnicity and gender. This is explored in Chapter Five, working across 'race' and culture, with some practical ideas to prompt that personal exploration.
- *Avoid making assumptions as to what intervention will work best and how it should be delivered without supporting evidence.* In Chapter Three the dangers of blanket approaches which ignore gender differences are considered in detail. Chapters Eleven and Twelve discuss evaluation, encouraging the practitioner to be reflective both in terms of service delivery but also in relation to their own practice development.
- *Have the ability to understand and incorporate the perspectives of others.* In Chapter Five, in Figure 5.1, the 'iceberg model' offers a means of exploring the thoughts and feelings of others as a way of understanding their perspectives.

The list above is not exhaustive. This chapter may have helped readers to identify other operating principles which flow from the key concepts. The reader is now encouraged to get into the detail of subsequent chapters while seeing the links between them and their origins in risk, responsivity and diversity.

Part Two
Diversity

THREE

Women offenders

Introduction

In 1981, one of the authors and two colleagues set up a social skills group for women, adapting materials designed for young male offenders written by Priestley and McGuire (1978). One participant commented:

> We would all like the group to continue with more proper discussions ... and less silly games now that we all know each other. (Unpublished evaluation, 1981)

In 2006, anecdotal feedback from practitioners delivering programmes aiming to cater for women, either as part of a predominantly male group or in a women-only context, highlighted how little had changed in 25 years:

> We don't have any women's groups as such but we always ask them if they mind joining a male one. If possible the policy is to have at least two women. It's always good to have a woman in the group as she often 'mothers' the men. (Comment from male tutor, general offending programme, 2006)

> This programme is very female-oriented but sometimes when women are very upset because of emotional problems we haven't got time to deal with them as we have to stick to the programme. (Comment from female tutor, acquisitive crime programme, 2006)

These comments about the experience of groupwork interventions with women offenders suggest that methods were, and still are being, used which were designed for a predominantly male offending population, methods which favour structured activity over discussion and reflection within positive relationships. There may also be a tendency, particularly in mixed groups, to perpetuate the traditional characteristics and roles of women.

It could be argued that what is at issue here is merely a question of the style of delivery, and that the content of offence-focused programmes simply needs to be delivered in a manner which is more likely to engage women.

However, even when interventions are designed specifically for women, it is difficult to target the work flexibly enough to retain a focus upon offending, and also address what are often regarded as welfare or lifestyle needs. These needs may include experience of abuse and violence, mental health problems and the demands of parental responsibilities, all of which are commonly significant in the lives of troubled women and can affect how effectively they engage with interventions or sustain positive change in their lives. Moreover, as this chapter will show, such needs are often linked with women's offending choices. An ongoing issue for researchers and practitioners is to distinguish between needs which constitute dynamic risk factors specifically related to offending and those which are more a part of the context of that offending and likely to be significant in terms of desistance (Hedderman, 2004c; Porporino and Fabiano, 2005; Blanchette and Brown, 2006).

Such long-standing issues about services for women offenders are at the heart of this chapter and pose a challenge for practitioners who need to try to respond to diversity while retaining the focus upon risk, especially of reoffending.

Before moving into the detail of the chapter it is worth considering briefly *the research and criminological landscape* relating to women's offending. The issues raised and themes that emerge shape approaches to women offenders and account for some of the particular tensions likely to be experienced by practitioners. Against this backdrop, the authors will then go on to consider *how women experience the criminal justice system*, explore *current understandings about women and their offending* and consider research into *the most promising approaches to working effectively with women offenders*. The pieces will then be brought together to offer *a broad paradigm for intervening* effectively.

Setting the scene: research and criminological perspectives

It is acknowledged by researchers across disciplines, and indeed across cultures, that men offend more than women. Gelsthorpe (2004: 13) describes this as "one of the most persistent and universal findings in criminological research". Acceptance of what Walklate (2004: 1) refers to as this "empirical reality" that "crime is committed disproportionately by males" has meant that women have not, until recently, attracted significant attention of their own from mainstream criminal justice researchers. Research into offending has focused upon the majority group: White male offenders. In writing about evidence-based practice, comments about women's offending behaviour can be lost within the general picture. Sometimes comparisons are made between men and women, but often with little analysis as to the reasons for differences in either the extent or the characteristics of their respective offending behaviour.

Researchers have not in the past been helped by the fact that criminal behaviour in women is relatively rare. There has not been the volume of offenders to provide the wealth of statistically significant evidence that has shaped work with male offenders. Heidensohn (2002) draws attention to the consequences of this both for research and for women offenders themselves:

> Women's low share of recorded criminality is so well-known that it has significant consequences for those women who do offend. They are seen to have transgressed not only social norms but gender norms as well. (Heidensohn, 2002: 504)

Two implications flow from this statement. First, researchers, criminologists and practitioners still argue about the roots of female offending and, as a result, offence-focused interventions designed for the majority population of White male offenders have tended to be 'tweaked' to cater to women at the superficial level of their femininity rather than redesigned in light of an understanding of their offending behaviour (Porporino and Fabiano, 2005).

Second, decisions about women offenders can be influenced as much by who they are, or are perceived to be, as by what they have actually done. In a sense their welfare needs (poverty, domestic responsibilities) or personal characteristics (physical or mental health, personality) can serve to "neutralise their criminal culpability" (Rumgay, 2004b: 104). Sentences and subsequent interventions tend to be a response to individual needs or characteristics rather than focusing on offending behaviour.

However, there are now expanding opportunities for researchers to access and scrutinise data. For example, since the 1991 Criminal Justice Act (Section 95), the Secretary of State in the UK has been required to publish data about women and other minority groups of offenders in order to promote services which do not discriminate. Such data complements and confirms research findings already available in North America about the characteristics of women offenders and their specific offending patterns and how these differ from male offending (see McIvor, 2004; Walklate, 2004; Blanchette and Brown, 2006).

Nevertheless, the picture of women's offending remains relatively incomplete, raising as many questions about gendered patterns of offending and the place of motivation as it suggests practical ways forward (Davies, 2002). Consequently, there is as yet no unified, or unifying, body of research relating to women offenders. The questions raised are the focus of much criminological debate as academics seek to interpret the available data.

Until the latter part of the 20th century, criminological studies focusing upon women and their offending were relatively rare (Heidensohn, 2002). With the increasing influence of feminist thought in the 1970s, the subject began to attract serious and focused academic attention (see Smart, 1976) and for some it was then that feminist criminology really began to take off (Snider, 2003).

The range and complexity of theories about women's offending which have been generated by this increased attention, along with the increased availability of data mentioned earlier, has been described extensively and effectively elsewhere (see Naffine, 1995; Gelsthorpe, 2002; Walklate, 2004; Blanchette and Brown, 2006). This book aims to highlight some key themes in criminology which can determine how data is analysed and understood, with a view to developing theories to inform practice.

Criminologists, especially those with a feminist perspective, responded to perceived discrimination and ineffectiveness in the traditional response to women's offending (see Smart, 1976). This field of feminist criminology has produced three broad approaches to research that are relevant here:

- **Feminist empiricism** which aims to develop a scientific understanding of women as the 'missing subjects' of criminology (Naffine, 1995), recording the detail of their lives as both offenders and victims. It emphasises equality and objectivity.
- **Standpoint feminism** which emphasises the difference of women's experience and stresses the importance of knowledge drawn directly from women's experience. It has led to "the notion of work done by women, with women, for women" (Walklate, 2004: 45).

- **Feminist post-modernism** is, in a sense, both a reaction against these two perspectives and also draws upon the work of both. It rejects the idea of a unitary reality, favouring complexity over certainty, valuing "plurality, diversity, difference and openness" (Gelsthorpe, 2002: 114). It promotes diversity and resists easy or 'off the shelf' explanations for individual behaviour.

Each of these theoretical perspectives has a place in helping practitioners to think through why women offend and make decisions about the content of work and the manner of its delivery.

It might also be unwise to disregard the traditional approaches to work with women, those that lead to an emphasis upon welfare and relationships and which feminist criminology sought to move away from. Recent research into women's offending does, ironically, support the notion that women's behaviour is often rooted in relationships, and in the context in which they live their lives. To ignore the significance of these influences when working with women would be a failure of responsivity.

In summary, these broad theoretical approaches suggest that:

- offending behaviour should be understood in a research-based, systematic and neutral way;
- women's personal and relationship needs must be acknowledged and given attention;
- women's life experience should be valued and positively developed.

Furthermore, the uncertainties which still surround women and their offending, despite increased availability of data, also provide opportunities for practitioners to contribute to the developing body of practice wisdom in this field.

Activities and reflection 3.1

Consider your own work with women offenders:

- How far does it reflect the main theoretical perspectives outlined above?
- Do you have a particular view about women and their offending which influences your approach?
- How does this show itself in your work?

Women's experience of the criminal justice system

The broad picture emerging from more recent data is that women are now accounting for increasing proportions of officially recorded crime, although the overall volume of crime committed by women in the UK still remains small by comparison with men. A research review of young offenders in the late 1990s found that, "although the rate ... [of offending] ... is always higher for males, the ratio is now only about a third of that observed 40 years ago" (Rutter et al, 1998: 278).

Official figures suggest that the female prison population rose by 173% between 1992 and 2002 (Home Office, 2003). These rises in the number of women entering custody may not be due entirely to a rise in the volume of offending alone. Other influences upon the figures may include increases in the number of women who are brought before the court in the first place, the length of sentences imposed, and appearances for drug offences that may attract heavier penalties. These factors may be influenced in turn by changes in political and social attitudes (discussed in HMIP, 2005: 4). The underlying general trend is, however, one of increasing female offending.

Within the general picture there are more specific differences between groups of women. For example, with respect to drug offences, 41% of all women prisoners in 2002 were sentenced for drug-related offences. When the focus is upon the population of Black women prisoners that proportion rises to 75% (Home Office, 2003). There are also differences within the profile of this 75% in terms of both age and ethnicity, including a relatively high number of women coming from overseas. This suggests that Black women's experience and the context of that experience may be different again from their White counterparts.

Understanding the experiences of Black women offenders is also likely to be less developed than understanding about women's offending in general. Their experience "remains subsumed in the experience of black men and homogenised with the experience of white women" (Chigwada-Bailey, 2004: 183). When seeking to work effectively with this minority within a minority, practitioners will need to draw upon both the broad research into female offending covered in this chapter, and also upon what is known about responding effectively to issues of culture, 'race' and religion (see Chigwada-Bailey, 1997, 2004; also Chapter Five in this book).

In the context of the underlying trends outlined above, researchers have drawn attention to differences in sentencing patterns, and to inequalities in sentencing options and the availability of alternatives to custody (Hedderman and Gelsthorpe, 1997; Lyon, 2002; Home Office, 2003). It is possible to draw out the following themes in terms of perceived sentencing disparities between men and women:

- Overall, women are treated more leniently than men with some significant exceptions. For example, drug offences tend to attract heavier penalties in specific instances (Hedderman and Gelsthorpe,1997).
- Recent rises in the women's prison population may in fact be due to more severe responses to less serious offences (Home Office, 2003).
- It has also been argued (Carlen, 1983, 2002) that characteristics of individual women might attract harsher treatment from the courts. Similarly, Malloch (2004: 386) argues that "women's behaviour and self-presentation is often used to depict them as 'respectable', 'bad' or 'inadequate' based on hierarchies of social value".
- There appears to be a reluctance to impose fines upon women, possibly because many have family responsibilities (Hedderman and Gelsthorpe, 1997; Home Office, 2003).
- Magistrates seem to distinguish between 'troubled' and 'troublesome' offenders, with women tending, historically, to be placed in the former category, leading proportionately to more frequent use of community supervision (see Home Office, 2002c).
- Patterns of female offending create an impression of relative 'harmlessness', with violent offending being a rarity (Kemshall, 2004). There is also a risk, therefore, that women commiting exceptional offences may attract exceptional penalties.

In essence, the research raises the question of how far the sentencing of women may be influenced by factors which go beyond the offending behaviour itself.

Smart (1976) described the experience of women passing through the criminal justice system. She provided a picture of a sentencing process which sought to regulate the behaviour of those who have acted contrary to accepted (and arguably traditional) societal norms, to confirm "certain cultural understandings of female behaviour" (Smart, 1976: 45). That regulatory process would involve not just the sentencer/decision maker, but also the offender, and the practitioner. All participants bring to the process a cluster of values, behaviours and attitudes which may reflect accepted norms or, conversely, appear to conflict with them and require regulation. These attitudes, particularly in the case of women, will have an impact upon decisions made, services offered and, indeed, the responses of offenders to both.

Smart's analysis remains relevant to our understanding of contemporary responses to female offending. Hudson (2002) explores similar issues asserting that:

> The same circumstances … will be constructed differently by probation officers, magistrates and others with the power to punish, and will appear as mitigating or aggravating, according to the woman's race, sexual status, appearance, demeanour and lifestyle. (Hudson, 2002: 41)

Activities and reflection 3.2

Consider the experiences of two or three of the women with whom you work as they have progressed through the criminal justice system.

- What key decisions were made from arrest through to sentence?
- What attitudes of any of those involved might have influenced those decisions?
- Were there any significant issues associated with the individual's status as a woman?

If you are not currently working with women offenders you could apply these questions to cases that appear in the news.

The challenge for all involved in the sentencing process is to make decisions which reflect what Halliday (2000: 20) described as a "consistency of approach" rather than "a uniformity of outcome" and which clearly promote the principle of transparency. This approach would not be one which is weighted by subjective value-laden judgements about women who behave anti-socially.

There is an imperative to understand women and their offending, with a view to using resources more effectively. In the UK the NOMS expressed an aspiration that "stakeholders … ensure that their policies, interventions and services are made more appropriate to meet the needs and characteristics of women offenders" (NOMS, 2005: 3). It recognised that women's offending needs can no longer be catered for as part of general provision, whether in one-to-one relationships or groupwork settings.

In order to respond more effectively to women offenders, practitioners need to consider the following:

• understanding women's offending behaviour
• promising approaches to work with women offenders.

These are now considered in turn.

Understanding women's offending behaviour

At the risk of oversimplifying what is a complex picture, and one which is explored in detail elsewhere (Heidensohn, 2002; McIvor, 2004; Walklate, 2004), a number of broad trends emerge from data relating to the patterns of offending associated more commonly with women's offending:

• Women in the UK are in the minority in all types of offending behaviour (Burman, 2004).
• Acquisitive crime accounts for over half of the incidents of female offending (Home Office, 2003; see also figures gathered by the Scottish Executive in 2000 and quoted in Burman, 2004).
• Theft is not only the most common current offence for women but is often the first conviction. For example, with the notable exception of women trafficking drugs from abroad, who are often older and criminally less experienced (HMIP, 2005: 6), women drug offenders often have previous convictions for theft and forgery (Home Office, 2003).
• Consistently less than 1% of women offenders are convicted of burglary, compared with 4% of men (Home Office, 2003: 8).
• Women have much lower rates of involvement in murder, serious violence and professional and organised crime.

If broad trends in women's offending are reasonably easy to identify, the complex networks of reasons which underlie these trends are less easy to describe. There are ongoing discussions within the research literature about what dynamic risk factors are most closely associated with female offending.

There is some consensus (Hedderman, 2004c) that dynamic risk factors are broadly similar in both men and women: poor or limited cognitive skills, anti-social attitudes and feelings, weak social ties, difficulty with self-management, drug or alcohol dependency, poverty and negative family or social circumstances. What may differ is their level of importance, their prevalence, the way they interact with each other and the mechanisms which support that interaction (Clark and Howden-Windell, 2000). Such interactions may differ at different moments in an individual's criminal career.

Some dynamic risk factors may also serve a different purpose in the lives of women by contrast with men (Porporino and Fabiano, 2005). For example, in terms of basic skills, numeracy, as opposed to literacy, difficulties were found to increase the risk of offending in women, particularly when associated with negative familial and social circumstances (Parsons, 2002). For the practitioner the question is why should this be so? In terms of assessment, for an individual offender, the answer lies in the detail of their life experience.

To help the practitioner make sense of the influence of and interaction between dynamic risk factors as they relate to women's offending, the dual concepts of the *criminal career* and *pathways into crime* are considered here. They also have implications for both an understanding of the diversity of need and experience of individual women, and the responsivity of work done and services offered.

Consider first the *criminal career*. This concept, and the research underpinning it, is addressed in more detail in Chapter Four.

From the point of view of women offenders two aspects are significant: the length of the career and the nature of onset, persistence and desistance factors. Research (Hedderman and Dowds, 1997; Home Office, 1998b, 2003) suggests that women in general tend to start offending later and to both peak and stop earlier than the majority of male offenders. Furthermore, the preponderance of male offending is in early adult life, by which time many young women have begun to desist.

This apparently short but intense criminal career may be connected to the causes of women's offending, in that a majority of female offending takes place in the developmental period of their lives when they are beginning to explore and establish long-term relationships and take on social or family responsibilities.

The factors which seem to be distinctively female are those which make women vulnerable to offending choices in the first place, the onset factors, and which may also determine the nature of those choices. These tend to be associated with long-standing contextual dimensions of an individual's life, either reaching back into their past experience or linked to the social and relational networks which may sustain them in the present.

Rumgay (1996) and others (for example, Lyon, 2002) have argued that women's personal difficulties and welfare problems are inextricable from an understanding of their offending. Women are influenced to a greater extent than men by factors relating to their financial management, drug misuse, relationships and emotional well-being. Amongst the female prison population, both in the UK and North America, women report high levels of previous experiences of abuse, involvement in significant drug use and mental health problems (Home Office, 2003; HMIP, 2005; Blanchette and Brown, 2006).

These factors are not exclusive to acquisitive crime, the major strand of female offending. For example, in writing about violent women offenders there is a prevailing assumption that "the majority of violence perpetrated by women is interpersonal violence" (Fitzroy, 2001: 8), in other words embedded within their social or family context. (A more detailed discussion about women and violence is contained in Chapter Nine.)

How far these issues constitute dynamic risk factors, the extent to which they are evidence of a woman's vulnerability, and how far they are part of a wider picture relevant both to engagement (responsivity) and supporting change (desistance) will differ from woman to woman.

Take, for instance, the influence of relationships, so frequently mentioned in relation to women offenders; an example of this is that women are more likely than men to have a partner or child convicted of offending (Hedderman, 2004c). How far this is a direct dynamic risk factor is open to question. Certainly in terms of abusive relationships, in adolescence and adulthood, there is evidence that such relationships increase the incidence of depression, emotional problems, alienation and self-harm (Gardner, 2001). They are also linked with addiction (De Cou, 2004) and susceptibility to further victimisation. There also seems to be some agreement that this latter aspect of relationships may play "a role in the onset of criminal offending" (Blanchette and Brown, 2006: 9; see also Hedderman, 2004c) but the links to recidivism or persistence are less clear (Clark and Howden-Windell, 2000; Hollin and Palmer, 2005).

For some offenders a continuing abusive relationship may reinforce the cognitive deficits which can be associated with an offending lifestyle, such as poor reasoning and problem-solving, and contribute to a reduced sense of self-efficacy. The criminal partner in the relationship may even exert direct and overt pressure upon them to commit offences. Each woman's experience is different. While research provides some broad indicators about what to look out for, it also reinforces the need in the current climate of knowledge to take a case-specific approach in practice.

The same caveat applies to identifying desistance factors in relation to women. It seems, for example, that women tend to show more remorse for offending (Mair and May, 1997). This is associated with reconviction rates (Clark and Howden-Windell, 2000) and is an acknowledged desistance factor. However, based upon her analysis of this and other studies, Hedderman (2004c: 232) argues that some of the anomalies in the detail of the research also suggest that, for some women, regret may coexist with a more 'self-serving' and pragmatic approach to offending. This suggests that some elements of an individual's life can operate both as potential risk factors and as positive protective factors. For practitioners, the ambivalence inherent here could be a fertile area for motivational work (Porporino and Fabiano, 2005).

In a risk-oriented system there may be a tendency to overlook or underestimate the importance of positives coexisting alongside the negatives. Ward and Brown (2004) remind practitioners to take a balanced approach and actively seek to identify, value and develop such strong desistance factors as stable partnerships, and positive investment in familial or social responsibilities.

Finally, to some extent the dynamic nature of age can contribute to desistance and the ending of the criminal career. For many women, the types of positive change required for desistance (a developing sense of social responsibility, along with complementary supportive friendships based on common interests) are likely to coincide with early adulthood for many young women (Paludi, 2002).

While the idea of a criminal career can help the practitioner to consider the developmental nature of female offending and to recognise how risk factors can change with time and circumstance, the second concept provides a framework within which to consider in detail how risks and needs interconnect at the point of the offence. It can also help to refine the distinction between dynamic risk factors and wider welfare needs.

Throughout the body of the literature the notion of female pathways into crime is commonly discussed (McIvor, 2004; Rumgay, 2004a; Shaw and Hannah-Moffat, 2004). *The framework for offence-focused assessment* (Figure 3.1), with its sense of journeying, has a particular resonance with that notion. It brings together what research indicates are the most prevalent offence-related needs of women in a manner which begins to suggest how these risk factors impact upon choices and behaviours, and also how they interconnect with each other. This sense of interconnection and interdependence of need is a recurring theme in writing about women's offending (Hipwell et al, 2002; McIvor, 2004).

Figure 3.1: Offence-focused assessment – the individual journey to the offence

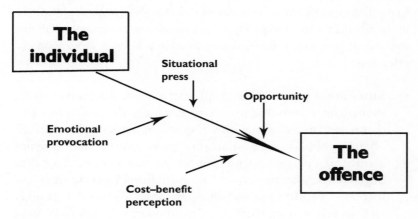

Source: Kelly and Wilkinson (2000)

This framework, derived from a model originally formulated by Rutter et al (1998: 311), was adapted initially by Kelly and Wilkinson (2000) for a youth justice context. It emphasises the need to pay attention to individual predisposing risk factors, internal influences (feelings and thoughts), and the external situational factors which can influence behaviour. The impact of the internal and external and the interaction between them can account for the specific circumstances of the offence(s).

Starting with the beginning of the journey, the *individual factors*; include learnt behaviours, vulnerabilities and dispositions.

It is widely accepted that, in general, a history of previous offending is a good predictor of future offending for women as well as men (Home Office, 2003; Hedderman, 2004c).

That most female offending is acquisitive may suggest poverty as a predisposing individual factor, along with other aspects of impoverished backgrounds. Data about the experiences and needs of women in prison (HMIP, 2005) reveal a high level of poor physical and mental health, experience of domestic violence and sexual assault, and drug or alcohol dependency. Many women entering the prison system are also mothers and primary carers. Their opportunities to solve problems more appropriately may also be hindered by poor academic achievement, a further individual risk factor. A Home Office study (2000c) found that 14% of women entering prison lacked basic and work skills and were also primary carers of dependent children.

Individual pre-existing risk factors are, however, no guarantee of an offence taking place. These factors will interact with a range of more immediate, specific influences on an individual's journey, culminating in the offending episode. As Figure 3.1 shows, these influences fall into four categories, and are applied here to what is known about women's offending:

- **Situational press**: refers to specific, individual responses to the immediate environment or circumstances that offenders find themselves in, insofar as this response is associated with their offending. For women 'situational press' may include ongoing abusive or coercive relationships, a current or escalating drug dependency, unexpected and unusual financial difficulties and increased family responsibilities. In order to avoid a 'blanket' welfare-oriented approach, the practitioner will need to be wary of drawing generalised conclusions about the potential pressure resulting from such problematic situations.
- **Emotional provocation**: for example current depression or other mental ill-health, stress, desperation, anger or resentment.
- **Opportunity**: which will include available targets or victims, as well as having the skills to undertake a criminal activity. For many women offenders their individual experience of life may determine the range of opportunities available to them. Statistics show that not only is theft and handling the most prevalent type of offence amongst women, but, within this offending, theft from shops is by far the most frequent expression of this behaviour. Furthermore, in terms of violence, Fitzroy (2001) indicates that women are unlikely to harm people with whom they do not have an interpersonal relationship.
- **Cost–benefit perceptions**: which are the calculations that individuals make about the benefits of offending, set against the risks of detection and its consequences. Hedderman's suggestion (2004c: 239) that female offending is often "a rational response to restricted opportunities, social inequality and poverty" supports this idea. The immediate gains of an offence outweigh the potentially negative consequences, perceptions of which can also be limited by a narrow frame of reference. Within this specific context the offending makes sense to the offender.

The interaction between the individual and these influences, at a given moment, comes together in *the offence*: the end of this particular journey. This systematic assessment of the individual pathway to the offence, and the way in which different influences interact and are played out, provides a foundation for interventions which constitute a more positive pro-social pathway forward.

Offence-focused assessment is not, however, simply about the 'journey'. The detail of the individual's offending behaviour gives clues about the important external and internal influences upon them and consequently an insight into both the wider context of the offending and issues relating to their motivation to change.

Activities and reflection 3.3

Think about a woman who you do not as yet know very well. You are beginning to unravel the detail of her offending behaviour. This offending may be set against a background of onerous family responsibilities and difficult relationships, or she may be coping well within the limitations upon her. Be cautious about jumping to conclusions about how her life experiences are connected to her offending.

Use the framework for offence-focused assessment to analyse this woman's specific and individual offending behaviour.

- How might the common experiences of women who offend have specifically influenced her offending choice?
- How might you go about exploring this with her?
- What questions might you ask?
- Does this framework help you begin to separate life experiences closely connected to the offending from more general characteristics of the woman's life?

Promising approaches to work with women offenders

There is still a paucity of rigorously evaluated programmes of intervention specifically targeted at women offenders. Data are now being gathered about the extent and content of women's offending and the sentences imposed upon them. However, and perhaps not surprisingly, understanding about effective interventions lags behind. It was only in 2004 that the NOMS launched its Women Offenders Reduction Programme (WORP) in England and Wales. Its main focus was to:

> ... improve community-based provision for women offenders and make sure that it is tailored to meet their

needs, so that courts are encouraged to make greater use of community disposals for women offenders and custody is only used as a last resort. (NOMS, 2005: 3)

The first annual review of the WORP acknowledged that, while "there is still a long way to go before gender becomes an integral consideration in … policy development", there is evidence of:

> … a greater awareness now that achieving gender equality in the criminal justice system is not about treating women offenders the same as men but about recognising the differences between the factors which affect why women offend and making sure that there are the right interventions and services in place to address those factors. (NOMS, 2005: 4)

This awareness of the particular needs of women is an essential prerequisite for developing practitioner responsivity in this area of work. Practical diversity goes further than general awareness. The message for anyone working effectively with someone different from themselves is to pay attention to the detail of each individual's life experience.

In terms of the interventions most likely to have a positive impact, the following common themes emerge:

- It is important to incorporate a women's perspective and be relevant to their life experience; to look, as Roberts (2002: 112) suggests, "through the women's window". There are gender-specific differences in the socialisation of women, which have an impact upon the offending opportunities open to, and choices made by, women. The research into women's pathways into crime and their individual journey to the offence is important here. Understanding the individual's offending behaviour and the context in which it occurs is fundamental to determining the content of any interventions.
- While it is certainly true that acquisitive crime remains the most common female crime (Home Office, 2003), the practitioner will need to be careful to avoid the stereotype of the woman as victim of poverty and economic marginalisation, leading, in some circumstances, to an approach which justifies rather than challenges individual women's responses to their difficult life experiences. Each individual's motivation will differ in terms of the function that their offending behaviour fulfils.

- Several sources (Farrall, 2002; Roberts, 2002; Batchelor and Burman, 2004; Rumgay, 2004b) point to the need for a comprehensive, holistic approach to the design of programmes, an approach which is able to take account of and meet the multiple interconnected needs often associated with women's offending. A holistic approach will also take account of powerful needs and strengths not directly associated with the offending but crucial to promoting and sustaining the life experiences which may make an individual more (or less) vulnerable to offending choices.

- To reflect these interconnected and interdependent needs women should be helped to access a range of mainstream community resources (NOMS, 2005:14). A coordinated multi-agency approach could be beneficial with access to a "strong network of community resources relevant to the needs of women" (Roberts, 2002: 123).

- Work with women should start with taking proactive steps to encourage engagement, both by paying attention to the content and methodology of programmes, and also by overcoming the barriers to initial involvement and working to sustain motivation over a period of time (NOMS, 2005: 8).

- There is some evidence that women respond more positively to methodologies which are collaborative rather than linear/ hierarchical (Morgan and Patton, 2002), and staged and cumulative, incremental rather than immediate, change, reflecting their progress through the system.

- There should be a focus upon beliefs supportive of offending through approaches that explore the notion of rational choice (explored further in Chapter Ten), and complementary development of skills to arrive at realistic solutions to problems (Home Office, 2003: 2).

- It is important to differentiate between the needs of adult and younger women as research suggests that they have different offence-related needs (Batchelor and Burman, 2004). There has been acknowledgement by the Prison Service in the UK, for example, that it is not appropriate to house young female offenders with adults.

Implications for practice

For everyone working within the criminal justice system, the challenge has been described as:

The need to develop an understanding of women's offending behaviour that is able to acknowledge women's oppression in the broad social fabric of their everyday lives, but still name women's agency and make women accountable for the ... crimes they choose to commit. (Fitzroy, 2001: 26)

It is important to resist stereotypes of women offenders which see them as victims of their circumstances, influenced largely by their various relationships with the world and their role within it. Such stereotypes can lead to a welfare-oriented approach, underestimating or overlooking individual agency and choice. A balance needs to be struck between offence-related needs and wider lifestyle issues. The practitioner will need to recognise the links between the two domains, delivering appropriately targeted interventions designed to produce real change in relation to the former, as well as contributing to the alleviation of the stress and influence of the latter.

The approach to work with women offenders suggested here has case management at its heart and reflects key themes suggested by research and described earlier. These have also informed the development of several groupwork programmes for women offenders (Thomas and Jones,1998; T3 Associates, 2002).

Effective work with women is characterised by two strands of complementary work which need to be managed and synchronised in a staged manner throughout a period of supervision; offence-focused work and responding to, developing and sustaining responsivity. It is important to bear this in mind whether you are delivering the range of interventions yourself or have access to specially designed programmes and services for women offenders and are, therefore, acting as a case manager.

Sequencing and timing, coordination and balance, are likely to be significant from the outset, influencing the effectiveness of the two key aspects of face-to-face work with women: assessment and interventions.

Assessment

Assessment informs sentencing decisions and provides the foundation upon which appropriate interventions are built. It will be concerned with both the offending episodes and any aspects of the individual's life which might affect her ability to engage with services offered. It is, as is reiterated elsewhere in this book, about having an eye for detail.

An essential dimension of the assessment process is the practitioner's own honest awareness of the values and attitudes which may shape their interactions with, and their judgements of, the individual. Attention must be paid to the methods employed to engage the offender in the assessment process. The assessor works at the gateway into criminal justice services and needs to behave in a way that contributes to alleviating "existing discrimination and … not … to its continuance" (Kemshall and Wright, 1995: 23).

Activities and reflection 3.4

Before starting an assessment of an individual, consider what you are bringing to the interaction:

- Be aware of your own attitudes, shaped as they are by such individual characteristics as gender, age, life experience and values.
- Consider how the individual offender might perceive you as the assessor. What effect might this have on your relationship with the offender?
- How can you overcome this and any practical concerns which might hinder engagement?

In terms of the information required and how that should be interpreted, assessors may often need to take account of the formal assessment tools implemented in their professional setting. However, an understanding of key factors influencing women's offending and, more importantly, how they interconnect will help practitioners to analyse and interpret that information. The framework for offence-focused assessment (Figure 3.1) is useful here in helping the assessor to distinguish between direct dynamic risk factors and wider responsivity issues, either personal and internal to the individual or related to the external context in which offending has taken place.

Assessment will also identify practical obstacles, with a view to ensuring safety and developing motivation. This may involve addressing at the same time immediate 'welfare' or practical issues which are likely to impede the individual woman's commitment to offence-focused work, alongside facilitating understanding of her offending choices. Assessment will also point towards ongoing support and post-programme work which will be linked to establishing appropriate partnerships and access to specialist services.

Finally, some attention to the individual's history and pattern of offending – their criminal career – can help determine the level, intensity, timing and specific purpose of interventions.

Interventions

Interventions will be based upon a shared and detailed understanding of the individual's offending choices. It will recognise the emotional and relational context of women's offending. The professional working relationship, either in group or individual sessions, should model positive relationships which encourage the constructive expression of emotions and actively value individuals (Trotter, 1993; Cherry, 2005). Above all, the focus or content of the work should be rooted in the individual's experience, so that learning can be easily practised and reinforced. Thus while offence-focused work is likely to include skills development to improve social and instrumental functioning, it will do so in a manner that recognises "existing strengths and competencies" and means something to the individual: she will "see the point" (Porporino and Fabiano, 2005: 3).

In terms of promoting desistance from offending, ongoing personalised support has been found to be particularly valuable to both young offenders and women. Research into the value of mentoring suggests that mentoring for female offenders would "prove a useful tool in supporting the women generally and helping them to reduce the areas of their lives where they are most at risk" (Walmsley, 2001: 14). Whether through formal mentoring arrangements, or by facilitating access to mainstream services in the community, the practitioner will need to pay attention to methods of supporting the individual woman's positive reintegration into the community, and reinforcing learning and progress. These could be through formal partnerships, local women's organisations or friends and family members. Successful reintegration is about promoting desistance and positive social relationships.

Practice Tool 3.1 reminds the practitioner of the dual strands of work at each of the two stages of a programme of supervision and prompts thinking about activities which might be appropriate as work proceeds.

Practice tool 3.1

Assessment

Offence-focus:

- Have you identified the characteristics of this individual's pathway into offending, the factors which cause them to persist and positive features of their life which could support desistance?
- Do you have a clear picture of contextual, situational and personal factors which influenced them?

Responsivity issues:

- How committed is the individual to changing her behaviour and what might impede her? What work needs to be done to develop motivation and reduce barriers to commitment?
- How can you ensure a sense of safety (for example, by addressing issues of victim-hood, childhood abuse, domestic violence)?
- What practical support may be needed?

Intervening

Offence-focused content:

- What skills do you intend to develop in the work with the individual woman?
- How will you explore attitudes, beliefs and feelings, helping her to develop more positive emotions and thoughts and build upon personal strengths?
- Are the methods collaborative and inclusive?
- What practical opportunities are there to reinforce change in the 'real' world?

Sustaining engagement and promoting desistance:

- Are you alert to any problems (immediate or ongoing) which might affect the individual's involvement in the offence-focused work?
- What positive relationships are already available to the individual?
- What other networks or services might you use to enhance positive social relationships?
- Does the individual have access to positive mentors, either formal or informal, for example, family members or friends?

Conclusion

In general, women's offending is less frequent than male offending. It is mainly at the less serious end of the spectrum, and acquisitive crime constitutes the largest proportion of known offences. There also seems to be some association between acquisitive crime and drug use. This wider picture has shaped the services for women offenders, particularly formal offence-focused programmes. It is important, however, for practitioners to avoid stereotypes about women and offending and to remember that each person's situation may be different. Awareness of these differences can influence the effectiveness of interventions, whether in a groupwork or one-to-one setting.

General research into effective interventions should not be ignored when working with women offenders. Indeed, responsivity is a fundamental principle of the effective practice agenda alongside the emphasis upon offence-focused work (Andrews and Bonta, 1994; Home Office, 1998).

Work with women offenders requires practitioners to take a detailed and multidimensional approach to responsivity, extending its application beyond simply the design and delivery of offence-focused programmes. Achieving a detailed understanding of individual pathways into crime, of the barriers to engagement and of appropriate routes into desistance requires active participation from the offender throughout.

The process has to be meaningful and inclusive if the content of interventions is to be effective and relevant. Furthermore, there are some recent and powerful arguments about the need to reclaim the community dimension and pay more attention to the social and personal circumstances which influence individuals. This is a prerequisite of effective work with women offenders at whatever stage they find themselves in the criminal justice system.

FOUR

Young people who offend

Introduction

Offending is often associated with younger members of the community, predominantly young adults (McNeill and Batchelor, 2004). Much of the original research into 'What Works' was conducted upon cohorts of male offenders between the ages of 17 and 21 (Roberts, 1989; Andrews et al, 1990; Lipsey, 1992). Evidence-based practice, therefore, started with young offenders, and those age-specific principles have, ironically, been applied widely across the adult offender population.

In this chapter youth will be loosely defined as young people between the ages of 10 (the age of criminal responsibility) and 21 (the point at which young offenders formally enter the adult prison system), the main emphasis being upon work with those in the middle of this age range.

The peak age of offending in 2000 was 15 for women and 18 for men. Rates of offending begin to decline significantly after the age of 25. By 35 people are less likely to be found guilty of, or cautioned for, indictable offences (National Statistics Online, 2006).

This statistical 'bulge' in offending provokes questions about how far young people *per se* are prone to delinquency or, conversely, how far the way society treats its young people criminalises behaviour which is sometimes part of the process of individuation to 'grow into' adulthood. Other questions that arise include why and how youth and crime are associated, how to work within formal organisational frameworks with individuals who are often particularly prey to uncertainty and disorganisation, and how to accommodate the multiple needs of young people whilst retaining a focus on their offending behaviour. These questions are relevant not simply to those who work within the formal youth justice system, but to anyone working with offenders where their youth and maturity is an issue.

In this chapter the focus is upon the challenge for practitioners of understanding and addressing the fluid dynamics, the mercurial nature, of a young person's journey from adolescence to adulthood.

Consequently, the chapter is not specifically about how to work with young offenders as defined by statute (for example in the 1998 Crime and Disorder Act), or about the system within which that work takes place, although there is considerable contemporary debate about both (see Smith, 2003; Squires and Stephen, 2005; Goldson and Muncie, 2006). It is clear, however, from this debate, relevant research (Barrow Cadbury Trust, 2005) and commentary (Burnett and Roberts, 2004; Muncie, 2004) that the history of work with young people who offend exemplifies some of the key practice issues, described in Chapter Two, that are addressed in this book, namely the need to balance:

- risks and needs;
- control and care;
- punishment and treatment;
- actuarial, technical approaches and dynamic personal engagement.

Arguably, these issues flow from the tension between 'freedom' versus 'control' or liberalism versus authoritarianism (see also Pickford, 2000; Newburn, 2002; Muncie, 2004; Fionda, 2005).

The balancing act takes place against a backdrop of the diversity of individual young people's experiences as well as the risk factors they share. The authors will seek to explore youth, both as a lens through which to view and understand the interrelationships between dynamic risk factors influencing offending behaviour and as an aspect of responsivity which should shape how interventions are designed and delivered. They will encourage practice which is youth-aware, informed by an understanding of:

- adolescent and development issues as they can relate to offending and as captured by the concept of the criminal career;
- the complexity of needs often associated with offending by young people, using as a basis for discussion a research-based practical framework for holistic assessment;
- the significance of maturity in terms of key life transitions and the development of influential attitudes and values.

Whilst policy makers and commentators may occupy definitive, and often opposing, positions along liberal–authoritarian, care–control spectrums, the practitioner needs to steer a more balanced and measured course. This is based upon a detailed, rounded understanding of specific behaviour and the context in which it takes place. This understanding then informs responses which are youth-appropriate.

The chapter will consider briefly the historical, philosophical and organisational contexts which provide the setting for face-to-face work and reflect upon some links between age and specific types of offences. It will then go on to focus on the two key aspects of practice:

- **Assessment** informed by adolescent and development issues. This will take into account maturity, the stage the individual is at in terms of his or her offending career, and the range of influences which have shaped behaviour. Some potentially helpful theoretical or research-based approaches to assessment will be considered.
- **Interventions** which respond to the complexity of young people's needs and seek to balance appropriately the elements described earlier.

Youth and crime: historical, philosophical and organisational perspectives

Newburn (2002: 533) observes that the history of youth justice has been one of "competing philosophies, approaches and ideologies".

This history has been described (Pickford, 2000; Muncie, 2004; Fionda, 2005) and key themes widely debated as responses to youth crime have developed over the past quarter-century. Such themes include:

- The difficulty of defining the parameters of youth (Barrow Cadbury Trust, 2005).
- The consequent difficulty of ascribing responsibility for young offenders and unhelpful "inter-agency conflicts and rivalries" (Muncie, 2004: 269).
- An emerging consensus that multi-agency approaches are more likely to be able to meet the complex needs of young people (Audit Commission, 1996).
- The belief that multi-agency teams, taking a coherent, coordinated and holistic approach to services, would help to "fuse the justice and welfare approaches" (Pickford, 2000: xxxvii).

The culmination of research and debate, especially in the political arena, was the 1998 Crime and Disorder Act. As well as leading to the redesign of the youth justice system, placing at the heart of it multi-agency YOTs, it also formally drew the line between child/youth-focused and adult-focused services at age 18.

The justice system now treats everyone 18 and over as adults, but "some people mature earlier than others and nearly everyone matures at different times in different stages of their lives" and "the transition to adulthood is variable and dependent upon a wide range of circumstance peculiar to each young person" (Barrow Cadbury Trust, 2005: 9–11).

This difficulty of pinning down when children can be considered fully formed adults is reflected in how society grants its rights and responsibilities. Between the ages of 15 and 25, in contemporary Britain, individuals are gradually accorded a range of rights and responsibilities associated with becoming an adult (Muncie, 2004).

The range and number of responsibilities represented in legislation implies an expectation of young people that they make a major shift from dependence and subservience to independence and autonomy during this period. This shift is staged and not confined to a specific moment in time. Over several years, they become increasingly responsible for their own welfare and decision making. This significant but prolonged shift, or transition, coincides with higher volumes of offending within that age group and has been described as an 'age–crime' curve (Home Office, 1998b). Successfully managing transitions, becoming a 'grown-up', may be associated with increasing desistance from crime. What Melrose (2004) describes as 'fractured' transitions can be linked to problems such as substance use. Melrose's work is discussed in more detail in Chapter Seven.

Not only is the notion of youth difficult to squeeze into crude age-delineated parameters, but the formal parameters themselves have been influenced by an ongoing tension in society's views on why young people offend. This tension is often described by writers in particularly evocative language. Are young offenders "devils or angels" (Fionda, 2005), "deprived or depraved" (Muncie, 2004: 49), "artful dodgers or feral youth" (Shore, 2006)? Shore's description of the tension also captures the sense that society has always been worried about its young people, at least for the past 150 years. *Oliver Twist* alone bears witness to that (Dickens, 1838). Adults, parents or professionals, strive to provide young people with "the freedom to fulfil their potential" alongside enough "control to instil discipline" (Newburn, 2002: 533).

As in any adult–child relationship, society can swing between the liberal and disciplinarian approaches, or try to be both at the same time. For some the redesigned youth justice system was a distinct shift towards the disciplinarian, bringing "tougher social discipline ... rather than more broadly preventive social policies" (Squires and Stephen, 2005: 17). Three key points emerge from this discussion:

- The boundaries of youth are hard to define universally.
- Offending behaviour and significant life transitions appear to coincide.
- Legalistic approaches to addressing youth offending neither fit easily with the fluidity of 'growing up', nor with the variety of philosophical beliefs society has held about young people and how to help them mature.

Debates about appropriate responses to youth and crime have tended to focus upon the organisational (the law and the system) and the technical (the benefits or pitfalls of actuarial tools and evidence-based programmes). Increasingly, however, the debate has begun to include the quality of relationships in relation to enhancing effectiveness (McNeill, 2006). Eadie and Canton (2002) suggest that it is the interpretation by individual practitioners of some of the formal requirements of the system, such as assessment tools, which determine whether they become managerialist in impact, driving and constraining the process, or whether they usefully enhance professional practice, with all the skills and knowledge that this implies.

The individual practitioner is at the interface between the offender and the 'system'. They have the responsibility of ensuring that, within the broad legal framework of accountability, young people are treated not simply on the basis of their age, but in a manner which recognises that "appropriate responses ... will vary with an individual's maturity and particular circumstances" (Barrow Cadbury Trust, 2005: 13).

Age and crime: statistical perspectives

A self-report study by East and Campbell (2000: 12) demonstrates that broad figures showing "the prevalence of offending by age conceals differences between age groups as to the nature of offending: the types of offences committed by a young teenager are different from those committed by someone in their late 20s". They identify some of these differences (2000: 12-13), in relation to young male offenders:

- Comparatively high rates of offending among 14- to 15-year-olds reflected their involvement in fights, buying and selling stolen goods, theft and criminal damage.
- By 17, property-related offending was declining and fighting increasing.

- In the 18–21 age band fighting increased significantly, theft declined but buying and selling stolen goods increased and fraud and workplace theft began to be significant.
- Post–21 there was a marked decline in all offending and a particularly sharp fall in criminal damage and violence.

These differences raise a number of issues. There may be some correlation between the opportunities open to young people at different stages, or in the social contexts within which they move. The patterns relating to violence may also point to particularly stress-inducing times in the transition from childhood to adolescence, and then from adolescence to adulthood. At such times young people appear to be both more reliant on relationships outside the family, as well as posing more of a risk to others by virtue of increased anxiety, aggression or recklessness within those relationships. They may also be more at risk of self-harm and suicide (see Chapter Six which explores this in detail). Finally, the purpose of the offending behaviour and the dynamic risk factors which influence it may differ at different developmental stages (for example, the changes in patterns of violent behaviour described above).

If particular types of offences are considered more closely, there are further differences in behaviour across the age range. For example, different types of vehicle crime seem to be associated with younger offenders. Research (Home Office, 1993) has suggested that aggravated vehicle taking is predominantly an offence of the under–21s, with the peak age being 15–18, the period during which young people are seeking greater mobility and independence, whilst still being too young to drive legally. In contrast, targeted car theft seems to be the province of the over 18s and can continue after the age of 25. These findings tend to confirm an association between age and types of offences.

The precise nature of the association between factors associated with age, the process of maturing and offending behaviour is an important element of any assessment of a young person. Factors which are highlighted as particularly relevant during this 'ageing' process may include changing family and personal relationships, education and employment opportunities, and the developing sense of identity (see discussions in McNeill and Batchelor, 2004; Barrow Cadbury Trust, 2005). How these factors reinforce each other, and how directly they influence particular behaviour in a specific context, are key questions to be addressed in any comprehensive assessment of a young offender. The question becomes more intricate still in relation to Black and

Minority Ethnic young people, and assessment would need to recognise some of the complexities explored in Chapter Five.

Activities and reflection 4.1

Consider a young person (between the ages of 10 and 21) with whom you are working or whom you know personally:

- What did he/she do?
- Where is he/she in terms of 'growing up'?
- Is he/she experiencing any problems relating to changes in responsibilities, expectations or circumstances which may be connected with his/her age?
- How do the answers to any of these questions help your understanding of his/her behaviour, positive or negative?

Assessment

The aim of the assessment of young people who offend is to understand their offending behaviour in the context of:

- their age, maturity and the implications of both for what is expected of them and how they rise to these expectations;
- their lifestyle and opportunities;
- the "diverse array of economic and cultural realities" (Muncie, 2004: 42) which shape both their attitudes and their opportunities. These will include the impact of race, gender, sexuality and disabilities upon an individual's life experience.

The quality of the assessment will be dependent upon the practitioner's understanding of the youth dimension. Jenkins (1998), writing about engaging with young people who sexually abuse, stressed the importance of collaborative, interactive and motivational methods.

Motivational interviewing techniques (Miller and Rollnick, 2002) can be useful here, particularly the principle of empathy, which captures the importance of recognising and accepting the "individualised meaning" (Muncie, 2004: 42) that the young person attaches to his or her life and behaviour. The practitioner will aim to draw out the individual's story, as it has meaning for him or her, and avoid imposing an adult, impersonal, 'professional' interpretation too early in the process.

Young people's lives are complex in terms of experiences, relationships, emotional intelligence and self-knowledge, particularly at key developmental and transitional stages. They are likely to have a variety of shifting networks with the world outside the family, with whom ties are consequently loosening: friends, teachers, employers and social groups. Dynamic risk factors will neither be constant nor unchanging (see Day et al, 2004). Assessment needs to recognise:

> ... how critical and significant the private elements in ... individuals' lives are, the emotional roller coaster they are going through, issues about forming and breaking relationships, certain kinds of health issues ... issues to do with their wider families at particular moments. (Williamson, 2005: 2)

In this context, assessors will need to:

- Draw out the detail of the story of the offence – the criminal event.
- Look beyond the offence to embrace the individual's whole life experience and consider how this either reinforces offending patterns or has the potential to promote desistance – the big picture.
- Try to determine how well established the pattern of offending is and how integral it is to the life of the individual.
- Analyse and make judgements through the lens of what is known about adolescent development, the journey from childhood to adulthood.

The outcome will be an understanding of how individuals develop modes of interacting with the world, and how integral to these interactions are offending patterns of thinking and behaviour. Frameworks offered here emphasise the interactive and dynamic patterns of influence which are a particular feature of 'growing up'.

The first framework for *offence-focused assessment* is described in Chapter Three and focuses upon *the criminal event*. The notion of a journey also conveys the sense of an individual story. The framework is easily adapted to be a creative and visual way of helping the young person describe and make sense of his or her behaviour. Used alongside the searching questions which are described in Chapter Ten, it could provide the multidimensional understanding of the offence which should be at the heart of the assessment. The framework gives clues about key external and internal influences upon the individual, as well as suggesting important patterns of thinking and responding to the outside world.

The wider key influences upon a young person who offends, *the bigger picture*, can be broadly defined under four headings:

- past experience and history which can increase his or her vulnerability to offending choices/opportunities;
- the community in which the individual lives;
- his or her immediate social circle and lifestyle;
- his or her internal world.

Figure 4.1 breaks down these four domains of influence even further. The diagram was designed initially to show the core components of the Asset assessment tool for young people who offend (Baker et al, 2002). It is also a powerful image of the complex network of influences which may result in offending behaviour in its own right. It represents the most important dynamic influences (changing and changeable) that research has indicated could affect young people for the worse (risk factors) or the better (protective factors). It also incorporates the static

Figure 4.1: A framework for the holistic assessment of young people who offend

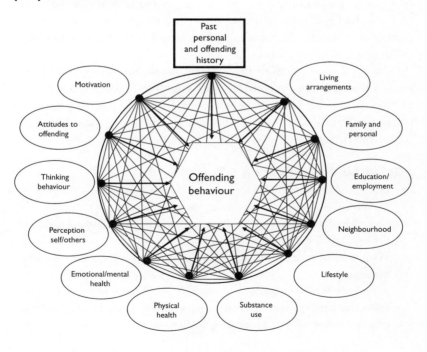

Source: Adapted from, and printed with the permission of, Baker et al (2002)

factors (past and unchangeable) which might increase an individual's statistical vulnerability to future offending. The framework is offered here as a format for a multifaceted assessment that is particularly appropriate to young people.

The shape of the framework reminds the practitioner that:

- assessment should be rounded and holistic;
- some factors are more important than others (the bold arrows);
- factors interact with each other creating a web of complex relationships of which even the individual is unaware (the spider's web of fine lines).

For example, a young person may steal from local shops both because of a need for money, linked to the family's financial status, and because of being influenced by friends. The individual's choice of friends may in turn be affected by being unemployed or excluded from school. Neither the family situation nor the exclusion from work or education is likely, in itself, to lead directly to the offending. In combination, however, with the influence of peers and particular patterns of thinking and behaviour, they are likely to have a significant, reinforcing effect. In this case the assessor needs to gather information about the range of individual risk factors, but to do so "in a way that is also alert to connections, inter-relationships and the strength of links to offending" (YJB, 2003: 31).

Figure 4.2 is a version of the original assessment framework. It has been adapted to be jargon-free and visually accessible to a young person. It can be used creatively to engage the young person in unravelling the 'spider's web' of influences which may have led to his or her offending.

Activities and reflection 4.2

- In an assessment meeting with a young person, try using the child-friendly framework as a basis for your conversation.
- Record your information on the framework and mark the interconnections between influences.
- What are the most important areas to work on to address the offending behaviour?
- What aspects of the individual's life, possibly linked to his or her welfare or safety, also need attention to create a more positive context, supporting any offence-focused work and promoting desistance?

Figure 4.2: A child-friendly assessment framework

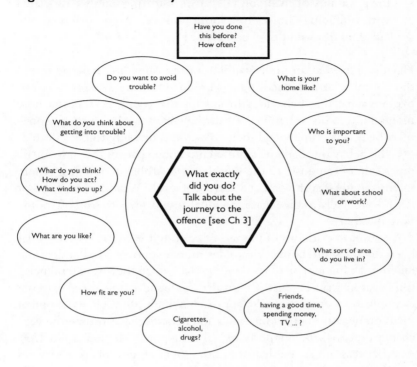

Source: Callahan et al (2004: 37)

Taking a more holistic approach, going beyond the offending focus, may also remind the practitioner of less problematic aspects of an individual's life, the positive or protective factors which can be overlooked. These factors, which have been linked to the development of resilience (Rutter et al, 1998), are important aspects of assessment since they can give the promise of positive growth and support desistance. By identifying and developing positive aspects of an individual's life the practitioner may be contributing to:

- a reduction in the sensitivity to risk through increasing ability to resist offending choices and the influence of others;
- a reduction of risk impact by increasing potential alternative sources of protection such as improved parental supervision;
- reduced negative and increased positive interactions;
- promotion of self-esteem and self-efficacy;

- the possibility of changing a negative, distorting mindset associated with offending choices to a more positive, change-oriented one (adapted from Rutter et al, 1998: 211).

Having arrived at an understanding of the offending behaviour and the complex of influences which produced it, the assessor needs to explore what that behaviour means for the young person and how integral it is to his or her life. Was the behaviour a 'blip', a chance one-off which, with timely and focused work, is unlikely to be repeated? Has the behaviour become a more entrenched part of the individual's repertoire of responses to the world and its problems, requiring more intense and in-depth work at a variety of levels? What aspects of his or her life are likely to give that individual an incentive to stop offending now, or later?

A common criticism of the use of custody for young offenders has been that they often mix with older more experienced offenders and emerge at a higher risk of reoffending than when they were sentenced. One reason may be that a custodial sentence is the most extreme example of a correctionalist approach which, through its "implicit focus on negative behaviours, risks and deficits, may frustrate the very change process that ... [it purports] ... to support" (McNeill, 2006: 133). Another reason may be that, as Smith (2006) argues, 'blanket' services to offenders have tended to abandon the 'risk principle' propounded in the early days of the 'What Works' project, that is that the intensity of interventions should be proportionate to the identified risk of reoffending (Andrews et al, 1990). In other words, when seeking to work with young people it is important to understand where they are in terms of the development of their offending behaviour and to try to avoid treating the experienced and inexperienced offender in similar ways.

The concept of a **criminal career** is a reminder that patterns of dynamic risk factors and associated behaviour can change over the life history of an offender. The criminal career recognises the significance of the process of desistance and highlights the need for practitioners to understand why people stop offending, as well as the risk factors that maintain their offending. The most significant study, the Cambridge Study in Delinquent Development 1961–81, involved tracking a birth cohort's criminal activity from the 1960s through to the turn of the century. The study has generated extensive literature on the implications of the criminal career (West and Farrington, 1977; Farrington, 1996, 1997). There is debate both about the methodology of the research and the conclusions that it reached. Muncie (2004: 27) summarises the main concern about the study in terms of the narrowness of its focus on "lower-class criminality", upon officially recorded crime and on the individual rather than the "extent, causes and meaning of offending *per se*". These criticisms need not undermine the usefulness of the concept for practitioners. The criminal career provides a paradigm which emphasises the need to unravel how different factors influence individuals at different stages in the course of their offending life.

McGuire (2001) uses the concept to explore the development of car crime careers. His analysis is useful for understanding the potential influences on a young person involved in car crime. **Onset factors** are factors which increase a young person's susceptibility to offending choices and may be linked to early offending incidents. With respect to car crime these often include peer pressure, the need to be 'one of the crowd', risk-taking or trying things out, excitement, in the absence of other leisure activities, and status issues. At the outset stage car theft is often expressive. The thrill may be crucial.

Offenders may have been around car theft for some time as onlookers or 'apprentices', learning how to get into cars and perhaps 'allowing themselves to be carried'. Theft of cars requires certain technical skills or mechanical knowledge. It might be useful to understand where and how these were first acquired. Financial gain is unlikely to be a common motive, except perhaps when items are stolen from cars. In those instances offenders would also require 'know-how' in selling goods on. At this stage, timely intervention by the courts and practitioners

Figure 4.3: The criminal career

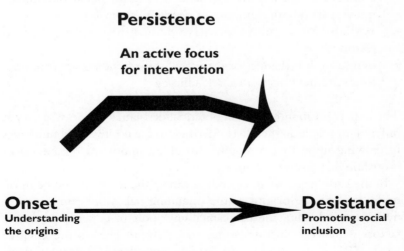

Persistence

**An active focus
for intervention**

Onset
**Understanding
the origins**

Desistance
**Promoting social
inclusion**

Source: Adapted from YJB (2003: 22)

may be enough to prevent the new behaviour becoming habitual and integral to the individual's life and indeed their own view of that life. Other research (Home Office, 1993) has also suggested that the earlier an individual starts car offending the more likely he (it is most commonly 'he') is to continue after the age of 25.

Persistence factors relate more to the purpose that the offending has come to fulfil over time and will form the basis of offence-focused interventions. Consider the 15-year-old 'joyrider' for whom this activity has become the main source of excitement, self-expression and social contact. He is likely to offend repeatedly and probably indiscriminately. His purpose is not to steal the best car, but the one that is most accessible. Sometimes the persistent behaviour evolves to such an extent that the young offender continues into adulthood, becoming life-course persistent. His motivation is likely to become less about excitement, and more functional in terms of mobility, gain or supporting other offending. Recent research associated with the earlier Cambridge Study (Farrington et al, 2006) suggests that there are few car thieves over the age of 25, but many who drive whilst disqualified or irresponsibly in terms of their consumption of alcohol and lack of concern for other road users.

Other (indeed most) offenders mature, giving up offending as one of the aspects of their 'growing up' or coming of age. Only 7% of the Cambridge cohort went on to become 'chronic' offenders for example (Farrington et al, 2006: v). The majority will have moved towards *desistance* for a number of individual reasons which could include:

- awareness of the negative consequences of the behaviour, for the individual and other important people in their lives;
- availability of more positive friendships and personal relationships;
- significant life changes or increased non-offending opportunities for excitement or positive self-efficacy.

The impact on an individual of potential desistance factors will vary at different moments in their lives. Alertness to the positives and timeliness in drawing upon their strengths can be an important dimension of motivating a person to change.

In the early stages of an offending career, the focus should be upon understanding the origins of the offending behaviour and diversion from future offending through capitalising upon the potential protective factors which can encourage desistance. Approaches to preventative work with young people are largely aimed at developing these protective or positive factors which can constitute incentives to refrain from offending behaviour. Debates about the ethics of the preventative agenda (for example, Squires and Stephen, 2005) are beyond the scope of this book. However, the positive emphasis of preventative approaches can be incorporated into face-to-face work with young people who have offended. They can be an antidote to the potentially negative focus of a predominantly offence-focused approach where the emphasis may be on risk reduction or management as opposed to developing the foundations for a positive future (Ward and Brown, 2004).

Persistent offending behaviour requires more intense attention to the meaning of the behaviour for the individual: the attitudes, circumstances and skills which sustain the behaviour, alongside the identification and development of protective factors. The latter will both reinforce change and form the basis of future desistance.

Whilst the concept of the criminal career is not to be confused with either the age of the individual or the stage that he or she is at in the criminal justice system, there is a sense that criminal careers are 'adolescence-limited' and tend to fall off during the mid-20s, with the exception of those who are described as 'life-course persistent' (Moffitt, 1993; Rutter et al, 1998). Maturity, in terms of both thinking and behaviour, may influence both how an individual becomes involved in the offending and whether he or she persists or is susceptible to timely interventions which encourage desistance.

Activities and reflection 4.3

Persistent offending behaviour is not dissimilar to a 'bad habit'. Think about one of your own bad habits (smoking, speeding, watching too much television, etc.):

- How did it start (onset factors)?
- What keeps you doing it (persistence factors)?
- What might have helped you stop early on?
- What might help you stop now (interventions)?
- What would motivate you to keep stopping (desistance factors)?
  (YJB, 2004)

The complex issue of *maturity* is a thread which runs through the comprehensive understanding of an individual's behaviour. The volume of rights and responsibilities accorded to young people over a 10-year period has been described earlier. How individuals assume or respond to them is a more complicated, individual process. It is not within the scope of this book to explore the vast literature about child and adolescent development. However, it is worth considering briefly the concept of moral development which is often associated with cognitive behavioural interventions (see, for example, Goldstein, 1999) and is a helpful framework within which to consider the maturity of individuals, at least in terms of their attitudes and thought processes.

The stages of moral development considered here were originally conceived by Kohlberg (1958, 1973) to explain the evolution of moral reasoning. His thinking was inspired by the work of Jean Piaget (Jean Piaget Archives Foundation, 1989). Kohlberg's theory holds that moral reasoning, which is the basis for ethical behaviour, has six identifiable developmental stages and that the process of moral development continues throughout the lifespan. It is not restricted to childhood or adolescence.

Interestingly, in undertaking his initial research, Kohlberg (1958) used moral dilemmas to determine which stage of moral reasoning an individual was using. This methodology is adapted by designers of cognitive behavioural programmes, who use the idea of applied moral dilemmas to explore how young people relate morally to their world and then help them develop what Goldstein (1999: 1) has called "pro-social competencies". Essentially, Kohlberg's stages of moral development have been adapted for practical application by a number of writers of programmes for use with young people (Goldstein, 1999) and, more specifically, young people who offend (Callahan et al, 2004). The stages are summarised here, with some practical examples, to give clues as to the level at which the individual is operating:

- Stage one (obedience): 'You do as you are told. If you don't you get punished'.
- Stage two (self-interest): 'What's in it for me?'.
- Stage three (conformity): 'If I do this other people will like or respect me'.
- Stage four (law and order): 'Rules are important, they help you judge who is good and who is bad. If I break the law then everyone else could have the right to break the law'.
- Stage five (human rights): 'The law represents our rules for living together so it is important to respect that'.
- Stage six (universal human ethics): 'While we should keep to the law, it is more important to uphold important principles like the importance of individual human life' (Goldstein, 1999; Callahan et al, 2004).

The first two stages are associated with childhood, dependence upon others and concrete external regulation; stages three and four are linked to the development of wider mutually supportive relationships, awareness of society and emerging independence of attitudes and beliefs; the last two stages involve a more abstract focus upon personal values, opinions and ethics. Whilst the detail of Kohlberg's work has attracted criticism as to its cross-cultural or gender appropriateness (Gilligan, 1982), for the practitioner his broad stages may give clues as to the intellectual or moral maturity of an individual young person.

If, for example, a young person of whatever age is significantly influenced by 'mates' and highly sensitive to what they think of him or her, their opinions may 'bend with the wind' in difficult situations (stage three). Thus, whilst it might be appropriate to help this individual to find a more pro-social group of friends, he or she may also need help in exploring beliefs and attitudes and developing independent 'rules for life'. As individuals move towards maturity (broadly, beyond Kohlberg's stage four), their journey is from the predominantly self-centred to a more other-centred way of perceiving and operating in the world. Of course that journey will be influenced by a range of life experiences, family circumstances, cultural disadvantages, inequalities of opportunities, acquisition of skills, educational attainment and intellectual abilities. It is the interplay between the developing interior world of the individual, the circumstances of their lives and the processes which bind the whole together which is the focus of assessment. The assessor will seek to "unravel different forms of criminality, the expressive and the instrumental" and to understand why "different types of behaviour [are] engaged in at different times" (Williamson, 2005: 2).

Practice tool 4.1

The following are the key elements of assessment.

A youth-aware assessor will need to reach an understanding of:
- *The event* – the detail of what was done (the journey to the offence).
- *The network of influences* (positive and negative) upon the individual in relation to his/her specific offence, patterns of other behaviour and the 'shape' of his/her life experience (the holistic assessment in Figures 4.1 and 4.2).
- *The meaning of the offending* and *how long* it has been a part of his/her life. How experienced are they in their offending? (Think about the ideas represented by the criminal career.)

> • *The individual's attitude to his/her behaviour:* why do they think that they committed the offence? (In listening to their answers refer back to the practical summary of Kohlberg's stages of moral development.)
> • Any wider *transitional issues.*

Interventions

Some young offenders will benefit from the multi-agency approach of YOTs, which aims to address offending behaviour within the context of a holistic assessment. This can also form the basis of referral to appropriate mainstream welfare services. Other offenders could, however, find themselves from the age of 18 in adult offending services where they are no longer treated as a discrete group and the level of support available to those under 18 drops away.

The content of offence-focused work in both settings tends to follow similar principles. These have been embodied in the Youth Justice Board's approach to effective practice as well as extensively applied in the Probation Service's accredited programmes. For young people it is how interventions are delivered, the methods and context, which matters, along with the attention that is paid to the influences which continue to shape their lives into adulthood. Williamson (2005: 13) suggests that practitioners should be "critical people at critical moments".

Broadly speaking, a youth-informed assessment will alert the practitioner to potential barriers to engagement in terms of maturity of thinking, literacy skills and lifestyle issues, all of which should influence how, where and when work is undertaken. Of even greater significance to young people is the nature of their relationship with the practitioner. A report by the Social Exclusion Unit (ODPM, 2005) identified four strands to effective interventions with young people:

• a holistic approach;
• the significance of a 'trusted' adult;
• needs- as opposed to age-focused services;
• skills development (thinking and practical).

These coincide with the types of interventions which would flow from the youth-informed assessment described above.

The Social Exclusion Unit report went on to highlight the characteristics that young adults considered most valuable in a worker (ODPM, 2005: 10):

- being fair and transparent, employing appropriate sanctions and incentives;
- continuity of support;
- being able to prioritise and meet the most immediate needs first;
- knowledge and experience;
- looking at the whole picture.

These characteristics are also similar to those encapsulated in the case management model described by Holt (2000), a model that is particularly apt in work with individuals experiencing multiple needs. This model is discussed in detail in Chapter Ten.

Such a case management model can operate in multi-agency teams and in settings where services need to be accessed from agencies external to the team. It can carry within it the individual young person's narrative of change, as they move through a range of targeted programmes and activities, and bind together the whole journey of supervision. It will build individual skills and knowledge or 'human capital' as well as developing more positive social and economic relationships – 'social capital' (McNeill and Batchelor, 2004; see also the discussion about these concepts in Chapter Eight).

McNeill and Batchelor (2002, 2004) emphasise the significance of the quality of the worker–offender relationship. They suggest that the worker needs to "sensitively and thoughtfully *individualise* the change process" (2004: 68), pointing to ways in which practitioners can promote change through their own professional behaviour:

- Building a belief in the offender that change is possible and sustaining that belief during interventions.
- Understanding the switching and vacillating nature (Burnett, 2000) of desistance from offending and being alert to small opportunities to support desistance.
- Providing active and participatory supervision in which offenders have a sense of being involved in setting goals, and then work jointly towards them, being clear about roles and responsibilities.
- Providing practical support and guidance and involving the offenders in problem solving.
- Demonstrating interest in the well-being of offenders and giving focused reinforcement and praise (Rex and Crosland, 1999).

These aspects of the practitioner's relationship are reflected in the methods encompassed by pro-social modelling which has been shown to be effective in preventing offending behaviour (Rex, 1997;

Trotter, 1999; Cherry, 2005). Research into effective relationships in juvenile secure establishments also reinforced the significance of the worker–offender relationship (Smith et al, 2000), highlighting the values which are important to young people in a practitioner: transparency, consistency, fairness, equality of access and achievability.

All of this implies the need for a collaborative approach which is young-person-centred with clear and realistic expectations and boundaries and which helps individuals navigate potentially difficult transitions by recognising, exploiting and developing "their competences, resources, skills and assets" (McNeill, 2006: 134).

Understanding the 'drivers' of behaviour (persistence factors) and the incentives for change (desistance factors) are two key aspects of assessing motivation. In exploring these influences practitioners could usefully use some of the motivational approaches discussed in Chapter Seven, with their emphasis upon exploring the meaning of behaviour, ambivalence and reluctance to change, and the need for small but manageable steps to change, clearly signposted and flagged up.

The notion of SMART targets (targets that are Specific, Measurable, Achievable, Realistic and Time-limited) is well-rehearsed in effective practice literature. The idea may be very familiar but it remains a useful way of simplifying (but not oversimplifying) and making accessible and understandable the work that needs to be done to achieve change. Furthermore, young people are more likely to engage with these targets if they have the characteristics of positively oriented goals (Ward et al, 2006). Such goals promote the development of 'human capital', personal attributes and skills alongside, or even instead of, goals which seek to contain, avoid or reduce risk or to focus specifically upon offence-related risk factors.

In the light of these considerations targets for young people need to be:

- specific to them and expressed in clear, understandable language;
- achievable in small measurable 'bites' giving a sense of increased self-efficacy;
- framed in positive terms, focusing where possible upon increasing the skills of self-risk management rather than simple risk reduction;
- relevant to their circumstances, reinforcing positives or even using positives as a medium for change;
- short-term steps to a long-term end.

With a holistic case management approach, it should be possible for the practitioner to identify with the young person targets that address attitudes associated with their offending, but framed in such a way as to take account of the context in which that behaviour takes place.

Consider, for example, a young person who is disengaged from education or employment by poor basic skills, highly reliant on and influenced by an offending peer group and who solves his or her related problems (no money, increasing substance use) through shoplifting, which seems the only option. This type of theft is also relatively acceptable as a 'victimless' crime. A short-term offence-focused target might be for the young offenders to be able to describe the consequences for themselves and other people of their offending. This might be the first step in motivating them to change their behaviour, identify more appropriate ways of solving their problems and, most importantly, acquire the skills to do so. The methods that could be employed might include the use of a mentor (thereby also addressing some of the relationship issues), or formal offence-focused programmes adapted to the literacy needs or maturity of the individual. Three things are important here:

- the case manager retains an overall vision of where the work is going (the ultimate goal);
- offence-focused interventions will be connected to the wider life experience of the young person;
- the 'small steps' will be part of a cumulative and sequenced process.

Wilkinson et al (2002) have explored the key features of the youth-aware practitioner and highlighted what have been the essential themes of this chapter. Some of the conclusions are encapsulated in a final practice tool; a quality checklist to test out the responsivity of work with young people.

Practice tool 4.2

A. In *assessing* young people, practitioners will:
- *Be aware of young people's perceptions, drawing out their individual stories.* How will you achieve this? What methods or skills will you employ?

- *Communicate in a way that is appropriate to young people, using creative and interactive methods.* How will you (without condescension) make a point of checking that the young person understands your discourse and idiom (and you theirs)? Will the atmosphere you create be likely to encourage a sense of worth or appear intimidating? How will you avoid jargon? How will you make your meaning plain? How will you make your active listening evident?

- *Have clear values and a purpose which are transparent and fair.* How will you convey your values and responsibilities? Are boundaries and expectations clear?

B. In their *interventions*, they will:
- *Model problem-solving.* How will you use systematic methods which seek to understand and unravel, rather than complicate?
- *Be solution-focused and encourage small steps towards change.* How will you set precise, relevant and understandable targets? How will you know that the young person understands them? How will you involve this individual in setting targets?
- *Give consistent feedback about behaviour.* How will you make time to review progress? How will you be specific in your observations about behaviour? How will you make your judgements appear transparent and fair?

C. In their *relationship* with the young person, they will be:
- *Open, active, optimistic and realistic, retaining a focus upon the positive factors which promote desistance as well as designing interventions which appropriately challenge offending behaviour (a tall order and not a counsel to perfection).* How will you find out how the young person experiences his/her working relationship with you?

Conclusion

The youth-aware approach promoted by this chapter embodies principles which have relevance to work with offenders across the age range, but particularly those who are entering adulthood. Each offender will have a unique story, representing a particular complexity of needs, influences and life experiences. Responsivity requires the practitioner to draw out the detail of these individual stories to ensure that, as far as possible, there is a "fit between the services offered and the abilities of [individuals] to engage with those services" (YJB, 2003: 59). The implication in terms of designing programmes of intervention is that, although there may be some core theoretical and research perspectives which shape responses to crime at a general level, practitioners will need to work creatively to adapt interventions to make them relevant, challenging and positive experiences for individual offenders. The aim is, as Goldstein asserts in his introduction to a programme for young people (1999: 12), to "maximise the likelihood that [individuals] will be adequately motivated to attend and benefit from [interventions] that their resistance to doing so will be minimised, and that the lessons they learn will endure and be available for future use in a wide range of real-world settings".

FIVE

'Race' and culture

Introduction

Making a risk assessment about an offender requires the assessor to gather information about potential risk factors and to think about how those factors interact with each other, and with the behaviour of concern (Baker, 2006). As considered in Chapter Two, risk factors are based on findings about groups of offenders; being those variables that have been found to be associated with the likelihood of offending behaviour (McGuire, 2002b). The precise causal connections for any individual offender have to be considered for that individual in context (Kemshall et al, 2006). This process is not unproblematic because of the danger that, when considering offending behaviour, variables are wrongly ascribed causal status (Murji, 1999; Shaw and Hannah-Moffat, 2004), the substantive causes being ignored or underestimated.

Misattribution or oversimplification of the causes of offending behaviour are themes that influence the experiences of Black or Minority Ethnic offenders within the criminal justice system (Bowling and Phillips, 2002). This is not unique to these offenders, a misunderstanding of cause and effect is possible for any individual. Difficulties can be identified, for example, in work with women offenders and this was discussed in Chapter Three. Challenges to practitioners in making accurate and holistic assessments across 'race' and culture are, however, compounded by a number of influences, including lack of knowledge. "If little is known about women offenders, even less is understood about the qualitative differences between white and non-white offenders" (Shaw and Hannah-Moffat, 2004: 101).

Differences of 'race' and culture may also cause more anxiety and self-doubt in the practitioner than other areas of practice, to some extent because of those gaps in knowledge. Judgements are also being made in a politicised context. Again this is not unique to this aspect of practice; however, the social and political context around 'race' and culture is often heightened (Davis and Vennard, 2006).

Despite this, practice across difference in 'race' and culture has to retain clarity of purpose. The role of the practitioner fundamentally remains that of assessing risk and seeking to intervene in ways that minimise risk of reoffending and harm to others. A lack of knowledge does not just distort and limit understandings of risk factors, it also potentially affects responsivity (see Calverley et al, 2004).

The authors are not immune from doubt and write as White British women, influenced by their own 'race' and cultural backgrounds. Even writing that sentence gives pause for thought. The writers are not in the habit of thinking of themselves as having 'race'. This is a relatively modern concept that often carries with it beliefs that superficial physical features signify much more noteworthy differences. 'Race' as a signifier of difference is associated with classifications and hierarchies in society and with resulting power relationships (Hall, 2005). While the readers of this book would hopefully be committed to challenging racist assumptions, everyone is affected by them, not least by the 'taken for granted' way many of those of us who are White will view ourselves. This chapter reflects on how understandings of 'race', racism, culture and identity have changed and developed (Tizzard and Phoenix, 2002), and on how those differences remain highly significant for an individual's experiences, including their experiences of the criminal justice system. It is intended to encourage an open, but self-critical, discussion of work with offenders who have diverse patterns of 'race' and culture, by practitioners who themselves are diverse. It will have its own strengths and limitations. Similarly, each reader will bring with them their own identity and history and this will make a difference to how the chapter is read.

Two perspectives the authors hope will influence the reading of this chapter are:

- That racialised identities, that is, how 'race' and culture affect an individual's understanding of themselves and of their place in the world, are dynamic and changing over time (Bradley, 2003). Similarly, our knowledge and understandings are continually changing. Practitioners have to hold on to a principled and thoughtful response, while being willing to change and develop their own thinking and practice.
- Practitioners and offenders embody many differences. It is important for practitioners to see work across difference as an opportunity not a threat. Practitioners who are able to communicate effectively and with sensitivity are likely to have personal qualities and use skills that are important for good practice much more generally.

Challenges will be different for every practitioner because of their own backgrounds and experiences. All practitioners will face challenges, however, and this chapter seeks to help them think through their responses. The chapter considers the impact of language. Readers are asked to be reflective and critical in their acceptance of terminology, considering from the outset how they understand the terms being used and how the use of language affects understanding.

Throughout the chapter there will be a focus on identity or self-concept and how that is informed by differences in 'race' and culture (see McGuire, 2000; Tizzard and Phoenix, 2002; Bradley, 2003; Hall, 2005). There is also a consideration of the social and political context, where disadvantage and discrimination are associated with those differences (Modood and Berthaud, 1977). The chapter goes on to examine the implications for offending behaviour, drawing on a body of theory and research (see Bowling and Philips, 2002). This is then explored further in considering implications for practice.

This chapter can of course only 'dip a toe' in the water of understanding the range of potential differences that might underlie encounters between individuals in the criminal justice system and the range of discriminatory and potentially abusive behaviours that might be associated with those encounters. It seeks to explore some ways of thinking about those experiences that might be helpful. In doing so the suggestion is, as with other areas of practice but, perhaps, even more crucially here, that the practitioner requires self-awareness and an appreciation that they are part of the process they are seeking to analyse and understand. (See Chapter Three for a similar discussion about gender.)

Activities and reflection 5.1

Reflect on your own identity and how this might impact on your reading.

- Take a blank sheet of paper and write on it the two words 'I am' 20 times on 20 separate lines. Then complete each of those sentences, thinking about all the elements that go together to form your self-concept.
- Look back over the list and reflect on the origins of your ideas about yourself; what concepts have you drawn on, which elements are most important to you, which are fixed and which might change, which involve you in relationships with other people.
- Think about how this might influence you in reading further.
(Adapted from McGuire, 2000: 105)

Communicating and thinking clearly – the importance of language

Clarity of communication is essential both for the accurate assessment and management of risk and to support responsive relationships between practitioners and offenders. Debates over the use of language have seen groups of practitioners and of theorists taking up opposing positions. Over time language has played a significant part in helping to form, as well as reflecting, an appreciation of all of our experiences in living and working within an increasingly diverse community.

Tuklo Orenda Associates (1999) give extensive suggestions about the meaning of particular terms that help to navigate some of those sensitivities. They discuss, for example, the use of the term 'Black' as a political statement underlining the commonality of experience, most particularly racism, of African Caribbean and South Asians in British society. Dominelli (2006) reinforces the significant impact of racialised relationships that are normalised around ideas of superiority and domination. This use of the term 'Black' is in contrast to the use of it, in this chapter, as an indicator of individuals of African and African Caribbean descent. Although the authors have chosen to use 'Black' in this sense they remain aware that its use in a political sense is also important for many individuals, from a range of communities, seeking to face up to the impact of racism within British society.

It is essential whatever convention of language is adopted that the shared experiences among minority ethnic communities, in a predominantly White society, are recognised and that the impact of racism as the key to much of that commonality remains at the centre. It is, however, also important to acknowledge the diversity of experience within and between those communities, including their different experiences of racism, which is itself influenced by differences in social class and by gender (Durrance and Williams, 2003; Davis and Vennard, 2006).

The terms 'ethnicity' and 'minority ethnic groups' are used as terminology that is broader than 'race' describing differences in groups which both have a sense of themselves as a group and which are perceived externally as distinct (Bowling and Philips, 2002). This is not without its difficulties, however, in that ethnicity is often used as a substitute for 'race', while at the same time obscuring the impact of racism. It also tends to suggest that the only minorities are non-White and that only those non-White minorities have ethnicity, thus obscuring the importance of other cultural identities. White people also have ethnicity and it cannot be assumed that their ethnicity is unproblematic.

For example, minorities within the White majority such as the Irish and more recently the growing numbers of Eastern Europeans have problematic experiences within British society (Kushner, 2006).

'Race' and culture – the social and political context

Attention has been paid to the experience of Black and South Asian migrants, the impact of racism and disadvantage on that experience and the effect this has on their involvement in crime and with criminal justice agencies and processes. A consideration of Black and South Asian offending has often been politicised, with major attempts at understanding being made in response to incidents that have received significant attention in the media. The Scarman report (1981) in the wake of the Brixton riots is an example, highlighting as it did the impact of deprivation on minority communities. The Macpherson report (1999) into the death of Stephen Lawrence is another. These reports developed the concept of institutional racism:

> ... the collective failure of an organisation to provide an appropriate and professional service to people because of their colour, culture, or ethnic origin. It can be seen or detected in processes, attitudes and behaviour which amount to discrimination through unwitting prejudice, ignorance, thoughtlessness and racist stereotyping which disadvantage minority ethnic people. (Macpherson, 1999: 634)

This consideration of Black and South Asian involvement with the criminal justice system has taken place against a backdrop of political attention to immigration and to 'race' and, more recently, concern about the growth of international terrorism and the West's response to it. Within this political context, debate over the years about 'race', ethnicity and society has been characterised by a tendency to take up polarised positions. Crime has been no exception as it can be used to argue wider social and political positions. It has, for example, been considered that differences in rates of conviction are either because Black people are more likely to commit crime, or because they are unfairly treated by the criminal justice system. Such a polarisation can be unhelpful, distracting attention from the complexities both of offending and of the experience of living within this community as a member of a minority ethnic group.

An overemphasis on Black and South Asian offenders distracts attention from the experience of victimisation of these communities and individuals (Bowling and Phillips, 2002). The politicised context has also led to a drive for simple solutions to complex problems, a common experience for those working in criminal justice. Reports like Scarman (1981) and Macpherson (1999) have tended to be looked to for definitive answers, rather than regarded as contributions to a developing understanding.

Ethnic identity is multifaceted, ever developing, and both personal to the individual as well as influenced by society. When group identity is threatened, however, that sense of development is weakened and groups may respond by withdrawing from, or even attacking, others. These processes do not just affect minorities but are equally applicable to dominant groups (Hall, 2005). Ray et al (2002), investigating racially motivated offenders, suggested that a risk factor for this behaviour is the development of groups of excluded working-class White males who are uncertain of their own identity. They respond with violence towards other ethnic groups, whom they perceive as being to blame for their difficulties.

Focusing more explicitly on 'race' on the other hand helps to recognise the potential impact of racism, but also carries with it the danger of over-problematising Black and South Asian people. There is a danger that, in people's minds, 'race' becomes the obvious reason, or risk factor, for social disorder and other causes are ignored (Murji, 1999). If 'race' is viewed as problematic that view will influence the questions asked by research and therefore the nature of our developing knowledge (Barn, 2001).

Any individual, in this society, working with the diversity of offenders and communities, requires an accurate understanding of each person's culture, as well as of the impact of racialised perceptions and responses to that culture. Thinking about culture (including religion) helps to emphasise the variety within communities, including their positive attributes. An emphasis on culture can, however, divert attention from the ways in which perceptions of 'race' may still impact on how those cultures are treated by others. If understandings are simplistic, responses are likely to be so too, making it more difficult to analyse risk factors and to understand how to help individuals benefit from resulting interventions.

Modood and Berthaud (1997) discuss findings that suggest that the extent to which religion is central to self-definition in ethnic groups varies, with it being so for the majority of South Asian people. White people and those of Caribbean and Chinese origin are much less likely to have a religious affiliation. Within this broad picture there are, however, many individual variations and differences. The Home

Office Citizenship Survey (O'Beirne, 2004: xi) "indicates that religious affiliation and ethnicity are very closely inter-linked and therefore, both should be considered together rather than separately in policy and research work. It also indicates that religion is relevant to debates on socio-economic circumstances, self identity and discrimination". Macey (2001) suggests that some of what is interpreted as linked to the Muslim religion is actually reflecting particular forms of that religion, originating from particular geographical regions, for example, in Pakistan. Some of the forms and practices are therefore cultural as much as religious, just as might be said for Catholics of Irish origin. The faiths of other South Asians may be treated as of less importance, because their political significance seems less, thus overlooking their potential significance to individuals. Wilson (2004) highlights the growth of interest in Islam within criminology, in contrast to other religious affiliations.

As is true for other aspects of culture, religious affiliation and observance will also change. British socialisation appears to reduce religious affiliation over time for many groups. This is not universal as is demonstrated by its growth amongst Muslims in recent years. The function a religious identity serves for the individual also needs to be understood. Miller et al (1996: 10, cited in Modood and Berthoud, 1997) suggest that for Jewish individuals "religious observance is a means of identifying with the Jewish community, rather than an expression of religious faith". The meaning of that identity alters over time as the context, internationally as well as within this country, changes.

Other themes are emerging in the context of the growth in levels of immigration from Eastern Europe and the rise in newer Black groups, such as the Somali community. The terms in which that debate is conducted are reminiscent of previous debates about Black and South Asian immigration. However there is a significant difference in that some of those groups are White and some of the hostility to new immigration can come from minority ethnic groups now settled within British society. There are implications, both subtle and more overt, that again groups within this society are seeing other groups as inferior because of their ethnic origins and differences in language and culture.

> **Activities and reflection 5.2**
>
> • Take a few minutes to think about the area in which you live and/or work.
> • Do you know what different ethnic groups live within the area? Where does your knowledge of those groups come from?
> • If your knowledge is limited, how might you go about changing that?

Findings about 'race', ethnicity and the criminal justice system

In considering the relationships of ethnicity, offending and the criminal justice system two areas of particular significance are:

• Statistical information, often gathered by government, suggests that patterns of representation of minority ethnic communities in the criminal justice system require analysis and understanding.
• There is a responsibility to provide services that are meaningful to the diversity of experiences represented by offenders.

Much of the information about Black and Minority Ethnic offenders is based on statistical information which has largely been structured around notions of 'race' and ethnicity. There is not enough evidence from studies exploring in depth the experiences that underlie the statistics, or the meaning of those experiences for the individuals concerned. Statistical information tends to submerge the individual and draw our attention from the dynamic and diverse range of roles and identities represented within those statistics. This information should not be ignored, however, but used as a starting point to expand understandings and clarify what other questions should be asked.

Statistics gathered by the Home Office (2005b) suggest that Black and other minority ethnic groups are disproportionately represented in the criminal justice system. Black people are, for instance, six times more likely to be stopped and searched, three times more likely to be arrested and seven times more likely to be imprisoned than White people (Home Office, 2005b). The British Crime Survey (2001/02) suggests, however, that Black people aged between the ages of 10 and 25 are no more likely than White people to commit offences and are significantly less likely to use illegal drugs, with the highest rate of illegal drug use found in mixed race groups (Aust and Smith, 2003; Melrose, 2004). Much of the information gathered by government classifies all Asians under a general heading. This obscures the differences between communities, specifically the experience of Pakistani and Bangladeshi communities, who have higher offending and incarceration rates (Spalek, 2006).

These differences between ethnic groups occur at different points in the system. A study on young offenders suggests that there is no evidence of significant differences in the likelihood of Black, Mixed Race, or White youths receiving a custodial sentence; however, South Asian males are more likely to receive such a sentence. Black males are more likely to get a longer sentence. South Asian males are less likely to receive a community disposal than White offenders and more likely to be fined (Home Office, 2005b).

It is also important to take account of the fact that Black and Minority Ethnic offenders are also victims of crime. Salisbury and Upson (2004) suggest that Black and South Asian people are more at risk of becoming the victims, although much of the reason for that appears to be the younger age profile of those communities. They are, however, at greater risk of personal crime and of racially motivated victimisation. South Asian and Black offenders in prison also report a high level of racially motivated incidents, both from other prisoners and from staff (Nacro, 2000).

How does the criminal justice system disadvantage Black and Minority Ethnic offenders?

Bowling (2002) stresses the importance of interpreting statistics in the light of what they tell us about a criminal justice system, rather than simply assuming that they reflect the behaviour of Black and South Asian offenders.

An offender will be convicted in only 2% of all offences that are committed and only a sixth of offenders who are convicted and sentenced receive a custodial sentence. "Overall, fewer than one-third of 1 percent of all offences that actually occur will result in a custodial sentence" (Bowling, 2002: 83). There are therefore ample opportunities for the agencies that make up the criminal justice system to influence outcomes by their decision making. There is a process of attrition as individuals move from the commission of an offence, to a complaint by the victim, detection, charge, sentencing and the experience of that sentence. Bowling (2002) suggests that for Black and other Minority Ethnic groups the likelihood of being 'filtered in' is greater at each step, although cautions that the experience of South Asians is complex, with Pakistani and Bangladeshi offenders having different experiences from those of Indian origin.

Influences on Black and South Asian experiences of the criminal justice system may include patterns of 'stop and search', the types of offences committed by individuals from different groups, and the social class, age and experience of poverty and disadvantage that are often associated with ethnicity. Patterns of sentencing, including assessments of risk, the influence of reports by the Probation Service and decision making about release may also be significant, although findings always have to be interpreted with care. A study into parole board decisions (Moorthy et al, 2004) found that South Asian and Chinese offenders were more likely to be granted parole than Black or White prisoners, but that seems to be accounted for by their characteristics such as stable family homes which are associated with successful release on parole.

The issue of 'stop and search' has attracted a lot of media attention. Of particular concern is whether differential rates are evidence of institutional racism, as suggested by Macpherson (1999). This has supported the polarised debate discussed earlier in this chapter (Waddington et al, 2004); in the case of 'stop and search', between a belief that the figures show discriminatory police activity, and a belief that some groups are more involved in crime than others.

In fact, reality is more complex. While it is not possible here to rehearse all of Waddington et al's statistical debate, it is useful to consider some of their examples. The figures have compared ratios of 'stop and search', with the ratio of different groups within the population as a whole. This is misleading. In fact, there are differences in the numbers of some groups found in public places, and therefore available to be stopped and searched. This presence on the streets may be because of poverty, the relative youth of some communities and cultural dimensions associated with certain groups. If the numbers of 'stop and searches' are compared with those available to be stopped, rather than proportions within the community as a whole, the bias disappears. This does not mean that there is not a problem to be addressed, or that institutional racism does not exist, but that our understanding of what it means needs to continue to develop.

Newburn et al (2004: 693) found that "there was a striking disproportion in the use of strip-search powers against African Caribbean arrestees in the police station", suggesting that policing is unequally experienced. Waddington et al (2004: 911) point out that, "It has emerged that those who are antagonised by being stopped and searched object most strongly, not to the exercise of this power, but to the manner in which it is exercised". Perceptions of harassment and deliberate provocation by police during such encounters may feed into a process of alienation from authority. These perceptions emerged in

Wilson's (2004: 322) study of young Black men "it made me feel mad that only the black boys were getting stopped".

The Home Office report into the impact of the Stephen Lawrence Inquiry (Foster et al, 2005) found that, while significant improvements had taken place, there were ongoing difficulties with police officers feeling under scrutiny, particularly about 'stop and search'. The report suggests that whatever organisational responses have been made, individuals making decisions are still not doing so confident in their ability to be fair and unbiased, or in the fairness of the context in which their decisions are being made.

The experiences of minority ethnic individuals in the prison system are also of concern, a recent expression of this being the Zahid Mubarak Inquiry (Keith, 2006) into the death of a young South Asian man at the hands of a racist cell mate. Dominelli (2006) discusses the way in which prison staff contributed to his victimisation, by failing to listen to his concerns. Wilson (2004: 326) found that young Black men in custody perceived prison officers as more likely to abuse their power than police in the community. This is illustrated by the following quote: "If I was out on the street they wouldn't even dream of saying some of the things that they say to us in here".

A Home Office study (1994b) found differences in Black and South Asian experiences in custody with a higher proportion of South Asian than Black offenders reporting racial incidents from other prisoners, while from staff the proportions were reversed. This suggests that perceptions of Black men as aggressive and challenging are affecting their treatment by staff and by other prisoners, with the former seeing them as a threat, the latter as forces to be reckoned with. In contrast, South Asian men are seen as less threatening to authority but more vulnerable to abuse and this may be compounded by religious intolerance, particularly of Muslims (Keith, 2006).

There are suggestions that the Probation Service also responds to minority ethnic offenders in ways that can be problematic. Arguably in recent years the attention given by the Probation and Prison Services to accredited programmes has been, in part, at the cost of attention being given to the diversity of offenders. The impact of this has been varied. In some ways the development of accredited programmes has highlighted gaps in service provision, drawing attention to the experiences for Black and Minority Ethnic offenders. In other ways this approach to service delivery can make it harder to see the offender as an individual and can encourage an approach that fits the individual to the intervention available, rather than responding to difference (Durrance and Williams, 2003).

Calverley et al (2004: 5) looked at some of the experiences of Black and South Asian offenders on probation and found that "all three minority ethnic groups [Black, Asian and mixed heritage] showed less evidence of crime-prone attitudes and beliefs, and fewer self reported problems than relevant comparison groups of white offenders". This suggests that minority ethnic offenders receive the same community sentences as White offenders who have higher levels of criminogenic need.

Hudson and Bramhall (2005: 735) looked at how probation officers assessed White and Asian offenders in reports, and found that:

> Assessments of Muslim Asians incorporate and reinforce entrenched stereotypes of the strengths of family networks in Asian communities and newer stereotypes of aggressive behaviour by young Asian males. We are suggesting that the close-knit family which exerts strong influences on the behaviour of Asian youth is so prevalent an image that it is the first resort for explanations of Asian crime – any aspects of criminality or lack of criminality.

They believe that probation officers want to deliver a good and fair service but suggest that discrimination effects can come about through "nice people" doing their jobs (Mavunga, 1993, cited in Hudson and Bramhall, 2005: 737). For example, a practitioner might be so concerned to understand the family experience of an offender that he or she overemphasises its causal relationship with offending behaviour. Power (2003: 259) suggests that the processes designed to combat discriminatory practice fail in reports on groups like Irish Travellers, despite evidence that they are more likely to be imprisoned than other groups.

Activities and reflection 5.3

It is very hard to admit to preconceptions but do your best to be honest with yourself. Think about a Black or Minority Ethnic group you are familiar with:

* What beliefs about that group do you hold?
* How do they make a difference to your contact with individuals from that group?

The impact of discrimination on individual identity

An understanding of Black and Minority Ethnic experiences of victimisation, which for a long time were overshadowed by images of Black people as offenders, has developed more recently, given momentum by the Lawrence murder and growing attention to racially motivated violence (Macpherson, 1999). This development has also necessitated a reflection on White ethnicity and the cultural context within which racially motivated offending occurs (Hall, 2005).

Other commentators have concentrated on the meaning of offending behaviour for different groups. Frosh et al (2002) in a study of the development of boys in modern society found that images of masculinity were very important to help boys maintain a difference from girls and that they tended to value qualities such as 'coolness', a casual attitude to school work, dominance and control. Some boys were seen as more masculine than others and these perceptions were racialised and class conscious. Boys of African Caribbean descent presented as the most likely to embody these characteristics. These images of Black identity may influence teachers and of course the Black pupils themselves. Bowling and Phillips (2002) discuss the development of an image of Black criminality influenced by these subtle processes. Not all boys who adopt these postures, or behaviour, necessarily become offenders. Others, however, start to perceive that type of adolescent bravado as a threat or challenge and too easily slip into 'reading' criminality or delinquency into those groups.

This can be contrasted with the development of South Asian criminality. Frosh et al (2002) also give an account of the perception of Asian boys which is very different, with a more conformist and passive stereotype. The reality of South Asian experiences and others' perceptions of them is changing however. Young South Asian men growing up in this society start to reject that stereotype of passivity and to cultivate an image more like that traditionally associated with African Caribbeans. Bowling et al (2002) draw on the work of Desai (1998: 298): "the so-called 'Asian Gang' is a product of a particularly British form of working class masculinity", making links between the development of minority identities and the consideration of White male working-class culture and its links with racism.

The experience of a probation project in Camberwell (Durrance et al, 2001) suggests that Black young people may turn to consumerism as a route to social acceptance, a route that in itself may increase the likelihood of offending in communities with limited legitimate access to jobs and financial rewards. There is, of course, nothing unique here as it reflects the struggles of some White working-class people who have sought the material goods and perceived social recognition that their background and class may have prevented them attaining.

Identity is often rooted in a sense of sameness and belonging with others and, because of that, individual and group identity can be threatened by difference. When a group perceives itself to be under threat, it affects the behaviour of individuals within the group and their responses to others. This makes the rejection of others and a closing of cultural boundaries more likely (O'Hagan, 2001) and, in turn, influences the development of behaviour. More gang-based identities among young people, for example, create the potential for clashes between groups and increased opportunities for offending behaviour.

When differences between groups are linked to hierarchies of power then the potential oppression and discrimination, both personal and institutional, become greater (Dominelli, 2006). If those hierarchies are threatened then members of the dominant group may seek to reassert their superiority, a process which finds one expression in racially motivated offending (Hall, 2005). As is considered further in Chapter Nine, such offending is also influenced by gender and social class.

Activities and reflection 5.4

Revisit your thoughts about your own identity:

- What groups do you see yourself as belonging to?
- Are those groups in a secure position in society or under threat in some way?
- How does it affect how you think about that group and about others?

Women's experiences

There is a danger that Black women's experience is discounted, being assumed to be covered by attention to 'race', or to culture, or to gender, ignoring the specific interaction between all of these elements. Black women are over-represented within the prison system. Chigwada-Bailey (1997) argues that race, gender and class are three forces that create a greater potential for bias against women. When working with women offenders, it is suggested that the practitioners look "through the women's window" (Roberts, 2002: 112, and quoted in Chapter Three). When working with Black women it is important to remember that their 'window' on the world is likely to be shaped by experiences linked to both gender and 'race'.

Bowling (2002) also identifies the relative lack of attention paid until recently to domestic violence within Asian communities. Minority groups are not alone in wanting to avoid facing some unpalatable truths. This reluctance may be heightened because of a sense that they are under threat and therefore cannot afford to be self-critical (see Shoham, 2005). These processes may affect the extent to which domestic violence within particular groups comes to the attention of the criminal justice system and how it might best be addressed.

Risk and responsivity

The ability of offenders to respond to the interventions on offer will be affected by their perceptions of the individuals delivering those services. The Home Office Citizenship Survey 2003 (Home Office, 2004b) found that individuals from minority ethnic groups saw a range of organisations as discriminatory, including the police and the Prison Service. However, a study of Black and Asian offenders under supervision by the Probation Service found that their experiences of supervision were broadly favourable and that they generally described probation staff as acting fairly, but described the police as less so (Calverley et al, 2004).

This chapter encourages practitioners to respond more sensitively to difference, in order to ensure that the service provided is risk focused and responsive to individuals. What can individual practitioners do to ensure that they assess and manage risk effectively and work responsively across differences in ethnicity? How can a common standard of good practice amongst individual practitioners be ensured?

Sale (2006: 28), in the context of a discussion about child protection in faith communities, draws on the opinion of a training officer who suggests that "practitioners either over-intervene or under-intervene because they don't fully understand cultural differences. When they go into families and do assessments they are at risk of allowing stereotypes to get in the way of decision making". In a similar vein, Weber (2004) talks about the difficulty of making judgements about the difference between culturally-appropriate behaviour and behaviour that is problematic.

Practitioners therefore face the substantial challenge of being sufficiently knowledgeable and self-aware to avoid stereotyping and making assumptions. In order to make accurate and equitable judgements about risk practitioners should bear in mind that:

- Minority ethnic offenders, like other offenders, will be resistant to change. They will find the process of change threatening and the worker may ask them to think about areas that are painful and challenging. Practitioners have to be careful not to fall into stereotypical interpretations of resistant behaviour or running away from holding those offenders responsible for their own problematic behaviour.

- Some staff in criminal justice agencies may find that much of their direct experience with minority ethnic people centres around contact with offenders and that they lack alternative images and understandings with which to balance this experience. Hassan and Thiara (2000) include the following comment from an offender which illustrates this point: "there's no point for a person who has never associated with a Black person or Asian to come to us. If they have only associated with Black people in prison they don't really know about Black people". Lea (2000) talks about the impact on the policing relationship of the restricted contact between many police officers and ethnic minority populations.

- Practitioners have a responsibility to seek to expand their knowledge and experience of lives different to their own. It is perhaps even more important that a strengths-based approach is adopted (Ward and Brown, 2004) so that Black and Minority Ethnic individuals and communities can contribute to the process of desistance.

In order to avoid making assumptions practitioners need to understand and engage with attitudes, patterns of thinking and the individual's emotional response, not just with immediately observable behaviour. Face-to-face practice should as far as possible be based on skills deriving from research. Some writers, however, criticise dominant theories and skills as unresponsive to diversity, for example, cognitive behaviourism (Shaw and Hannah-Moffat, 2004). Skills and understandings deriving from those approaches can help practitioners to work well with Black and Minority Ethnic offenders, provided that practitioners remain questioning and focus on their ability to 'perspective take' by seeking understanding of the experience of those offenders. One very widely quoted and helpful model, 'the iceberg', arising out of a cognitive behavioural approach, can be used to analyse the individual's experience in context (see Figure 5.1).

The following example helps to illustrate the application of this model to the experiences of Black and Minority Ethnic individuals. The Black self-development programme at the Camberwell Day Centre

Figure 5.1:The 'iceberg'

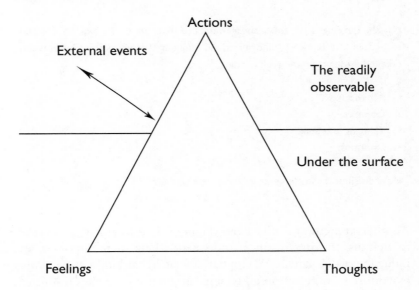

of the Inner London Probation Service (Durrance et al, 2001) stresses the ways in which the experiences of racism may lead to cognitive distortions among Black people about themselves as individuals, and about other Black people. The internal dialogue of Black offenders, their self-talk, will be affected by racist experiences. They may show learned helplessness (Petersen et al, 1995) as a response to an environment in which racism has meant that they receive inconsistent and biased feedback and responses from others.

This process is also acknowledged in the writings of one of the foremost social learning theorists, Bandura (1997), who discusses the ways in which dominant groups justify discriminatory social practices by blaming the disadvantaged for their maltreatment. He suggests that these justifications are potentially more damaging than simple open hostility, and that members of a devalued group may come to believe the negative characterisations of themselves.

Practice tool 5.1

Use the headings from the 'iceberg' model to think about the experiences and responses of a Black or Minority Ethnic offender that you know. Put in some detailed evidence under each heading.

- Behaviour.
- Context.
- Thinking and beliefs.
- Emotions.

How do all of these elements influence each other?

Another strength of the 'iceberg' (Figure 5.1) is its equal applicability to helping the practitioner understand their own responses and influences. O'Hagan (2001) emphasises that, in working across cultures, practitioners must be careful to separate their own beliefs from their response to others. He suggests that some may have negative beliefs and attitudes towards religion in general, or a specific faith.

Practitioners have a right to hold their own beliefs about religion and all of these beliefs can be held to be valid. However, they have to question whether their own beliefs impede the delivery of a service to those for whom religion is important. For those practitioners who are themselves religious, do their beliefs impede their response to those of a different religion or to whom the absence of a faith is important? Practitioners without religious beliefs should seek to understand why and to what extent they are of such significance to others.

A secular-based approach to anti-discrimination emphasises ethnicity over religious identity, but for some this may not be enough. O'Hagan (2001) suggests that for many individuals religious beliefs are the core component of their cultural identity and from this they derive self-esteem, a strengthening of family and community bonds and sources of support when under threat. Religious values and principles may, on the other hand, sometimes encourage harmful behaviour, if, for example, they stress the superiority of a particular religious group over others, but they remain a potentially significant source of pro-social beliefs.

Practice tool 5.2

Look at an example of a risk assessment tool.

- What information about religion does it seek directly?
- For an offender whose religion was of significance what other sections of the tool might be helped by information about this?
- What sorts of questions would you use to gather that information?

Bandura (1997) also draws attention to the responsibility of members of a dominant group to act in ways that affirm the self-worth of others. Everyone, staff and offenders will be helped if they are able to cultivate skills and competencies that will sustain a positive sense of self-belief, rooted in pro-social behaviours. This is the basis for many interventions with offenders, and is not specific to those from minority ethnic groups (Trotter, 1994; Cherry, 2005). For minority ethnic individuals and their communities strategies should be in place to empower them to develop pro-social behaviours and provide pro-social models. Individual practitioners should reward positive attributes in devalued groups, and also support access to societal rewards and resources (Farrall, 2002; Durrance and Williams, 2003).

Self awareness and reflection on practice is important when working with difference and the following Activities and reflection box will help this process.

Activities and reflection 5.5

- Are there any offenders or groups of offenders that leave you as a practitioner anxious, less sure of your skills?
- How does that anxiety impact on your thoughts and behaviours?
- How do you use your power in this relationship and how might that be perceived by the offender?
- Black and Minority Ethnic offenders are a small proportion of their communities, the vast majority leading law-abiding lives. Do you overgeneralise about them to the exclusion of acknowledging those who do not offend? Adapted from Ahmed (1990) and Tuklo Orenda Associates (1999).

The next practice tool suggests ways in which practitioners can evaluate their practice to help ensure the effectiveness of their interventions.

Practice tool 5.3

The following can be used as a checklist against which to consider an individual case.

The assessment:

- Does the assessment reflect an accurate understanding of the offender's self-talk and beliefs and how they may have been affected by the impact of racism?
- Does the assessment pay careful attention to the causal links between risk factors and offending behaviour?
- Does it overemphasise any aspect of the offender or their life, for example their 'race' or culture, to the detriment of a more complete picture?
- Does the assessment of risk balance public protection with the needs and rights of the individual?
- Does the assessment emphasise the strengths as well as the problems and needs associated with particular cultures?

Interventions:

- Does the intervention plan reflect a process in which the offender has been actively involved?
- Does the work with an offender support them in overcoming obstacles, including those posed by racism?
- Does the intervention develop coping skills and self-efficacy?
  Adapted from Ahmed (1990) and Tuklo Orenda Associates (1999).

Conclusion

In a context where there is a lack of knowledge, the task for practitioners is to develop their own knowledge base and challenge their taken-for-granted thinking. Important strategies for practitioners will include collaborative approaches with a diversity of colleagues, as well as with local communities.

The small proportion of Black and Minority Ethnic people who become persistent offenders, like others, will be helped to change by practice that addresses risk and is delivered with responsivity. This involves an accurate assessment of dynamic risk factors that is particularly careful about attributing causation. Black and Minority Ethnic people should be provided with culturally aware, positive and pro-social contexts and opportunities to help develop an identity and sense of self-worth that is rooted in something other than offending behaviour. Practitioners should be sufficiently secure in their own identities to be able to value and respect differences. This will be enhanced if they are practising in a context that supports relationships with individuals, which are rooted in the details of their experience and which seek to develop the positives in them and in their communities.

Part Three
Responsivity

SIX

Mental disorder

Introduction

Many studies identify the prevalence of mental disorder amongst prisoners and other offenders (Hodgins, 2000; Lynch and Skinner, 2004). People who develop major mental disorders are more likely than those without such disorders to commit criminal offences. However, the link between offending and mental disorder is unclear and offending is not necessarily a consequence of mental disorder.

McInerney and Minne (2004: 43) suggest that "mentally disordered offenders have special problems; their offending places them apart from other psychiatric patients and major mental disorder separates them from most offenders". The populist tendency to see crimes committed by people who are either 'mad' or 'bad' results in mentally disordered offenders being seen as doubly deviant. Mentally disordered people remain among the most vulnerable and marginalised in society (Silver and Miller, 2002; Lynch, 2005; Nolan, 2005), yet many see this group as justifying more restrictive approaches and having fewer civil rights than the rest of the population.

Instead of seeing that only a small number of mentally disordered offenders pose a serious risk of harm, there is a tendency for all mentally disordered people to be regarded by society as high risk. However, as Blackburn (2004: 298) notes, "mentally disordered offenders are a heterogeneous group" and whilst "there is little disagreement that the mental health needs of offenders are a challenge for rehabilitation, there is less agreement on whether mental disorder is a risk factor for criminal or harmful behaviour".

Practitioners should always pay attention to mental disorder as a potential risk factor, especially when combined with substance abuse or anti-social thinking and behaviour. However, although it is not possible to state for certain that mental disorder is a dynamic risk factor there is an assumption (Andrews, 1995) that mental disorder also affects responsivity and will therefore need to be incorporated as part of interventions.

There is widespread agreement that people suffering with mental health problems are not best served by being locked up in overcrowded prisons; however, statistics show an alarming prevalence of mental disorder in prisons (see, for example, Bebbington, 2005). Research by the Office for National Statistics in 1997 identified that 7% of sentenced men, 10% of men on remand and 14% of women in both categories had a functional psychosis such as schizophrenia or bipolar disorder in the year leading up to their imprisonment, in comparison with the figure of 0.4% for adults in the general population (Fryers et al, 1998; see also Singleton et al, 1998). The huge rise in people being sent to prison in the last decade, 85,000 in 1996 in comparison with 112,000 in 2002 (Home Office, 2004a), has created prison overcrowding which puts particular pressure on those with mental health problems. Not only can overcrowding exacerbate symptoms of disorder but also staff may be too pressured to provide appropriate care and to pass on information about the vulnerability of, or problems posed by, particular individuals.

For criminal justice practitioners there is limited practical guidance and training to help them recognise the indicators of mental disorder initially and then to understand the causative links between the disorder and the individual's offending behaviour. Practitioners who have developed knowledge and expertise in working with offenders as a generic group frequently do not have the professional expertise to intervene appropriately at the level of the mental disorder. Consequently, they will need to collaborate with others to ensure that both offending and mental health needs (which may be closely linked) are attended to in order to ensure both reduction of risk (of reoffending and harm to others) and relief of symptoms.

The approach taken in this chapter is to consider current definitions of, and approaches to, work with mentally disordered offenders, with the practitioner acting as assessor and case manager. The intention is not to provide expertise in direct intervention, but to provide a basic understanding of mental disorder, particularly its interrelationship with offending, to help identify when specialist assistance is required and to promote the role of offender manager as a practitioner within a multidisciplinary context. Also, practitioners need to ensure that services are delivered in ways which enable offenders with a mental disorder to engage with services (responsivity).

This chapter also includes a section on the subject of suicide and self-harm. Although included in this chapter for practical purposes it should be noted that while some people who commit suicide or self-harm are mentally ill, many are not. Offenders are often under pressure and stress when going through the criminal justice system and practitioners need to be alert to the risk of suicide and self-harm.

Definitions

The 1983 Mental Health Act defined 'mental disorder' as "mental illness, arrested or incomplete development of mind, psychotic disorder and any other disorder or disability of mind". As Blackburn (2004: 298) notes "these are legal categories and not diagnostic terms". The government has introduced a number of mental health Bills with a view to updating the current mental health legislative framework, particularly in relation to compulsory treatment for those who pose a threat to public protection but who are unwilling to receive treatment voluntarily. However, to date, these have not reached the statute book because of the controversial nature of some of the proposals (see, for example, Mental Health Alliance, 2006).

Definitions of mental disorder vary but they frequently include genetic, lifelong conditions, chronic or episodic mental illness and severe personality disorders. All are related to potentially difficult behaviour patterns that can, when unmanaged or untreated, bring individuals to the attention of the criminal justice system. The conditions themselves can vary both in severity of symptoms and impact upon the behaviour of individuals.

Mental illness is taken to mean conditions that are susceptible to psychiatric diagnosis and are treatable by mainstream health services. They may produce symptoms such as disturbed perceptions and faulty reasoning, which in themselves lead to anti-social behaviour. People diagnosed with *personality disorders* suffer personality traits that lead to persistent patterns of abnormal behaviour which may prove difficult and threatening at times (Bowers, 2001).

For the purposes of this chapter, therefore, the term 'mental disorder' is assumed to encompass both mental illness, and personality disorder. Practitioners are very likely to encounter individuals suffering from mental illness or demonstrating signs of personality disorder. It is helpful, but not always possible, to distinguish between these two broad strands, as interventions may differ. The former attracts more significant medical input, being viewed as more susceptible to 'cure' or management of symptoms. The latter tends to generate more psychological responses and there are questions about the intractability, and consequent treatability, of conditions within the definition of personality disorder (Blackburn 2000; Hodgins, 2000). However, significant numbers of persistent offenders are found to have personality disorders and as such pose a challenge to work with. They are therefore looked at specifically later in this chapter.

Activities and reflection 6.1

• Think about your own feelings towards people with a mental disorder. What fears do you have about working with this group of people? What might you do to counter those fears?

• Are there gaps in your knowledge about local mental health services?

• How will you overcome these knowledge deficits?

The tasks of the criminal justice practitioner

Assessment

Assessors need to be able to identify when an offender's mental state goes beyond the usual unhappiness, stress and poor levels of coping into a condition that may be liable to psychiatric diagnosis. Ultimately, a referral to a community mental health nurse (CMHN) will assist diagnosis, but the practitioner can do much to explore the situation through simple, direct questioning (see web page of Directgov for an explanation of the various specialist roles in mental health services, www.direct.gov.uk).

Most practitioners undertake assessments of offenders with the assistance of risk assessment tools. These 'tools' aim to guide the assessor through the process of analysing behaviour and emotional well-being, by encouraging them to be alert to indicators of mental ill-health such as difficulties in coping and social isolation, feelings of self-harm or suicide, and current and previous psychological or psychiatric problems. Assessors are also prompted to ask questions about disturbed patterns of thinking, attitudes towards others in society and interpersonal skills. Information about the offender's mental health may also be revealed from other responses to questions; for example, the offender may be misusing alcohol or drugs to alleviate the symptoms of mental illness or the current offence may be significantly different from previous offending. Assessors therefore need to make sense of the whole picture.

Offenders frequently evidence poor problem-solving skills, impulsivity and a disregard for the needs and rights of others (McGuire, 1995, 2002b) but, in their more extreme forms, these disturbed patterns of thinking may suggest the possibility of a personality disorder. However, these indicators will also frequently apply to those suffering from mental illness. It is therefore crucial that evidence of mental disorder is not automatically associated with a propensity for offending. As in any assessment of an offender, it is important to be as precise as possible about the link between the mental health of the individual, their specific offending behaviour and the risks they may pose. The assessment will be strengthened by accessing information from other sources, for example, their GP, particularly the circumstances surrounding the current or previous offending.

When faced with an offender who seems to have some sort of mental disorder, the practitioner's task is primarily one of screening to identify when a more thorough assessment of the offender's mental state by a CMHN or psychiatrist is required. Although an assessor can be aware of some of the indicators of mental disorder, they still need to ask the 'right' questions and be alert to verbal and non-verbal cues.

A number of obstacles to assessment can be identified, for example:

- Mentally disordered offenders often experience a complex range of problems and it can be difficult to distinguish mental health concerns from these other difficulties (Hodgins, 1995).
- Alcohol and substance abuse can produce symptoms which mask the indicators of mental disorder.
- Offenders may be reluctant to acknowledge symptoms.

Thus for the assessor it will be important to remember that screening for mental disorder is not a precise process. Practitioners also need to be aware of what services can be accessed to support both the worker and the offender through this course of action.

Wix and Hillis (1998) developed the following guide and checklist to support the frontline practitioner in clarifying their thoughts about mental disorder and guiding subsequent actions.

Mental disorder: some signs to be alert to

Anxiety and phobias:

- Faster heartbeat and quick short breaths.
- Sweating.
- Giddiness and/or fainting.
- Tension, aches and pains.
- Headaches.
- Dry mouth.

Depression:

- Having low moods for long periods.
- Losing appetite or weight.

- Feeling tired.
- Being unable to sleep, or waking up early.
- Losing interest in usual hobbies and activities.
- Losing interest in sex.
- Avoiding other people and being irritable.
- Poor concentration.
- Feeling persecuted.
- Feeling guilty or even suicidal.

Bipolar disorder (previously known as manic depression):

- Being overactive and very excitable.
- Poor judgement, for example, spending more money than you can afford.
- Not thinking straight.
- Believing yourself to be someone you are not and overestimating what you can do.
- Disinhibited behaviour such as being overfamiliar with a stranger.

Schizophrenia:

- Hearing critical or abusive voices.
- Excessive preoccupation with religious ideas.
- Believing that someone is following or persecuting you.
- Believing your thoughts and actions are known or controlled by someone else.
- Excessive fear and disturbed behaviour.
  (Wix and Hillis, 1998)

Practice tool 6.1: Being alert to signs of mental disorder and acting appropriately – a quick reference checklist

Observe behaviour:

- Is it similar to any of the common signs of mental disorder given in the above guide?
- Has it changed from previous observations?
- Have other people noticed or reported changes to you?

Assess the situation:

- Make a list of features you have noticed which concern you.
- Have the person's circumstances changed recently, for example, recent traumas, stresses, illness, family/social problems, court appearances, criminal charges?
- Imagine yourself in their position to see if you can see their perspective.

Assess the person:

- Approach the person in a non-threatening manner.
- Ask them if they are experiencing any problems and let them know that you have noticed they seem less contented recently.
- Ascertain if they are comfortable with your enquiries.
- If they are not comfortable, allay their anxieties, discuss with colleagues and seek advice.
- If they are comfortable, ask them if they are feeling anxious, depressed and worried about anything and whether they would like to talk to you about it.
- Listen carefully and reflectively to their responses and try to form a picture of their situation as they see it.
- Reassure them that you will try at least to find ways to help.
- If they have no insight or appear to think nothing is wrong, do not disagree with bizarre thoughts or confront ideas.
- Respect ideas and feelings expressed and ensure a professional approach towards confidentiality.
- If you think/feel that there may be elements of mental illness you need to obtain a psychiatric assessment. You will need to ask permission to obtain help from the GP or local mental health services.

Action:

- Discuss with your supervisor.
- Decide if the local GP needs to be involved.
- Refer to local psychiatric services.
  (Wix and Hillis, 1998)

Assessing mental disorder in a multicultural context

Research into the way mental illness is assessed and managed has led to a growing awareness that ethnicity, cultural background and 'race' are critical factors affecting decisions made by professionals and the way in which services can be accessed. K. Bhui (1999: 89) suggests that "mental health professionals, user movements and academic observers have long been concerned that psychiatry in this country embodies an oppressive system of care which persistently disadvantages minority ethnic communities". He notes that medical and psychiatric training has tended towards identifying "diseases of immigrants" and "culture bound syndromes" rather than promoting awareness of the complex reflexive relationship between culture and illness. K. Bhui (1999: 94) acknowledges that the last 10 years or so have seen a radical restructuring of adult mental health services aiming to provide "a comprehensive, culturally appropriate and less restrictive environment whilst targeting those with severe mental illnesses". However, racial inequalities still exist within the mental health system (Vige, 2005) and many Black and Minority Ethnic individuals 'fall out of care' through non-compliance and end up in contact with the criminal justice system.

In Chapter Five the challenge of working across 'race' and culture is explored. Issues raised there are of particular relevance to the assessment of offenders where mental health issues are inextricably linked to their experience of oppression/discrimination. Arguably, definitions of mental disorder are themselves culturally specific, and this can make the assessor's decision-making role particularly significant if cultural stereotypes are not to impede appropriate access to resources. A lack of clarity about the links between mental disorder and cultural or ethnic diversity can lead to confused and discriminatory assessment and decision making (see Department of Health, 2005;Vige, 2005).

Assessing normality for any individual involves reference to their individual, social and cultural context rather than making simple assumptions from their presenting behaviour and appearance. H.S. Bhui (1999: 93) proposes that probation officers (although this applies to most criminal justice practitioners) occupy "a pivotal position in the criminal justice system because of their role in assessment, diversion, management and treatment of offenders and so are in a position of either reinforcing or redressing the discrimination in the system".

For the practitioner, the challenge is to recognise the individual's diversity and the context of their behaviour, as well as specific behaviours/thinking patterns which may be indicative of mental disorder. It is important not to confuse the two as subsequent decisions may then be muddled and inappropriate.

Practice tool 6.2: Assessing mental disorder in a multicultural context

When assessing an individual and to improve responsivity you should ensure that:

• You recognise and identify clearly diversity issues for the offender and for you as the assessor.
• You try to inform yourself about the range of treatment that may be available both within the formal psychiatric services and the wider community.
• If using an interpreter, it is helpful to work (if possible) with someone who has previous experience of working with mental disorder. If no such interpreter is available, more time will be needed beforehand to establish how information can best be conveyed without distortion.
• You match decisions/referrals to the needs of the individual – try to avoid a blanket response.
• You are alert to possible obstacles to the individual accessing services (for example, language, perceptions of social stigma).
• You begin to develop packages of interventions which reflect cultural/ethnic diversity in terms of staff, community and methods.

Practitioners have much to contribute to local mental health services particularly in terms of expertise in assessing the risk of reoffending of an individual, and the person's offending history contained in case records may provide a useful source of information.

Following assessment the best outcome for the offender who is severely mentally ill may be through diversion from the court process. This depends on the availability and criteria of any diversion schemes in your locality.

Diversion from the criminal justice process

In 1990 the Home Office issued a circular, 66/90, which advocated that mentally disordered offenders in need of psychiatric treatment should receive assistance from health and social services, wherever this was identified and as soon as possible. There was recognition that prosecution was not always in the public interest. In response to this circular a number of diversion schemes were initiated in different parts of the country, but 15 years on practice between areas differs greatly. A parliamentary question in the House of Lords in February 2006 identified that at that time there were 139 local schemes in operation across England and Wales which allowed mental health assessments to be undertaken in order to provide the court with information about the offender's mental condition and any treatment that may be appropriate (Lords Hansard, 2006). A survey (NACRO, 2005: 5) of court diversion and criminal justice liaison schemes identified that almost a quarter of providers felt that mentally disordered offenders were a low priority for agencies in their area.

Chronic bed shortages in mental health provision can lead to a slow response from local services resulting in the offender's remand in custody overnight, and some disordered offenders are not detected by such schemes. It is important for practitioners to be aware of whether any form of diversion scheme operates in their area and how to initiate intervention if required.

Diversion of the offender from the criminal justice process may not always be the best outcome for the offender. Sometimes it may be appropriate for an offender to be held responsible for the consequences of their behaviour, for example, someone who is in a stable or 'well' period but with a permanent condition such as schizophrenia. Furthermore, diversion from the court process may preclude them from a full assessment of other risk issues and the opportunity to access a wider range of resources as part of a court order. Again, this judgement needs to be made in consultation with mental health specialists through careful consideration of the needs of the individual but also with regard to the public protection issues that arise from the person's risk of offending.

Intervening with mentally disordered offenders
Planning and prioritising

The practitioner needs to develop a plan which identifies key areas of work in terms of offender manager tasks and specialist involvement and resources. It should be recognised, however, that the needs of mentally disordered offenders may well be the same as those of non-mentally disordered offenders and that, providing their mental health is stable, cognitive behavioural programmes may be appropriate, if delivered within a multi-agency framework (Fleck et al, 2001).

Criminal justice practitioners are frequently seen as having a key role in minimising risk and acting as a bridge between the individual and mental health services. The task of the practitioner is to maintain an appropriate balance between mental health needs and the risk of harm and reoffending that need to be addressed or managed. As Blackburn (2004: 302) suggests, "the goals of intervention should be as much 'offender focused' as 'offence focused'". In addition, it is important that, in seeking to address the mental health needs, the courts do not impose statutory supervision that is excessive in terms of the seriousness of the offending.

Intervention – determining priorities

Effectiveness when working with mentally disordered offenders requires treatment to control symptoms, monitoring of their behaviour and focused efforts to achieve the change required to enable successful reintegration into the community. This will involve regular communication with others involved in the care of the offender. This model, adapted from Kemshall (1998a) (see Figure 6.1), attempts to match the severity of mental illness symptoms with the level of risk of harm and reoffending. It guides the practitioner in terms of frequency of contact, focus for intervention and the need to involve mental health 'partners'. The focus and actions of the practitioner in Figure 6.1 are in bold type. So, for example, with a lower risk offender with severe symptoms of mental illness the priority would be to get appropriate treatment for the illness through referral to mental health services and possibly, but not necessarily, by diversion from the criminal

Figure 6.1: Matching practitioner contact with severity of mental illness symptoms and risk of harm and reoffending

	Severity of mental illness symptoms	
	LOW	**HIGH**
HIGH Risk of harm and reoffending **LOW**	Persistence and/or danger may not be linked primarily to mental illness **Work focused on offending** **Surveillance/monitoring** **Frequent contact with supervisor**	Persistence/danger may be connected to mental illness **Work focused on offending and treatment for condition** **Surveillance/monitoring** **Frequent contact with supervisor and mental health services**
	Beware deterioration of mental health condition **Monitor for signs of escalation** **Less frequent contact**	Appropriate intervention with focus on health needs **Diversion from criminal justice system** **Monitoring** **Referral to mental health support services**

Source: Adapted from Kemshall (1998a)

justice system. The practitioner would monitor the offender's progress, encourage compliance with medication and basic self-management and access other community resources, for example housing, to support their rehabilitation (Hodgins, 2000).

The above model helps to establish focus and priorities for contact but effective case management based on the following principles is particularly helpful for mentally disordered offenders:

Regularity of contact − contact needs to be predictable in terms of frequency and location to help provide structure and certainty for the offender. Appointments need to be sufficiently frequent to allow deterioration in mental health to be detected swiftly.

Boundaries − the offender needs clear and consistent boundaries as to what constitutes appropriate behaviour and contact. This may require invoking enforcement procedures as part of managing their behaviour.

Focus and nature of contact − it is important to promote responsiveness and a shared sense of ownership of work together. This will counteract feelings of hopelessness and passivity in the offender and create optimism for change. They also need to feel that the worker−offender relationship offers a safe place where feelings of self-doubt and uncertainty can be shared.

Mentally ill offenders − Care Programme Approach

The 1983 Mental Health Act (Section 117) placed a duty on health and social services to provide aftercare for patients who have been compulsorily detained and subsequently discharged from inpatient treatment. The Care Programme Approach (CPA) was introduced in 1991 because there was serious concern that mental health patients were being discharged without formal planning of aftercare arrangements (Houlders, 2005: 115-19).

The CPA framework has four core elements:

1. Systematic assessment of the needs of the patient and their carers.
2. A care plan to meet those needs.
3. A key worker to monitor and coordinate the care plan.
4. Regular reviews.

Although the CPA was designed to coordinate health and social care arrangements it is recognised that other agencies need to be included in meetings as part of the decision-making process.

The Reed review (Home Office and Department of Health, 1992) identified that "there should be core teams of professional staff for ensuring that mentally disordered offenders are properly assessed and receive the continuing care and treatment they need". Subsequent reviews of the CPA approach (Department of Health, 1996) have emphasised that all mentally disordered offenders, including those detained in prison, should be supported through this framework, although, as Bebbington (2005: 7) notes, "the development of secure forensic psychiatry services has failed to reduce the number of severely mentally ill persons in prison".

As part of the CPA the care plan should normally be developed together with the patient and carers but will take into consideration the victim perspective (if available) or that of the victim's family and the risks posed by/to the individual. It must take account of public protection issues and this may involve the services of the victim contact officer. It also has to reflect the ethnicity, religious and cultural needs of the individual by ensuring the treatment plan makes use of appropriate support systems within the community (Houlders, 2005).

More recent changes in legislation (the 2004 Domestic Violence, Crime and Victims Act) have strengthened the duties of victim contact officers in relation to the victims of some mentally disordered offenders who have been diverted from the prison or court system into treatment through hospital orders and given them equal rights with other victims of serious crime (see Section 69 of the 2000 Criminal Justice and Court Services Act, and Probation Circular 42/2005 [2005a]). This pertains to victims where the patient was sentenced or transferred to hospital after 1 July 2005.

Multi-Agency Public Protection Panels (MAPPP) deal specifically with public protection issues and the needs of victims and their families when planning for the return to the community of high risk mentally disordered offenders and this may result in their being subject to restrictions by the Home Office or court. These requirements will form part of the care plan and will spell out both the arrangements for safe return of the mentally disordered offender to the community and also the tasks and responsibilities of each person involved in this process.

A diagnosis of mental illness does not render the practitioner peripheral to the offender. Although mental health services will be providing treatment to remedy symptoms, practitioners should see themselves as integral to the process. They should feel confident in their own knowledge base and take an active part in interagency collaboration which is essential to the effective management of mentally disordered offenders.

Interagency multidisciplinary working

The mental health of a mentally disordered offender may deteriorate rapidly; it is therefore essential to monitor their behaviour regularly, discuss progress and have clear systems of communication with other professionals involved in the provision of services to the individual, be they CMHNs, psychologists or psychiatrists. This communication should aim to support effective risk management and responsive intervention (see Turner and Colombo, 2005).

A number of mental health inquiries that take place after murders have been committed by individuals with a mental health history (see Reith, 1997: 67) identify weaknesses in interagency working arrangements. Practitioners have been found to be confused about what information may be shared between agencies, for example, prisons and hospitals. There would also seem to be insufficient understanding of the interface between mental health and criminal justice legislation and practitioners are reluctant to reveal what they do not know. Reith (1997) also suggests that too much weight is given to the needs and wishes of the individual at the expense of public protection. She emphasised that practitioners needed to be alert to signs of deterioration, for example, lapses in contact or self-care, and be ready to share those concerns. Reith (1997) was writing a decade ago and there have been significant advances in terms of formal arrangements for information exchange and decision making, but it remains incumbent on practitioners to make interagency collaboration effective.

Turner and Colombo (2005: 34) in their pilot study of the operation of a MAPPP suggest there is still "agency misalignment" with "agencies speaking different languages about risk ... different purposes to the sharing of information and ... conflict in approaches to the issue of client confidentiality". Their concern is that "practitioners appear more concerned with spreading the burden of responsibility than on making risk assessments about offender dangerousness" (2005: 34). They acknowledge the deep-rooted differences between agency groups in terms of values, professional training and experiences but stress the need for approaches which allow for a greater sense of shared accountability and information exchange, which is so central to managing risk.

Although writing about child death inquiries and interagency arrangements in child protection, Murphy (2004: 135) makes some useful suggestions as to how practitioners can increase their own effectiveness in the process of "working together".

> **Practice tool 6.3: Making interagency collaboration more effective**
>
> • Be willing to ask 'naive' questions, admit what you do not know or understand – this helps develop more shared perspectives.
>
> • Understand and value others' perspectives recognising differences in agency priorities and approaches. Do not get into competition as to whose perspective is more valid.
>
> • Be clear and communicate about your own agency's tasks and priorities. Do not promise to do things which you cannot deliver.
>
> • Practise in an inclusive fashion, move from 'I' and 'you' to 'we' in discussions. Be willing to share tasks such as chairing meetings and minute-taking. Do not always meet in one particular agency's premises.
>
> • Deal with conflict by clarifying why people do not agree rather than ignoring differences of opinion. Conflict, if managed appropriately, can be a useful source of different information and improve decision making.
>
> Adapted from Murphy (2004)

Some multidisciplinary teams work together sufficiently frequently to have time to iron out difficulties. However, criminal justice practitioners may well be required to attend and contribute to interagency planning in relation to mentally disordered offenders on an infrequent basis. It is important that they develop confidence and skills in contributing effectively to this process.

Antisocial personality disorders – background and intervention

Many persistent offenders who commit impulsive and anti-social crimes are found subsequently to have a personality disorder. There are competing explanations and categories of personality disorders, none of which receive universal endorsement (Bowers, 2001), but it is important to appreciate that offenders with disorders are a diverse group of individuals needing very different responses from the practitioner.

According to ICD 10 (one of the two largest schemes for diagnosing mental disorders) personality disorders are:

> ... deeply ingrained and enduring behaviour patterns, manifesting as inflexible responses to a broad range of personal and social situations. They represent extreme or significant deviations from the way in which the average

individual in a given culture perceives, thinks, feels and particularly relates to others. (WHO, 1999: 221)

Almost all personality disorders undermine good relationships with others and people are not described as having a personality disorder if their symptoms are regarded as minor or transitory (Stutterford, 2005). Research by Plomin et al (1997) indicated that personality disorders 'run in families' and that genetic inheritance is a major but not the sole cause of its development.

People with personality disorders often behave in ways that may be perceived as reckless and threatening. They can make contradictory demands on services and this may result in them being considered very negatively by psychiatric and other helping professions (Bowers, 2001: 2).

Severe anti-social personality disorders were historically referred to as 'psychopathic' but a new term is increasingly used for them and this is 'dangerous and severe personality disorder' (DSPD). This is a political rather than a clinical definition and the number of people in the UK classified as such is small. Home Office and Department of Health statistics in 1999 suggested that there were 2,400 DSPD people in the UK: 1,400 in the prison system, 400 in special hospitals and 300 to 600 living in the community (Bowers, 2001: 8). The high profile nature of some of these individuals, and the number in prison and special hospitals, has led to a specialist assessment and treatment service being piloted with a view to improving the mental health services for DSPDs and reducing the threat they pose to public safety. Severely personality disordered offenders, who currently live freely in the community, may subsequently become subjected to preventative detention or compulsory treatment in the future, although this continues to be a matter for public debate.

The treatability of personality disorders has been a source of considerable dispute within psychiatric services, which makes it harder to justify the use of sparse resources. Many people are pessimistic about the prognosis but "psychiatrists fall short of saying they are untreatable" (Hodgins and Muller-Isberner, 2000: 92; see also Blackburn, 2000).

Bowers (2001: 145) emphasises the importance of the attitudes of the professionals towards those with personality disorders, suggesting that it is those nurses who remain positive and able to see that "it is part of the sufferer's psychological make-up" who are most able to work effectively with this group. It is unsurprising, given the number of offenders who have personality disorders, that many of the techniques promoted by Hodgins and Muller-Isberner (2000) as being most effective with this group, are those already identified as most applicable to work with offenders.

> ## Practice tool 6.4
>
> The following checklist identifies approaches that have proved most effective with people with personality disorders. Case managers can use it to identify what is being done and by whom in relation to a particular individual. It may also be useful to highlight gaps in provision:
>
> * Using cognitive behavioural approaches.
> * Using positive reinforcement rather than punishment.
> * Helping them learn preventative measures.
> * Using relapse prevention strategies.
> * Monitoring and anticipating problem situations.
> * Planning and rehearsing alternative solutions to cope with problem situations with increasing levels of challenge and rewarding improved competence.
> * Working with significant others, for example, family, friends or maybe hostel staff, to promote and support change.
> * Organising maintenance and booster sessions after completion of programme.
>
> Hodgins and Muller-Isberner (2000: 101)

Experienced practitioners will appreciate the importance of nurturing the motivation to change, discouraging withdrawal from treatment programmes and ensuring a balance is kept between risk reduction and the promotion of positive ways of living (Hodgins, 2000). Personal interest and commitment on the part of the practitioner continues to be essential to the promotion of change and development in these often hard-to-reach individuals.

Dual diagnosis

'Dual diagnosis' or 'co-morbidity' are terms for people who have co-occurring disorders. This can mean people who have both a mental illness and a personality disorder or mental illness and a mental disability. However, it is more frequently used for those people who have both a severe mental illness and a substance abuse disorder (either alcohol and/or drugs). Since the early 1990s there has been increasing recognition that those with dual diagnosis have more negative outcomes in treatment than those with a single diagnosis (Drake and Wallach, 2000).

Both in the UK and in the US, the tendency with treatment has been to try to identify the primary disorder in terms of mental health or substance abuse and then tackle them in parallel or sequentially. This lack of appreciation of the interaction between disorders has resulted in poorer outcomes and frequent relapse on return to the community (Watkins et al, 2001). Integrated approaches to treatment, which tackle the disorders holistically, are increasingly being recognised as the route to improved outcomes. These approaches emphasise the importance of comprehensive, multidisciplinary treatments which build on outreach methods to improve, promote and sustain engagement throughout the process (Blackburn, 2004). Practitioners are encouraged to help the person build skills and supports into their life to sustain progress and prevent relapse. Osher and Kofoed (1989) propose a four-stage intervention model for use as a framework for intervention with dually diagnosed individuals. The stages of the model are: engagement, persuasion, active treatment and relapse prevention. These stages fit very closely with the principles of responsivity, ensuring that the practitioner encourages the offender's motivation and engagement throughout the intervention.

At the *engagement* stage the practitioner aims to understand the individual's own view, responding to behaviour and language in ways which promote a trusting and non-judgemental relationship. Interagency collaboration needs to begin at this stage to ensure that a comprehensive approach is adopted and a full assessment achieved. The *persuasion* and *active treatment* stages involve the practitioner in using motivational interviewing techniques (Miller and Rollnick, 2002) to help sustain reductions in substance misuse, attendance at appointments and adherence to prescribed medication. *Relapse prevention* is also vital to rehearse proactive coping strategies especially in the face of high risk situations and widen social and support networks to counter the person's vulnerability to slip back into old ways of coping. Unfortunately, progress towards integration of mental health and drug/alcohol treatments remains limited in the UK because of barriers at all levels: organisational, financial and professional. In view of this, it is particularly important that those engaged in supervision of offenders with dual diagnosis act as a link between treatment providers to ensure that the offender's needs are fully addressed.

Suicide and self-harm

The predominant concern of this book is reducing the risk of reoffending and harm to others; the focus of this section on suicide and self-harm, however, is to reduce the risk of harm to offenders themselves. All offenders going through the criminal justice system will be at a heightened risk of suicide and self-harm, although this section has particular relevance for work with women and young people (see some of the statistics included later in this section).

Self-harm

Self-harm is an expression of personal distress and is not an illness. This self-injury may take the form of cutting, scratching or picking at skin or at previous injuries, breaking bones and banging one's head. How people self-harm is not significant but why is more so. The National Institute of Health and Clinical Excellence (NICE, 2004) guidelines suggest that individuals who self-harm tend to be those who have yet to learn positive ways of coping with overwhelming feelings (www.nice.org.uk). Discovering that someone is self-harming can evoke feelings of shock, revulsion and maybe inadequacy in the practitioner but it is important that the service user is treated with the same respect, understanding and choice offered to anyone else. Dealing with episodes of self-harm is emotionally demanding and requires good communication skills and support. It is important to attend appropriately to physical symptoms and, except where injuries are largely superficial, encourage the individual to seek help from their GP or a primary care centre.

Ask for the individual to explain in their own words why they have self-harmed, ensuring that the discussion takes place in privacy. Try to assess the risk of further self-harm episodes; are they becoming more serious or more frequent over time? Inform other relevant staff and organisations of the outcome of this assessment. This is particularly important in institutions, for example hostels and prisons, where residents and inmates often experience stress and pressure from their environment and there may be regular changes of staffing. If you believe there is a significant and immediate risk then refer the individual to their GP or the emergency department of the nearest hospital.

It is possible to visualise self-harm and suicide as a continuum with deliberate self-harm at one end, moving through parasuicide (attempted suicide) to suicide at the other end (Kreitman, 1977). Many people commit self-harm on one or more occasions and yet do not move along the continuum towards parasuicide or beyond. However, some move along the continuum towards suicide, especially if the episodes of self-harm become less effective in reducing feelings of stress. Offenders on bail or remanded in custody are particularly at risk of suicide and self-harm. The strongest predictor of suicide is previous self-harm and those who have self-harmed within the previous year are 66 times more likely to attempt suicide than the general population (Ryan, 2003: 41).

Suicide and parasuicide

In the past 20 years the suicide and parasuicide rate has risen alarmingly in prisons. In 1983 the rate was 62 suicides per 100,000 average daily population and this had increased to 140 per 100,000 by 1999 (O'Grady 2004: 26). The suicide rate in the general population in 1999 was calculated to be 16 per 100,000. A comparative study of offenders in prison and offenders under supervision in the community identified similar rates of suicide among offenders in the community as for those in prison (Sattar, 2001). Although this suggests that characteristics of prisoners/offenders themselves largely account for the much higher suicide rate among offenders, the pressured existence within prison and the separation from friends and family is likely to exacerbate feelings of hopelessness and despair.

However, suicide rates vary between different sections of the population as a whole. A longitudinal study of 11,500 people who had attempted suicide over a period of 20 years (1978-98) identified that the risk of suicide is age and gender specific (Hawton and Fagg, 1988). The suicide risk is higher in teenagers and the elderly than it is in the general population with young men (aged 10 to 24) being 35 times more likely than the general population to commit suicide and similarly aged girls being 75 times more likely.

Practical guidance for engaging with someone who is potentially suicidal

Offenders may present symptoms or behaviours which suggest an increased risk of suicide. If the person is unfamiliar to the practitioner it is more difficult to assess the severity of the situation. As indicated earlier, self-harm and suicidal tendencies evoke intense anxiety in staff, and practitioners need to be able to talk with colleagues or a supervisor to gain guidance and support and, where appropriate, specialist help.

It is important for the practitioner to deal with the situation carefully in order to make an assessment.

The following section explores how a practitioner might sensitively explore the issue of suicide with an offender. Practice tool 6.1 (above) offers a framework which can easily be adapted for use here. The practitioner will need to use very similar skills to talk about subjects that may be painful or challenging for an offender, for example, violence or sexuality. It is important that a practitioner develops confidence and competence in tuning in to how an offender may be thinking and feeling in a situation. This is particularly useful as a means of understanding their perspective and also to understand the links between thoughts, feelings and behaviour (explored in more depth in Chapter Five in Figure 5.1, the iceberg model).

How readily the person responds really depends on the relationship but while their initial response may be guarded, they may find talking about their situation a source of relief. The person may reveal they have made plans to self-harm or commit suicide and these plans may include clear messages of method and intent. The following checklist (developed by Wix and Hillis [1998] for frontline practitioners) offers some strategies to reduce aggravating factors.

Practice tool 6.5: Strategies to reduce the risk of suicide and self-harm

- Encourage the person to participate in activities that involve other people and discourage isolated pursuits.
- Encourage the person to monitor medication, drug or alcohol use and discuss during contact with you.
- Emphasise the value of caring for themselves through a healthy diet, sleep, rest and social activities.
- Demonstrate that you are available to them by arranging regular contact times.
- Help to reduce stress levels by practical help, talking through concerns and giving support.
- Do not joke about issues of death or self-harm.
- Do not get into religious or philosophical conversation.
- Use positive reinforcement for any small signs of progress.
- Explain if you think they need further help and make suggestions appropriate to their needs; for example, GP, Samaritans, Community Mental Health Team, CRUSE Bereavement Care, youth counselling.
- In hostels it may be possible and appropriate to keep a closer 'watching brief' by arranging that the individual's room is near to staff and other residents

and through frequent day- and night-time checks. It may also be possible to remove objects of self-harm, supervise use of razors and involve the individual in group activities.

(Adapted from Wix and Hillis, 1998)

Conclusion

A disproportionate number of offenders are subject to a mental disorder; this may be mental illness and/or a personality disorder. Practitioners need a basic understanding of mental disorder to enable them to explore the links between the risk of the person's reoffending and harm and their mental disorder. Practitioners do not have to be experts in diagnosis but need to be able to identify when more specialist assessment and intervention is required. They also need to be alert to the risk of self-harm and suicide. Mentally disordered offenders are often portrayed as frightening and dangerous (Lynch, 2005) rather than marginalised and vulnerable. Practitioners need to be aware of diversity issues to ensure that their involvement counters rather than reinforces discrimination that exists in the system.

Effective intervention requires treatment to control symptoms, monitoring of offenders' behaviour and focused efforts to support the change necessary to reduce risk and to enable successful reintegration into the community. This involves taking a collaborative multidisciplinary approach with mental health and allied services. Clear systems of communication and arrangements for review need to be in place to ensure a rapid response should the offender's mental health deteriorate. While practitioners should give weight to the needs and wishes of the individual, these should not be at the expense of public protection.

Substance misuse

The first time I ever did it, I remember I had been out all day trying to get a graft the general way, the supermarket, anything I could [and] it just wasn't happening [so] five hours later I was nearly crawling back home and saw somebody drawing some money out of a hole in the wall and I grabbed his wallet. (A heroin user quoted in Allen, 2005: 368)

The individual quoted above fits a common perception of the substance-misusing offender: the heroin or crack cocaine user who engages in offending to fund a drug habit. This chapter seeks to explore in more depth what is known about the extent to which the misuse of drugs and/or alcohol is associated with offending behaviour and what is the nature of that association. The answers to those questions are more complex than might at first appear and will be used to suggest some practice implications for those working with substance misuse in a criminal justice context.

In order to make judgements about the risk of offending behaviour and to develop intervention plans addressing that risk, an individual offender is likely to experience an assessment process structured by risk assessment tools (Merrington et al, 2003; Moore et al, 2006). Both drug and alcohol misuse are dynamic risk factors for offending behaviour, included as part of a holistic assessment of risk. For those offenders where substance misuse is indicated, this risk assessment may be supplemented by specialist assessments focusing on the substance misuse in more detail. This chapter is not primarily addressing the role of the specialist drugs worker, but is aimed at the practitioner operating as an assessor, or case manager. The chapter takes the practitioner through a consideration of the social context of drug and alcohol use and their complex relationships with crime. It goes on to consider what is known about effective interventions, with a particular focus on responsivity and the motivation to change.

The chapter includes some separate consideration of drugs and alcohol, because research into the two is usually conducted separately and because the evidence suggests that the effects on behaviour are different. In criminal justice there are also distinct social, legal and service delivery contexts and the chapter addresses the implication of the coercive nature of treatment within those contexts.

What is meant by substance misuse?

The terminology 'substance abuse' or 'misuse' is important, in making clear that the person concerned is an active participant in the problem. This chapter is concerned primarily with psychological dependence and with patterns of behaviour associated with substance abuse, including offending behaviour. The terms 'addiction' and 'dependence' are both used in the literature in relation to serious alcohol and drug misuse. 'Dependence' is the term currently most in use (Harris, 2005) because, in part, it is seen as less stigmatising to the person concerned. Both terms can help to remind the reader that the misuse of drugs, or alcohol, can have a physical component, including increased tolerance for the substance in question and withdrawal symptoms following cessation of use.

There has been a move away from a reliance on a narrow medical model of dependency, assuming a biological compulsion as the most important influence. This approach tended to see the individual as largely powerless in the face of that physical compulsion, limiting the extent to which the individual could take responsibility for, and develop the self-belief that allows them to actively address, their problems (Harris, 2005). An understanding of dependent behaviour that locates it within a social and cultural context helps it to be seen as a response to environmental circumstances, influenced by individual characteristics. This is not to deny the importance of medically based treatments but to stress that, on their own, they are not enough and that an approach to treatment is needed that also emphasises individual responsibility for behaviour. This emphasis also fits with the focus of offending-related interventions, which also stress individual responsibility, supporting the increasing attention to substance misuse within the criminal justice system.

It is also important to see substance misuse by an individual as something that develops and changes over time (Brown, 1997; Melrose, 2004) serving different functions and having different meanings for individuals. Understanding those differences, and therefore being able to accurately assess the effect of substance misuse on an individual's offending, requires knowledge of the individual and of their context. The chapter begins to build a basis for that knowledge by looking at drug and alcohol use more generally.

Drugs and alcohol in society

The use of drugs and alcohol is widespread in the population. Surveys of young people aged from 12 to 30 suggest that 43% have used an illegal drug and that almost all 18- to 24-year-olds have drunk alcohol, with 10 per cent doing so every or nearly every day (Harrington, 2000; Goulden and Sondhi, 2001; Richardson and Budd, 2003).

Within this context, however, use of drugs is higher amongst offenders. Seventy-five per cent of serious and/or persistent offenders, in the Goulden and Sondhi (2001) study, were found to have used drugs at some time, compared to 25 per cent of non-offenders. Cannabis was by far the most widely consumed illegal drug, both in the general population and amongst offenders; however, offenders with higher levels of offending had a higher level of heroin and crack cocaine use than other groups.

Richardson and Budd (2003) found that frequency of drunkenness, rather than frequency of alcohol use, was most strongly associated with general offending behaviour, particularly involvement in fights. Frequency of drunkenness was also associated with illegal drug use, with 59 per cent of binge drinkers admitting illegal drug use.

There are also interesting findings about gender and drug use. Non-offending women have a lower rate of illegal drug use than males, whereas those women who offend have higher rates of misuse of drugs than do offending males. A study into prisoners' drug use and treatment found that White women prisoners had particularly high levels of drug dependency, usually involving opiates and sometimes crack cocaine (Ramsey, 2003). By contrast, women involved in the trafficking of drugs from abroad were not themselves drug users and the place of illegal drug use in their offending was not one associated with dependence, but rather with financial, or personal, survival (Bean, 2004; HMIP, 2005).

Engineer et al (2003), in a study of binge drinking, suggested four elements that need to be considered in identifying and analysing its impact on social disorder. The elements they suggest provide a useful model for assessors of substance abuse and any related offending behaviour:

- attitude and motivations
- social and peer group norms
- effects of drugs or drinking on mood and behaviour
- environment.

The following Practice tool suggests areas of significance that should be considered in information gathering and analysis about offending and substance misuse. At this stage you may want to use it to reflect. The remainder of the chapter adds detail to the content of this Practice tool and you may wish to return to it later.

Practice tool 7.1

Attitude and motivations:

- Why is the individual using the substance/s concerned?
- What motivates them to continue? For example, is it to cope with pressures, or in order to experience a high/get kicks?
- Do they use drugs or alcohol to give them the courage to engage in certain behaviours, including committing offences?

Social and peer group norms:

- What is acceptable or admired behaviour within their group?
- Are they responding to the norms of their group in relation to substances?
- Do they actively select peer groups that provide support and approval for their misuse of the substance concerned?
- How are these norms affected by gender or by ethnicity, for example?

Effects of drugs or drinking on mood and behaviour:

- How does their substance use impact on their mood and behaviour?
- What are the physical and psychological effects of the substance? For example, does it reduce inhibition, or give courage?
- Does it have a stimulant effect, or does it calm the individual down?
- Does it make offending or disorderly behaviour more or less likely? Is the individual using one substance or a combination, and how do different substances combine to affect mood and behaviour?

Environment:

- If abusing drugs how easily available are they?
- What are the pressures and triggers in their environment that increase the likelihood of substance misuse?
- Where is the individual engaging in both substance abuse and offending behaviours? Are they alone, or with others in social settings, like pubs? Are they at home?

- Are there particular circumstances or times of the day when substance abuse and offending occur?

A career of substance abuse

Longitudinal studies into offending behaviour provide important information about changing patterns of risk factors over the life history of an offender (Farrington, 1997). The concept of a criminal career, emerging from these studies, is discussed in Chapter Four. Dependency on either alcohol or drugs also follows a developmental process. If the individual is offending then the criminal career and the career of substance misuse (Allen, 2005) will run alongside each other. They may share some common influences and each can affect the other. In relation to substance misuse it is important to ask:

- How did their involvement begin? This may have important implications for preventative strategies, as well as helping to develop an understanding of the meaning of substance abuse in that individual's life?
- What keeps them abusing the substance/s concerned? What, in other words, are the current risk factors and how is their dependency developing? The idea of a career reminds the assessor to look for a range of causes of the behaviour both immediate and long term.
- What are the personal and situational factors that are associated with stopping, or reducing, substance use? Can protective factors be identified?

Melrose (2004) identifies five reasons for young people beginning to use drugs:

- Oblivion seekers – blocking out previous traumas.
- Acceptance seekers – because their friends are.
- Thrill seekers – curiosity and wanting a buzz.

And combinations of the above:

- Thrill and acceptance seekers.
- Oblivion and acceptance seekers.

Not all young people who experiment will go on to develop dependence. One way of understanding those that do is to see the individual as seeking to manipulate their subjective sense of happiness and well-being, gradually becoming dependent on one route (the addiction), to the exclusion of other sources of pleasure (Brown, 1997).

The transition from adolescence to adulthood is difficult for some young people and this is discussed in Chapter Four. Melrose (2004) uses the phrase 'fractured transitions'. Some young people's choices are constrained by circumstances making them more likely to follow lifestyles which add to any original social exclusion. Their ability to find happiness in socially acceptable ways, such as through educational attainment and satisfying personal relationships, is limited. These difficulties, which are risk factors for offending behaviour (McNeill and Batchelor, 2004), also make it more likely that the young person will begin to become involved in misusing substances. Not all young people who use drugs offend and many young people use drugs and alcohol without developing dependence, but for a particularly vulnerable group those first experiences provide them with otherwise elusive sources of happiness and self-worth. Allen (2005: 357) also talks about the idea of "critical moments", in particular sexual abuse and bereavement, as crucial in the move to participation in serious drug use, suggesting that Melrose's oblivion seekers may be the most likely to escalate into dependency. This is not inevitable, however. As Melrose points out, some vulnerable young people are also able to change their drug use over time.

For others, substance use increases and is accompanied by developing dependency. This, exacerbated by an involvement in offending, can affect the peers with whom the young person spends their time and further reduce access to socially acceptable rewards, particularly for those who lack protective factors like stable family support. Increasingly, the young person will gain access to those who supply illegal drugs and to means of obtaining cash from offending, enabling continued experimentation (Bean, 2004).

In the short term the use of substances helps to regulate negative feelings, producing either heightened states of arousal, or a relief of anxiety. The individual then becomes increasingly reliant on the substances to manage feelings. The time that this takes will vary for individuals according to physical effects and social context. For example, if the young person has access to experimentation with drugs, perhaps because of their involvement with other offenders, they may find that soon they experience a very significant positive effect on mood, so that these drugs supplant other substances as their preferred way of managing feelings. For others, who lack access, or who operate in a different social and cultural context, alcohol may prove the more reliable regulator.

A series of deficits in how the individual thinks about their use of substances helps increasing dependence to develop. The individual fails to recognise the escalating problems created by the misuse, which by now may be damaging personal relationships. They begin to live in a state of short-term crisis management, needing significantly higher exposure to achieve the same effects. Allen (2005: 365) talks about when individuals are "in deep" with drugs. This process is in part a physical one, rooted in levels of physical tolerance. It is also a product of unrealistic expectations and a decreasing psychological ability to tolerate normal levels of unhappiness. The individual's behaviour is likely to cause conflict in relationships, both personal and with wider society, but they may fail to see the addictive behaviour as the cause of those conflicts. They tend instead to see it as the solution to the negative feelings the conflicts leave them with, increasing its central place in their lives. Belief systems may already exist, or may develop, that support the abuse of substances and that are, in turn, reinforced by the individual's peers and social context (Brown, 1997; Melrose, 2004; Harris, 2005).

As this process continues the person increases their reliance on the addictive behaviour, as the primary source of positive emotions. The pathways within which this develops will differ for individuals and will be different for those who are abusing drugs and those primarily abusing alcohol. Timescales will vary. Progress into the criminal justice system is affected by the illegality of some substances, as well as by their physical and psychological effects. For individuals who abuse alcohol there is more social acceptance initially and it may be easier to maintain some normal social relationships alongside the abuse, altering the trajectories of the dependence and of offending behaviour (McMurran, 2002a).

Practice tool 7.2

The following checklist about the place of substance misuse in an individual's life can be used in addition to Practice tool 7.1.

- How did the individual begin abusing substances? Was there a 'critical moment'?
- To what extent do they and you understand the ways in which they use substances for reward and to manage difficult feelings?

- To what extent is their abuse of substances causing conflict with others and how do they manage those conflicts?
- What positive sources of support are they able to draw upon to provide them with pleasure and reward?
- What alternative strategies for managing difficult feelings have they developed?

Substance misuse and offending

The practitioner must assess to what extent the misuse of substances is a dynamic risk factor for offending and, if it is, what the precise linkages are for this individual? For some offences the linkage is embedded in the legal process itself, for drugs offences and offences of drink-driving, for example. Even for these offences, however, the assessor needs to understand patterns of cause and effect for that individual. Some offenders involved in the supply of illegal drugs, particularly at an organised level, may not themselves have a substance misuse problem and may have very different reasons for their offending, both economic and to do with status and masculinity (Crewe, 2006).

Budd (2002) offers the "three 'C's" as a way of understanding the potentially different relationships offenders may have with alcohol:

- *Causal*: alcohol misuse is directly and causally related to offending behaviour at the time of the incident, or in another direct way.
- *Contributory*: alcohol misuse is one of many interacting factors affecting offending behaviour, the exact role depending on the individual and on a number of social and situational factors.
- *Coexistence*: alcohol consumption occurs together with offending, because they have a common cause, rather than alcohol causing the offending, or *vice versa*.

Bennett and Holloway (2005) also stress the importance of clear thinking about cause and effect in relation to the links between substance misuse and crime, making the point that sometimes the connection may be no more than coincidental. They suggest a similar way of thinking about cause and effect for drug abuse and crime:

- *Causal*: drug abuse may cause crime, or crime may cause drug abuse.
- *Reciprocal*: drug abuse and offending are causally linked and mutually reinforcing.

Assessors need to understand these different patterns of connection, the nature of the relationships for each individual offender and how they may change over time and in different circumstances (Taxman, 2006). Some of what is known about drugs and crime and about alcohol and crime is now discussed separately.

Drugs

There is well–documented evidence of a link between illegal drug use, and in particular heroin and cocaine, and acquisitive crime (Bennett and Holloway, 2005). Allen's (2005) review of the literature and own research supports this link, but points out its complexity. For example, participation in acquisitive crime such as shoplifting tends to precede drug use, as seems to be the case with women drug offenders, whereas acquisitive crimes that are person related, such as street robbery, tend to occur after the perpetrators have become regular drug users. For many offenders crimes such as robbery are not the norm, but are resorted to when other offending options have failed, as is captured in the quotation beginning this chapter.

Studies into drug users in the community and into levels of drug use among prisoners suggest that heroin and crack cocaine use is particularly associated with acquisitive crime, including robbery and burglary (Stewart et al, 2000; Bean, 2004; Allen, 2005; Bennett and Holloway, 2005; Makkai and Payne, 2005).

For an individual, an understanding is then needed of the nature of this association, as discussed previously. The pressure to acquire funds to support a developing drug habit will be greater for those who have never accessed employment, or whose employment is threatened by their drug use. It may be that, in the early stages of their offending history, their motivations for offending were not drug related. However, as both careers develop the need to maintain a supply of drugs becomes more important and more central to the continuation and potential escalation of offending (Allen, 2005).

Abuse of substances may also be linked to the individual's self–concept, to their beliefs about themselves and about their relationship with the world they inhabit (Melrose, 2004). Status and a sense of belonging to a group can become associated with the use of illegal drugs and acquiring their supply can provide a sense of purposeful activity. Stopping drug use can, therefore, leave the individual with significant gaps in their sense of who they are and how they fit in the world. "Problem drug users tend more often to be unemployed and unemployed people tend more often to be problem drug users" (Leitner, 1993, cited in South et al, 2001). When there is a failure to develop a successful work-based identity, a drug-based lifestyle can provide an alternative.

Drug use may then make it more difficult for individuals to find employment, because of the demands it makes on their time and its impact on health and functioning. The time spent in a drug-based lifestyle leads those involved to fall behind peers in terms of the acquisition of work-based skills and experience. There is no simple relationship between unemployment and drug use, with cause and effect shifting over time and between individuals. However, finding stable secure employment helps to prevent relapse, since this promotes desistance from offending (South et al, 2001).

Drug use is therefore associated with a higher likelihood of reoffending for some individuals (Moore et al, 2006). It may also be associated with a higher risk of harm. There is a well-documented link between drug misuse and harm to the offender, including ill health and accidental overdose (Bean, 2004). There may also be a connection with serious harm to others. While Allen (2005) describes the reluctance of many drug abusers to engage in offences that harm others, this should not be seen as invariable. Offences that involve physical contact with, and threat to, individual victims inevitably raise the likelihood of serious harm. Nationally, the link between crack cocaine and aggressive and violent behaviour has been recognised (Home Office, 2002b). There is also the potential for harm to others in the supply of illegal drugs and in the organised and sometimes violent networks that support that trade (Bean, 2004; Crewe, 2006).

Alcohol

It is problematic levels of alcohol use, and principally drunkenness, which have been particularly found to be risk factors for offending behaviour, including an association with the use of illegal drugs. Even when other factors are taken into account, frequency of drunkenness is still an important indicator of offending and disorderly behaviour, particularly violent crime (Richardson and Budd, 2003).

Alcohol abuse is not linked to acquisitive crime in the way that illegal drugs are. This does not mean that, for individual offenders, getting money to buy alcohol cannot be a motivation. Alcohol abuse and the night-time economy are, however, linked to violent crime, with alcohol abuse associated with offences of disorder and violence around public houses and clubs (Budd, 2003). It could be that drunkenness acts as a disinhibitor, rendering violent behaviour more likely, but it is also likely that there are some shared causes, for example, peer group norms and expectations (McMurran, 2002a). It could also be argued that crime, or the desire to commit a crime, may be encouraging the use of alcohol, as an association is formed between heavy drinking and engaging in violent behaviour.

Completed OASys assessments suggest that alcohol misuse is not a good predictor of reconviction generally, but is a predictor of reconviction for offences involving serious harm (Moore et al, 2006). In addition, a review of the research indicates that there is a high provenance of alcohol abuse among men with histories of intimate partner violence and that a substantial proportion of perpetrators had drunk alcohol just before the incident. Intimate partner violence also tends to be more severe when alcohol is involved (Finney, 2004) so that alcohol is a risk factor for the violence and for the degree of harm associated with it.

Galvani (2004), in her research into the links between alcohol misuse and intimate partner violence, talks about the ways in which men's drinking is grounded in a traditional notion of accepted male behaviour, an understanding that, when fused with other beliefs about men's and women's relationships and male power over women, produces a more powerful effect than either would on their own. While alcohol may not be causative of partner violence, it heightens the risk in terms of likelihood and degree where violence and abuse are already present.

Assessment

Offenders who have problems with substance misuse, like mentally disordered offenders (see Chapter Six), present complexities for the delivery of interventions. Questions are raised about what to prioritise and how interventions addressing substance misuse and those targeting offending can support each other. In a criminal justice context what happens to an offender will also be determined by the facilities and orders available to the court (Bean, 2004).

For an individual, programmes of intervention should be informed by careful assessment of the links between substance misuse and offending. An offender may identify a problem with substance misuse that is not causally connected to offending and in those circumstances that need may best be met outside of the criminal justice context. Those involved in illegal supply at a significant level will have different reasons for their behaviour including opportunity structures necessitating different approaches (Crewe, 2006; Taxman, 2006).

The following discussions about assessment and interventions focus on offenders where there is a causal link between the substance misuse and the offending behaviour. They take as a focus the importance of responsivity. For those offenders with substance misuse problems, there are such powerful positives deriving from the abuse that engaging motivation becomes even more central to assessing and intervening successfully.

From the outset it is essential that practitioners remember the potential impact of their own behaviour. Practitioner skills play an important role in increasing the likelihood of an offender participating in treatment (Harris, 2006). Empathy rather than a confrontational style has been associated with greater success. Skills in reflection, open-ended questions and affirmation are important. The characteristics of the practitioner "can have a significant effect within a single session" (Miller and Rollnick, 2002: 7).

The process of information gathering and assessment should, therefore, be experienced by the offender as the first stage of engagement that will support the process of change. A structured approach guiding assessors' thinking and recording findings remains helpful (Merrington, 2004). However, such assessments may be taking place in situations of pressure, where time is limited. Practitioners need, therefore, to be skilled at understanding potential patterns of cause and effect and at asking questions that uncover those patterns efficiently. The assessment should also include attention to responsivity and the offender's state of readiness to change.

The model from Prochaska and DiClemente (1983) of the cycle of change has been very influential to an understanding of the complex process of change in addictive behaviour and raises concepts that are helpful in assessment. Alongside the work of Miller and Rollnick (2002) on motivational interviewing, this model suggests the skills needed when working with an offender struggling to change unhelpful behaviours. The cycle suggests that individuals move through a series of stages of change. These are: pre-contemplation, through contemplation, decision making, action, maintenance and moving to successful embedded change, or sometimes to lapse and relapse.

The first stage of pre-contemplation describes an individual who is not really engaged in thinking about changing. DiClemente and Velasquez (2002) suggest four different kinds of pre-contemplation: reluctant, rebellious, resigned and rationalising.

Practice tool 7.3

Use the descriptions below to think about the kind of resistance you are encountering with an individual offender.

Reluctant: those who are fearful of change – need careful listening and feedback.
Rebellious: those who put energy into resisting the idea of change – need the practitioner to help shift the focus of that energy.
Resigned: those who see themselves as incapable of change – need the practitioner to develop hope and remove barriers to change.
Rationalising: those who use argument and debate to prove that change is not necessary – need the practitioner to avoid argument and emphasise reflective listening.

As an individual is asked about their offending and their substance misuse, open questions and reflection can play a part in beginning to shift the balance of their decision making towards change (Fuller and Taylor, 2003). As part of the assessment process, offenders should be helped to understand the costs of their behaviour and the positive benefits of change. They are, however, likely to experience ambivalence about the process of change. They may engage in denial, seeking to minimise their responsibility for offending by a variety of strategies, including blaming others and sometimes drug and alcohol misuse itself. Denial serves to absolve them from the responsibility to take sometimes painful and difficult steps to change their behaviour (Spencer, 1999). In relation to substance misuse, practitioners can helpfully provide specific and personal information about the negative consequences of continuing misuse and about the supports available to help offenders. This could be included as part of a discussion about what interventions may result from an assessment. The practitioner should also acknowledge the positives of the addictive behaviour, so that the offender perceives them as realistic. This process will be built on as the assessment is used to develop a plan for an offender.

Interventions

There is growing evidence from evaluations of arrest referral schemes and from health services that brief interventions at a point of crisis can make a significant difference (Hopkins and Sparrow, 2006; Sharp and Atherton, 2006). These interventions combine assessment, feedback, education and advice and use motivational interviewing skills. They are important in themselves and also suggest that practitioners even in limited contacts with some offenders could make a difference to subsequent alcohol misuse. For higher risk offenders and for those offenders where brief interventions have not succeeded, then a more substantial plan of intervention over a period of time may be needed. How this plan is drawn up and implemented, as well as its contents, will be of significance.

Addictive patterns of thinking have rational and understandable elements, even though they may be linked to behaviour that seems damaging. Practitioners need to develop a personal style that is able to acknowledge the positive rational elements, without colluding with the addictive behaviour. This needs to be taken through to the process of setting and working on goals. Within a criminal justice context, objectives are often set with offenders that assume they are at the action stage, for example, to reduce their drinking, or stop using illegal drugs. If they are not at that stage then such an objective may not effectively address the reality of their thinking and behaviour and will be more likely to fail. The offender is then all too often blamed for the failure.

One example where attention should be paid to the detail of practice, therefore, is that of writing intervention plans and setting goals for individual offenders. As Merrington (2004) points out, structured assessment tools should be used to help set relevant goals, but should not be driven by the need to achieve national targets. They should instead be used to enhance professional decision making. An effective goal for an individual offender would recognise and match their place on the cycle of change. For example, an individual who is abusing alcohol but who has no, or limited, recognition of that as a problem is likely to resist goals framed in terms of reducing their intake. A more appropriate goal needs to be framed, perhaps addressing their ambivalence itself. A suitable goal for the offender (within an agreed timescale) might be to be able to explain to someone else the advantages and disadvantages, of their use of drugs or alcohol. Such a goal does not assume their commitment to change but, if skilfully managed by a practitioner, can be used to help them shift the balance in their thinking. They can be helped to recognise for themselves the reality of the impact of their behaviour.

This approach to change also recognises the importance of positive supports; like the literature on desistance more generally, and the 'Good Lives Model' which also suggests approach goals (Beech and Mann, 2002; Ward and Brown, 2004). This emphasis on developing supports and resolving difficulties in the way of the achievement of positive goals, also needs to inform the intervention. Burke et al (2006: 115) looked at service provision for prisoners with drug problems and found that many offenders felt that they could "only address their drug use once other more immediate concerns had been addressed". This same study highlights the importance of the links between the experience in custody and what happens in the community and some of the limitations in current provision.

Whether in prison or in the community, addressing substance misuse in isolation is likely to be less effective. Other individual and situational factors affecting the development of both the dependence and the offending need to be tackled (Lipton et al, 2002). Lipton et al's findings from a meta-analysis suggest that while questions remain about which approaches work best for different types of offender, programmes of intervention that included cognitive behavioural elements focusing on offending as well as drug treatment were the most effective.

Cognitive behavioural approaches should include specific reinforcement for positive achievements. The development of strategies and skills is also important, for example, how to engage socially without recourse to drugs or alcohol. It is crucial that the offender is helped to recognise the steps they have taken and the skills they have developed in taking those steps. They need to become increasingly convinced that the costs of change are worthwhile, in terms of positive outcomes.

It is also important to keep in mind the potential complexity of the link between the substance misuse and offending. Interventions, for example, must pay attention to underpinning beliefs and destructive ways of facing problems that have developed (McMurran, 2002a). For example, in relation to alcohol-related violence, beliefs that alcohol is to blame for the offender's violence have to be challenged. A tendency to focus on immediate, rather than longer-term, consequences and towards impulsivity may be central to offending and drug misuse. Skilful use of questioning is of great importance.

Practice tool 7.4

Here are some examples of Socratic questions given in McMurran (2002a: 233) to be used to challenge an offender's belief that alcohol causes them to be violent.

- Are you always violent after drinking?
- Tell me about the times when you have taken a drink and not been violent?
- What is it about those occasions that distinguish them from the times you are violent?

> Use those questions as a starting point and think about another unhelpful belief a substance misusing offender may hold, then write two or three questions of your own.

It is also important to recognise that for some offending behaviour deeper sets of belief may be involved, with significant motivations beyond those associated with the substance misuse itself. For instance, as already discussed in relation to domestic violence, alcohol use may be supported by a particular culture that also supports damaging attitudes to women. Those beliefs in turn increase the likelihood of violent behaviour towards a partner and any attempt at intervention would need to address those beliefs, as well as the alcohol use (Galvani, 2004).

Whatever programme of interventions is to be put in place to help an offender to overcome offending substance misuse, an individual's self-efficacy beliefs will be associated with success (Bandura, 1997). These beliefs help them to overcome ambivalence about change and to sustain that change over the longer term and in the face of obstacles, long after the effects of any initial physical addiction have ended.

Practitioners need to work to maximise the learning for offenders as they struggle with the process of change, no matter where they are situated on the cycle. Individuals can be helped to identify new thinking and behavioural skills and to see how they can use those skills in a range of contexts. The individual most likely to maintain change can be expected to have a strong sense of the skills they have acquired and some confidence in their ability to use those skills effectively; in other words, to have developed a good degree of self-efficacy (Bandura, 1997).

Danger points for relapse should also be identified and strategies for resistance supported. Because change is difficult, progress may not always be continuous. It is important that this is understood as an experience that can be learnt from, whether the individual re-engages with change immediately, or at some point in the future (Gorski and Trundy, 2000). It is also important that the offender is helped to develop strategies to manage potentially high risk situations. This thinking is particularly important for practice within a criminal justice system which emphasises enforcement.

The offender's social context is central. Even when successful change is initiated, if an individual is returning to the same peers and social context relapse is more likely. Self-efficacy beliefs will be supported by environmental changes – new peers and social arrangements, gaining employment, for example, and by the acquisition of relevant interpersonal skills, the setting of achievable goals and reinforcement for their attainment. Treatment for substance abuse must therefore include attention to broad-ranging interventions, including employment-based routes. It is not easy for drug users to find employment that is of a good quality. If they are to persevere with sometimes poorly paid short-term employment, in order to acquire some skills and a record of work (South et al, 2001), then they will need support from treatment providers.

The following Activities and reflection box gives the reader opportunity to think in some depth about what supporting someone through a process of change might mean. The chapter then goes on to think about the implications of doing so in a coercive context.

Activities and reflection 7.1

Think about a behaviour of your own that you have struggled to change. If you have tried to give up smoking or go on a diet those are good examples. What helped you move through a process of change? For example:

- What helped you begin to think seriously about changing and how did you overcome your ambivalence?
- What kind of goals did you set for yourself and were they realistic?
- What supports did you draw on?
- If you were successful, what helped you to succeed and can you identify specific self-efficacy beliefs that you acquired?
- If unsuccessful so far, what might help you in the future and what self-efficacy beliefs do you need to build?

Delivering interventions in a criminal justice system – the impact of coercion

Many of the large numbers of drug users within the criminal justice system will be least able to draw on personal and social resources to address their problems unaided. The system is therefore well placed to help tackle substance misuse (Kothari et al, 2002) and to expand the base of those being brought into treatment. Although consent must be given by the offender to be involved in treatment, it can be argued that that consent is in fact coerced, given the context, and that, therefore, offenders will be less likely to be motivated. There is evidence, however, that coerced drug treatment can achieve the same level of benefits as voluntary treatment (Hough, 1996). This evidence might alleviate concerns about coercion, in the light of the potential benefits. It seems likely that the extent to which this is true will depend, in part, on the ways in which services are delivered and their sensitivity to the individuals concerned.

The context may not however always be fully sympathetic to individuals' needs and to their level of motivation. It may be driven by targets and will also be influenced by the need for a criminal justice agency to be alert to the risks posed to themselves and others by offenders who misuse substances (McMurran, 2002a; Bean, 2004). If an offender is abusing alcohol and that abuse is linked with violence, then managing that risk must take priority and the rights of potential victims must be carefully considered. Working with substance misuse in a criminal justice context will therefore throw up additional considerations and challenges, aside from an understanding of the individual offender's willingness to change.

One major danger of a coerced approach to treatment is that it may produce confusion in the individual about the extent to which behavioural control rests with them, rather than with control mechanisms imposed by others (Harris, 2005). This would undermine an approach rooted in an understanding of motivation and the process of long-lasting change. There are potential solutions to this dilemma. Trotter (1999) points out that accurate role clarification improves outcomes for involuntary clients, in other words the worker taking time to explain their role and their dual function as both helper and social controller. This kind of clarity can ease the conflicts possible within a coerced approach, and can help the practitioner keep a clear focus on the management of risk, alongside attention to developing positive relationships.

Planning and managing interventions is equally vital. A report into the treatment of prisoners' drug use (Fox et al, 2005) reinforces the earlier point about the transition into the community. They suggest the importance of the following components of 'through' care:

*   timely assessments;
*   consistent collaboration in aftercare planning;
*   comprehensive referral system;
*   timely access to clinical assistance;
*   maintaining engagement and motivation at the point of release;
*   aftercare;
*   case management that cuts across agency perspectives;
*   a persistent and non-judgemental approach by staff;
*   housing support.

These elements will need to be overlaid with attention to the internal and external control of risk, particularly for higher risk offenders. Even high risk offenders need to feel that staff care about them as individuals. However, a non-judgemental approach has its limitations and practitioners need also to demonstrate clearly their disapproval of the harm caused by offending behaviour (Kemshall et al, 2006). For example, if working with a domestic violence perpetrator, attention must be paid to the linkage between beliefs that support alcohol abuse and those that support violence towards women (Galvani, 2004). Those working with offenders who are abusing alcohol should generally be alert for indicators of domestic violence.

There are challenges as well as supports to achieving this level of service in the current legislative and organisational context. For example, there continues to be a scarcity of treatment resources for alcohol misusers (HMIP, 2005). Closer relationships between health and criminal justice agencies are essential if the range of responses needed is to be made available to offenders. Interagency practice presents challenges and ongoing attention to communication between staff from different backgrounds, and clarity about shared understandings are crucial (see Chapter Six for a discussion on interagency collaboration).

Conclusion

Working with substance misuse within a criminal justice setting offers real opportunities to engage with those less likely to initiate change for themselves. It allows practitioners opportunities to make a difference to the harm caused by substance misuse to the individual and to others, not least by offending.

Responsivity presents particular challenges in working with offenders with dependencies. There is a need to pay attention to developing and sustaining motivation amongst those offenders who also misuse substances. This will be helped by an appreciation of the social context and an interagency approach; supporting problem solving and helping the individual set and achieve positive goals.

To succeed, the practitioner also needs to draw on a set of skills in interviewing and engaging offenders. They need to do so mindful of the potential impact of the involuntary nature of their relationship with many such offenders and the importance of reinforcing and supporting the responsibility of the individual for their own behaviour. An emphasis on taking responsibility fits well with a linked focus on offending behaviour and substance misuse and helps the practitioner also to be clear about the risks posed.

EIGHT

Basic skills

Introduction

There is widespread agreement across the developed world that links exist between poor educational achievement, unemployment and criminal recidivism (see, for example, the work of the European Offender Employment Forum which brings these threads together). In the UK, offender assessment tools, relating to both adult and juvenile offenders, identify education, training and employment as one of a range of potential offence-related needs requiring exploration and assessment. Once a practitioner has identified such needs in relation to a specific individual, these may then be addressed through employment and/or literacy and numeracy programmes tailored to the particular circumstances of offenders. For young offenders an emphasis is placed upon facilitating school attendance for all young people, sometimes irrespective of whether or not their educational experience is connected to their offending behaviour. The rationale for this almost universally applicable approach is that:

> The notions of 'literacy' and 'numeracy' are much more than the simple acquisition of 'basic skills' ... They are founded on the idea that the skills of communication and application of numbers are central to all areas of learning [and] are critical to enabling access, participation and progression in education, training and employment, as well as promoting personal development. (YJB, 2003: 11)

The broadness of this belief in the intrinsic value of education is rarely challenged. It is regarded as a fundamental right in many parts of the world, essential to both personal and societal development. The United Nations Children's Fund (UNICEF), for example, regards education as one of its four priority areas of activity in encouraging the "harmonious development of every child" along with health, equality and protection (UNICEF, 2007: 1).

This chapter explores the challenges and dilemmas for practitioners in the criminal justice system of promoting the acquisition of basic skills in a context where the emphasis is increasingly upon offence-focused work and the management of risk. The chapter will draw upon the increasing body of research, both national and international, which is beginning to enhance understanding of the links between poor basic skills, social exclusion, restricted life opportunities and the risk of becoming entrenched in an offending lifestyle. In doing so, it will explore the implications for practice of the twin notions of *human capital* and *social capital*, at the heart of which is education and, by inference, literacy and numeracy.

It will emphasise the importance of *basic skills* (or the lack of such skills) both as a potential risk factor contributing to offending behaviour and as a potential barrier to an individual's effective response to interventions. It will then explore promising ways of engaging with offenders experiencing basic skills needs, adapting offence-focused interventions to take account of these needs and developing and sustaining their motivation to take advantage of specialist services aimed at improving their skills levels.

Basic skills and offending: conceptual dilemmas

Despite the widely held belief in the value of education, the literature seems to suggest that, whilst links between education and subsequent employability and offending are strong, "little is known or understood about the relationship between [such factors as] schooling and criminal behaviour" (Lochner and Moretti, 2003: 1). Parsons (2002: 29) concludes that her study provides "the first set of insights into the relationships over time between poor literacy and numeracy and crime". YJB guidance (2003: 12) refers to a lack of clarity in the relationship between attainment and offending and speculates on only "likely associated links". Similarly, in reflecting on the experience of the Probation Service in addressing the basic skills and employment needs of offenders, Haslewood-Pocsik and McMahon (2004) intimate that links may be complex and indirect, and that skills deficits and poor employment prospects may interact with other social and environmental factors. Although they would suggest some strong possible connections, the language remains equivocal and speculative.

The absence of clear causal relationships and the complexity of a range of interconnected needs can present the practitioner with a number of challenges, not least of which is how to prioritise, sequence and coordinate interventions within this broad area of work in a context which increasingly emphasises offence-focused interventions and risk management. The central challenge which will be the focus of this chapter is "the question of determining the most effective strategies for responding to multiple problems presented by offenders" (Haslewood-Pocsik and McMahon, 2004: 130). This challenge is common to work described elsewhere in this book where practitioners not only have to work with complex multiple needs, but also balance the demands of a risk focus with a more needs-desistance-based approach, for example, work with women, young people, substance users and mentally disordered offenders.

To develop the skills of individual offenders, which are as much about their life in the world as their offending behaviour, is likely to require more than simple one-off interventions focusing on literacy, numeracy or enhancing their employment prospects. Arguably, practitioners will need to take a more strategic approach to this whole area of work, since deficits in what are described as 'skills for life' (Connexions, 2003) can compound other criminogenic needs, hinder the individual's ability to respond to offence-focused services, and stand in the way of the individual offender's reintegration into the community.

Valuing basic skills: useful definitions and key concepts

In the UK, basic skills have been formally defined as:

> The ability to read, write and speak in English or Welsh and use mathematics at a level necessary to function and progress at work and in society in general. (BSA, 2000: 3)

Even in this definition there is a suggestion that basic skills extend beyond literacy and numeracy. The spoken language is clearly associated with effective communication.

The practical implications of skills deficits range from simple daily routines such as telling the time, reading letters, instructions and directions and going shopping, to such complex activities as completing forms, communicating assertively with people in authority and any activity which takes an individual outside the world they readily understand and feel confident in.

Activities and reflection 8.1

Think about a life without literacy and numeracy skills:

* What would you be unable to do?
* How would this affect your daily life?
* What particular problems might this present someone in their contacts with the criminal justice system?

Research by the Basic Skills Agency (1997) identified longer-term practical consequences for individuals, including:

* higher rates of unemployment amongst those with low skills, both men and women;
* reduced earning capacity;
* increased likelihood of living in a disadvantaged area;
* more difficulty in progressing in employment through work-based training or promotion;
* poor general health and increased likelihood of depression;
* some groups in society already experiencing discrimination (for example, people with special needs, African Caribbean children and young people emerging from the care system) are more likely to find their sense of social exclusion heightened by basic skills deficits.

In his foreword to the UK government's 'Skills for Life' Strategy in 2003, the Secretary of State for Education at that time acknowledged the strength of these findings by asking his audience to "consider the wider impact that lacking such skills [literacy, language and numeracy] has on an adult's life". He stated that:

> Having poor essential skills means having a lower income and being less employable. It is not surprising that this condition compounds the problems of poor health, crime and living in disadvantaged areas. (Clarke, 2003, quoted in Connexions, 2003: 5)

Encapsulated within this brief comment are the two concepts which go some way to justify paying attention to basic skills deficits, both at a general societal level and in work with individuals: *human capital* and *social capital.* These are both associated with the principle of social inclusion, a key aspect of contemporary UK government policy.

There is extensive national and international research, reflecting upon and exploring these two concepts (for example, Coleman, 1990; Sampson and Laub, 1993; Putnam, 1995; Farrall, 2004). The concepts have particular relevance to an understanding both of individual pathways into offending and the social environment within which individuals move, and by which they are influenced.

Social capital concerns the network of social resources and relationships which binds people together and provides support and security. It has been defined as:

> ... a social asset which consists of social interactions, networks and network opportunities, which either people, groups or communities have, within a specific environment of mutual trust and reciprocity, and which are informed by specific norms and values. (Kemshall et al, 2006)

However, it is closely connected to **human capital** in that:

> Social capital relies upon (and in turn promotes) human capital. Human capital refers to the human skill and resources individuals need to function effectively, such as reading, writing and reasoning ability. (Rose and Clear, 1996: 22)

The inference here is that the development of 'human skills and resources' is valuable in facilitating the reintegration process and promoting social inclusion, both for communities and individuals. The significance of social capital has been highlighted by writers increasingly engaged in debate about the need to focus upon developing future resilience and desistance in offenders, which goes beyond a strictly offence-focused approach (see, for example, discussion in Bazemore and Erbe, 2004).

From a practitioner's point of view it is worth mentioning here that although these two 'commodities' can be connected and complement and enhance each other, they can exist and be developed independently of each other. Brennan et al (2006: 995) refer to social capital as the "social glue ... that binds people and enables them to cooperate more effectively", as distinct from the other resources, "financial, physical and human capital", that successful societies need. Developing human capital (individual skills and resources) falls more within the remit of the practitioner than promoting social capital, which resides more with those seeking to develop communities through policy or partnerships.

Such distinctions have entered debates about desistance from offending, including the promotion of resilience as part of the role of the criminal justice practitioner. Farrall (2004) makes a distinction between the development of the skills encompassed within human capital, and the wider challenge of working to develop an environment in which skills are relevant, sustainable in practice and form a bridge into stronger, more positive, pro-social relationships; in other words, the challenge of increasing social capital in the lives of offenders.

Nevertheless, it is hard to argue against paying attention to the basic needs of individuals in terms of their literacy, numeracy and related communication skills. The dilemma for practitioners is how central to their face-to-face work with offenders should this focus of concern be, especially in a climate where the more immediate emphasis is upon effectiveness in reducing offending and the assessment and management of risk to the public.

Basic skills and offending

There is now a body of research which supports the view that "improving skills and employment can have a positive impact on the incidence of re-offending, to the benefit of individuals, their families and communities, and wider society" by helping to "break the cycle of offending" (Home Office, 2005a: 12).

The picture emerging from research is that, in terms of the characteristics of offenders:

> ... the average educational achievement of offenders is lower than that of the general population. [Offenders] leave school at a younger age, have higher levels of truancy, suspension and permanent exclusion, and have fewer qualifications. (McMahon et al, 2004: 2)

Findings relating to the past educational and employment experiences of offenders in custody (Home Office, 2005a: 12) include, for example:

- 30% of prisoners were regular truants;
- 49% of sentenced prisoners were excluded from school;
- 52% of male and 71% of female prisoners have no qualifications at all;

- 67% were unemployed at the time of sentence;
- 76% do not have paid employment to go to on release.

In relation to the impact of basic skills interventions on future offending, a study undertaken in Canada by Porporino and Robinson (1992) found that there was a 33% reduction in recidivism among those offenders who completed an adult basic education programme in comparison to those who withdrew. This suggests the potential significance of improving basic skills levels and, with this, increasing the likelihood of successful rehabilitation.

The research quoted above tends to focus upon offenders in custody, a group that is easier to observe and quantify. In terms of the wider offending population it has been less straightforward to draw out clear messages from available data. Research relating to this population (Gendreau et al, 1996, cited by Blanchette and Brown, 2006: 86), suggests that "'social achievement' (comprised mostly of education/ employment predictors) is a strong predictor of recidivism". However, due to different assessment methods and lack of clarity about the definition of basic skills (McMahon et al, 2004; Blanchette and Brown, 2006) the nature of the causal relationship between basic needs and offending behaviour remains unclear.

The use in the UK of nationally recognised screening and assessment processes, such as the 'Basic Skills Agency Fast-Track 20 Questions' (BSA, 2004), is likely to contribute to a more accurate profile of the basic skills needs of offenders and, alongside other offender assessments, to open up the possibility of exploring in detail the nature of links to offending. Figures (McMahon et al, 2004: 21) emerging from the Probation Service's Basic Skills Pathfinder Programmes suggest that the number of offenders, assessed at pre-sentence stage, who experience basic skills needs in the field of literacy exceeds the estimated figure of 20 per cent of the entire adult population who have such difficulties. The figure for adult offenders is in the region of 30 per cent, with 30 per cent to 50 per cent experiencing numeracy needs.

The figures alone, however, merely begin to establish the broad incidence of basic skills deficits among the offending population and promising trends in addressing the deficits. As Parsons (2002) argues:

> ... it is equally important to unravel the links between poor basic skills and criminal activity. Is it that poor basic skills increase the likelihood of offending, or is having poor basic skills a symptom of the same cycle of deprivation that

exists for many of our society's socially excluded? (Parsons, 2002: 10)

If it were simply the latter, it could be argued that practitioners should be responsible for little more than facilitating access to mainstream services, acting as a broker between the offender and specialist agencies.

The picture is more complex, however. Parsons (2002: 29) herself concluded that "having poor literacy skills ... and poor numeracy skills directly increased the risk of offending". Evaluators of the Probation Service's Basic Skills Pathfinder Programmes hint at the nature of this increased risk, acknowledging that the causal link between skills deficits is not a direct one, but rather that "a lack of basic skills is related to other variables that are known to be correlated to crime" (McMahon et al, 2004: 3). Consequences, for example, of the poor employment prospects which tend to follow upon poor life skills, include limited "sources of legitimate income" as well as a lack of "potential psychological and interpersonal benefits" of work and value to the community (McMahon et al, 2004: 3).

Others have speculated upon further links between poor educational achievement and deficits in reasoning skills such as impatience in the face of problems and awareness of, and aversion to, risk (Lochner and Moretti, 2003: 27). It would be invidious to try to decide which comes first or is more significant – the problematic thinking and behaviour which can disrupt school careers and thereby the acquisition of basic skills, or the limited reasoning capacity and sense of self-efficacy which flows from not having basic skills. In either event, impulsiveness, anger, risk-taking and poor problem solving, intrinsic to impatience and riskiness, have long been associated with the types of dysfunctional thinking and behaviour which can lead to offending. These factors are routinely included in assessment tools used across criminal justice agencies.

A final aspect of skills needs, linked to the notion of social capital, is the way in which limited reserves of human capital (resources and skills) reduce the social capital of a community. Social networks are narrower, poorer and support the negative aspects of individual lives. Furthermore, those with lower levels of skill and achievement tend to socialise together, relying upon each other and reinforcing attitudes and behaviours. The development of basic skills can be viewed as a building block in the construction of more positive, supportive social relationships which, in turn, will provide 'oxygen' to the process of reintegration. Whilst this dimension of basic skills interventions remains somewhat speculative, it can suggest a challenge to more technical approaches to crime and offenders (see, for example, Maruna and Immarigeon, 2004).

To summarise, there appear to be some potentially significant interconnections between the development of basic skills and those domains of an individual's life which often constitute foci of face-to-face work with offenders:

- offence-focused cognitive behavioural interventions;
- associated problems, such as temper control or substance misuse;
- specific lifestyle problems, such as relationships or financial difficulties;
- reintegration into a supportive community network.

Implications for face-to-face work with offenders

Evaluations of the Probation Service's Basic Skills Pathfinder Programmes

Projects consistently refer to the important role of probation staff in motivating individuals to address basic skills needs. One key recommendation by evaluators was that:

> A pre-requisite to good motivational work ... is that they themselves are committed to the value of basic skills interventions and that the relevance of such work to Probation Service Goals is promoted by senior management and within training. (McMahon et al, 2004: x)

In light of the way basic skills deficits interconnect with and compound other recognised offence-related needs, practitioners should be confident that appropriate interventions in this domain are indeed relevant to 'Probation Service Goals'. As suggested above, increased attention is now being paid to the notion of desistance and its link to the reintegration of offenders into communities. Furthermore, reintegration has always been a recognised element of the effective practice approach to work with offenders (Chapman and Hough, 1998).

There is another implication for practitioners which goes beyond simply addressing skills deficits and promoting reintegration.

Evidence about the effective delivery of offence-focused programmes has also pointed to the difficulty of engaging some offenders in such programmes because of their literacy deficits. In terms of formal offending behaviour programmes the researchers conclude that:

> ... evidence suggests that for many offenders, the literacy demands of [the programmes evaluated] exceeded their literacy skills. There was also evidence that there were problems for some tutors in adjusting the delivery of programmes to accommodate the high literacy needs of some offenders. (Davies et al, 2004: 1)

The implication is that both content and delivery of work with offenders needs to be adapted to their basic skills level. Effectiveness is not just about what is done but how it is done. The 'how' is a key aspect of responsivity.

Moreover, the complexity of the interconnections between skills deficits and other risk factors does raise questions about where to focus first. For a case manager there are questions about prioritising and sequencing interventions and coordinating parallel processes. Which comes first, the offence-focused intervention or attention to basic skills needs? How can the impact of the latter be managed so as not to undermine the effectiveness of the former?

Whilst the evaluators of the Basic Skills Pathfinder Programmes are justified in emphasising the motivational role of practitioners in relation to both basic skills tuition and employment interventions, the practitioner's role goes further than that. Indeed, it captures what is one of the key themes of this book: how to balance the necessary emphasis upon risk and offending behaviour with individual needs and characteristics which may impede engagement and ultimately weaken effectiveness.

One dimension of this aspect of work is the need to collaborate with specialist partners to access appropriate services with the practitioner in a case management role. Practitioners will thus need to:

- Acknowledge and believe in the value of basic skills interventions, at a general societal level and in terms of the consequences for individuals and their offending behaviour (*knowledge and understanding*).
- Be alert to potential skills deficits and ensure both that appropriate specialist help is accessed and that other interventions are made accessible (*assessment*).
- Engage, develop and sustain the motivation of individuals in addressing their skills deficits (*motivation, incentives and support*).
- Facilitate positive partnerships with other professionals to support the longer-term reintegration of the individual into their community (*working with others*).

The range of activities which are implicit in these core case management task areas can be encapsulated in *the Three 'R's of Responsivity* in relation to offenders with basic skills needs:

- Recognition.
- Re-skilling.
- Reintegration.

Given the limitations of what is understood about the relationship between basic skills deficits and more specific offending risk factors, what follows is to some extent speculative, drawing upon some of the broad themes emerging from the research explored above.

Recognition

The practitioner's first task is, as ever, assessment. In relation to basic skills, the assessment focuses initially on the needs in their own right and identifying and overcoming potential barriers to engagement with other specialist services and programmes. Assessment can also help the practitioner understand the contribution of basic skills deficits in relation to an individual's vulnerability to offending choices and also the wider implications for how they live their lives.

This wider, more holistic approach will give indications of some of the features of an individual's life which may be sources of motivation and support, for example, family relationships, children, social networks and other skills (in order to cope with their lack of one set of skills individuals may have developed others to compensate). It may also suggest local gaps in social support and appropriate education and employment opportunities that could be addressed through building more formal partnership arrangements.

What is suggested here is a three-pronged assessment. At a specific level it is important for the generic practitioner to contribute to the identification of particular basic skills needs, the potential targets for intervention. Assessment of basic skills needs can be undertaken formally through specialist tools where available. To this end the Probation Service in the UK has worked in partnership with the Basic Skills Agency to adapt and implement the 'Fast-Track 20 Questions' screening tool. More informally practitioners should be alert to 'signs' and 'giveaways' which might suggest that basic skills are a problem. Warning signs relating to poor literacy or communication skills could include unanswered letters, missed appointments, poor concentration, avoidance of reading, misunderstanding of questions and the incorrect use of words. (For more comprehensive information see Connexions, 2003: Ch 4.) Generally the practitioner will not be undertaking detailed specialist assessments, but rather quick and broad screening assessments. This needs to be done with a 'light touch' however (Connexions, 2003: 80) and in the context of a genuine interest in the impact of any skills deficits upon the individual's life so far. Formal assessments apart, in routine contact with offenders, practitioners will need to recognise that some people may hide behind embarrassment and pretence with respect to their lack of skills. They may have spent many years learning to conceal their deficits and developing effective strategies to do so. While accepting that some pretence or avoidance of the problem is understandable, the practitioner needs to be willing to broach potentially difficult topics, using the same repertoire of professional skills and strategies used to explore other sensitive subjects associated with offending. So it should also be with the second strand of assessment, the focus of which is the individual's experience of learning, education and the development of their basic skills.

This aspect of assessment will give clues as to motivational issues and the most appropriate ways of delivering interventions. To achieve these ends the assessor will seek to draw out the individual's story and unpick what having limited basic skills has meant to them generally and in terms of their specific pathway into offending. Assessment is likely to be enhanced by using a collaborative approach, uncovering some of the obstacles to change and identifying incentives which might spur the individual to participate actively with any specialist interventions. Arguably, the biggest initial incentive to engagement might be to include basic skills interventions in formal orders of the court and this may be justifiable where a specific link can be made between skills deficits and offending. A more flexible referral system is suggested by practice evaluators, allowing for the importance of establishing a 'good working relationship' between offender and practitioner, particularly if they are in a case manager role. In any event it is in the initial stages that practitioners will need to focus upon motivation since "once access to tuition has been achieved ... the basic skills learning programme may become self-motivating" (McMahon et al, 2004: 70).

The practitioner will need to communicate the benefits of basic skills to an individual in the light of a real understanding of their life experience and with confidence in the rewards that are likely to accrue from active participation, in the short and long term. For example, in the short term they may be able to read to their children, and in the long term they may be able to access employment or play some other constructive role in their community. The latter, of course, begs the question about how to generate such opportunities and the type of partnerships that are set up both to rectify deficits and to reinforce and sustain learning.

A final prong of assessment is associated with the offence-focused interventions, usually running alongside the focus on basic skills development. At the very least, a practitioner, especially one in a case management role, will need to consider how far any skills deficits may affect the individual's ability to participate in offence-focused work, either in groups or on a one-to-one basis. If the materials used are paper-based, will the individual need mentoring support or tailored activities? Are the formal programmes that are available suitable at all to an individual? Might it be appropriate to start any basic skills tuition before the offence-focused work? After reflecting upon these questions the practitioner can then move on to consider how to design, deliver or coordinate appropriate interventions. In some senses this part of assessment is an extension of the attention to responsivity issues which all offenders should benefit from prior to embarking upon any programme of interventions.

Activities and reflection 8.2

In your initial contacts with an individual:

- Do you pay attention to how they communicate; the language they use; their understanding of your questions? Do you adapt your style of interviewing?
- How do you draw out the story of their lives, their routines, the way in which they spend their time, their experiences of education, training or employment?
- Do you consider how well they may be able to respond to formal interventions? Are the individual's communication and reasoning skills sufficient for them to be able to participate in these interventions?

Re-skilling

On the basis of the assessment, re-skilling becomes the focus. The practitioner's role now becomes more complex, requiring them to operate at two broad levels: face-to-face work with the individual, and working with others to deliver a range of interventions as effectively as possible. They also have to have an eye to both the short-term delivery of interventions and to embedding learning in the wider applicability/employability context. At this stage the emphasis is upon both supporting offence-focused interventions and the individual's engagement in basic skills work.

At the most simple level the practitioner will need to pay attention to facilitating good, appropriate communication, ensuring that they themselves are understood by individual offenders, both orally and in writing. Communication will be the cornerstone of other interventions and will encourage compliance. Evaluators (McMahon et al, 2004) emphasise the crucial role of the practitioner and the motivational, supportive and reinforcing relationship that is required to sustain individual commitment to the type of longer-term learning that is a feature of basic skills development.

In addition to this foundational relationship, the practitioner is likely to have a case management role and will need to liaise with specialist colleagues, in relation both to offence-focused and basic skills interventions. The liaison will be aimed at ensuring that specialists are adequately informed both about levels of need, the potential targets for intervention, and also possible incentives for, or potential barriers to, positive engagement.

It is also likely that, having identified key targets for intervention, there will be an important job to be done in coordinating and sequencing interventions so that they complement, rather than pull against, each other. Sequencing is not simply about ordering priorities but about balancing and juggling interconnecting priorities. In more complex situations the case manager will need to decide how priorities overlap, for example, will the individual need to achieve some basic skills targets before they are confident enough to participate actively in an offence-focused programme? If so, it might be necessary to determine how long it will take before a second programme of work should be introduced. There may also be practical issues about the availability of resources, for example, spaces on appropriate programmes or materials suited to the individual's learning capacity. Such issues may influence the timing of interventions and all the time the practitioner needs to continue to pay attention to motivation, particularly in the initial stages when the biggest 'push' is required (McMahon et al, 2004: 70).

In terms of the actual development of new skills, the practitioner has a role in preparing the individual for their tuition, however that is to be delivered, supporting them as it proceeds and reinforcing progress made. Some familiarity with the materials used and the approach taken will be essential in helping the individual visualise positively what is likely to be expected of them, in identifying and overcoming potential obstacles and in planning relevant and creative opportunities to reinforce learning.

Reinforcement may be as much about developing helpful relationships with family, friends or the community (building social capital) as providing those opportunities within the supervisory relationship. Indeed, given the fact that the enhancement of basic skills can be the foundation of lifelong learning, the practitioner would do well to pay attention to how an improved set of skills is likely to affect the offender's behaviour in their local environment and how they can be helped to continue with their learning after court orders end (see Chapter Eleven on evaluation and ending well). If basic skills interventions are confined to formal orders there can be a risk that not only will they lose interest but, in the event of further offending, they may need to start the whole process all over again. This latter situation has arisen in the prison context, where offenders may be more prolific or entrenched in their offending behaviour. Offenders find themselves caught up in what is termed the 'churn' effect (see, for example, the Select Committee on Education and Skills, 2005). This involves them moving from place to place with a consequent lack of consistency and continuity. Assessments are repeated and tuition is not followed through or built upon. An overarching strategy, systematic recording of progress and a planned 'exit strategy' are important components of supporting the re-skilling process.

Activities and reflection 8.3

- What basic skills resources are available in your area?
- How do you access them?
- What methods do they employ, in what type of atmosphere (formal or informal)?
- What level of support will individuals need to engage with basic skills tuition and then stick with the process?

Reintegration

Within the literature promoting desistance-focused or strengths-based approaches (Farrall, 2002; Maruna and Immarigeon, 2004; Ward and Brown, 2004; McNeill, 2005), there is an implicit critique of highly targeted 'What Works' programmes which tend to be focused upon clear and specific offence-related needs and whose effectiveness is measured by simple data collection, such as the use of reconviction statistics. Such measures are static and do not reflect the more dynamic and qualitative changes that can take place in the lives of offenders, changes which are likely to carry the individual beyond their offending into a more productive, pro-social relationship with their community.

McNeill (2005: 21) argues that "it is not enough to build *capacities* for change where change depends on *opportunities* to exercise capacities" (emphases in the original).

From the point of view of this discussion the implication for practitioners would be that the reintegration process, which creates the context for building and sustaining a momentum for change, takes basic skills development beyond the formal interventions to provide ongoing support and opportunities to embed learning in the real non-offending life of the individual. In a sense the notion of reintegration needs to be a thread that runs through the whole process of work with an offender.

While at an individual level the practitioner might be in a position to work with an offender and his or her family and to ensure that ongoing basic skills provision is available, the wider issue of employment opportunities is more problematic. Farrall (2004: 71) makes the case for what is effectively the strengthening of social capital to "become one of the aims of social and criminal justice policy" if it is to become "accordingly the focus of much of the work undertaken by probation services". In the absence of this policy emphasis, however, the practitioner still has responsibility not simply to support an offender through a programme of basic skills interventions but also to seek to maintain learning (McMahon et al, 2004: 65).

At the most basic level, and without necessarily engaging in in-depth family or relationship work, the practitioner can devise an ending strategy which:

- Identifies practical and high-frequency opportunities for the individual to practise new skills, for example, shopping, reading a newspaper, letters and children's books.
- Helps the individual to seek out ongoing support and understanding, perhaps by involving partners or friends who might already have been involved in helping out with the problem previously.
- Works with specialist colleagues to 'normalise' the learning process. If, for example, interventions have been one-to-one or delivered within a group of fellow offenders the individual could be encouraged to access more mainstream facilities.
- Explores with the offender local employment opportunities and actively support applications and introductions. Even though basic skills levels may have improved the offender's theoretical employability, they may also encounter difficulties because of their offending history or lack of work experience. The practitioner

can act as mentor, and occasionally advocate, without taking responsibility away from the individual.

The reintegration stage brings together all of the threads of supervision and recognises the importance of the positive change that has taken place, whether this has been in terms of offending behaviour or the acquisition of new life skills. The ongoing nature of basic skills development, as an aspect of lifelong learning, can form a bridge between the offender and their community and enhance the individual's desistance from criminal involvement.

The three 'R's and case management

The role of the practitioner in developing basic skills is essentially that of the committed, consistent case manager who ensures continuity and coherence of service and supports the consolidation of learning. Holt (2000) helpfully explores the role of the case manager informing the approach that is relevant here (see Chapter Ten for more detailed coverage of Holt's four 'C's).

Having identified and explored the three key elements of work with individual offenders, the challenge is then to bring them together into

Figure 8.1: The components of an effective programme of supervision

Targets for intervention — Offending behaviour — Case management managing risk

Behaviour linked to offending

Specific problem focus

Reintegration into community

Use of community resources

Source: Roberts (1995), reprinted with permisson

a coordinated programme of supervision. Roberts (1995) has illustrated how key aspects of work with offenders can be brought together within a programme of supervision. He argues that effective supervision will pay attention to all of the key aspects. Figure 8.1 is a framework which has been adapted from his work and is suggested here as a useful tool during the initial planning stages of a period of supervision, helping the practitioner to identify the range of interventions that may be necessary in both the short and long term. The model describes how effective interventions address a range of offending-related needs (targets for intervention).

At the 'sharp end' are the areas of work addressed by programmes, influenced by cognitive behavioural principles and delivered in groups, or in one-to-one supervision. These programmes address patterns of thinking and behaviour very closely related to persistent offending behaviour. Programmes may be directly offending related and/or may concentrate on underpinning thinking skills.

The second tier down includes issues which have close, but less direct, links with offending, including, for example, difficulties with education, or problems with substance misuse.

The third dimension relates to problems which may form part of the fabric of an individual's life and may undermine their progress.

At the bottom of the model are factors linked to the promotion of positive reintegration into the wider community, and also essential to the encouragement of desistance. Work in this domain aims to establish supportive and ongoing social networks. There may be overlap with areas covered in the middle of the model but the focus is on developing inclusion and looking towards relapse prevention.

The top two tiers of the framework tend to be associated with the development of personal skills and resources (re-skilling) and the bottom two with that of wider networks and resources (reintegration). The assessment of basic skills (recognition of needs and their impact) and consequent interventions to address deficits is relevant at all levels. Figure 8.2 develops the basic framework to show how basic skills needs can be integral to effective work with offenders. It suggests some examples of activities that might be appropriate at different levels of the model. Through assessment the practitioner will seek to identify the specific basic skills needs of an individual and understand how these needs interact with or compound other significant offence-related needs. Then, in addition to facilitating access to specialist services in education or training, the practitioner will go on to pay attention to both the implications for the individual of engaging with

Figure 8.2: A framework for integrating attention to basic skills into a programme of work with offenders

offence-focused work and solving other related problems (re-skilling) and to their positive reintegration and longer-term support.

Activities and reflection 8.4

Consider an individual with whom you are working and where you have identified some basic skills needs. Using the planning framework (Figure 8.2) as a point of reference:

- In the four domains suggested in Figure 8.2 what factors might have influenced his/her offending behaviour?
- What are the likely offence-related targets for intervention?
- How might poor basic skills interact with those factors and compound the problems associated with the offending behaviour?
- What other activities, in addition to basic skills tuition, would you undertake to support engagement, reinforce learning or promote ongoing development in relation to both basic skills and any offence-focused work?
- What supports or resources need to be put in place in preparation for the ending of your contact with the offender?

Conclusion

Roberts' (1995) original model (Figure 8.1) was designed to illustrate that effective programmes should include interventions at all levels of the triangle. It is not enough to offer good quality offence-focused programmes if individuals are not helped to overcome some of their wider difficulties which, in the short term, might hinder their involvement in that work (a failure in responsivity) and in the longer term undermine the positive impact of interventions. Applying this same thinking in relation to basic skills needs (Figure 8.2) it is the authors' suggestion that basic skills interventions can be more central to programmes of work than they have been in the past. More broadly, the implication is that it is important to address some specific, not directly offence-related, needs within the wider context of reducing offending, since to ignore these needs is to risk the long-term effectiveness of offence-oriented interventions.

Part Four
Risk

NINE

Violent offenders

Introduction

Working with violent offenders can be professionally exciting, offering real opportunities to understand, and potentially change, complex human behaviours. At the same time, work with violent offenders can be daunting. It carries with it an associated responsibility to protect the public from harm, in a culture that is increasingly risk focused, where that responsibility is carried out in a changing and pressured organisational context.

This challenge is increased because violent offending is so diverse. As Bush (1995) points out, criminal violence is not generally an isolated and distinct form of criminal behaviour. Many violent offenders engage in other types of offending. In order to make sense of this diversity it is important to understand patterns of violent behaviour and the risk factors associated with them, but it is also necessary to be able to relate this knowledge to the detail of the behaviour of particular individuals and their lives, lived out in particular sets of circumstances.

This chapter provides practitioners with an understanding of the range of violent behaviours and how they are developed and supported by social processes. It looks in more detail at some specific areas:

- Alcohol and violence.
- Women and violence.
- Domestic violence
- Racially motivated offending.

The chapter then looks at how best to intervene and engage with a violent offender and how to manage the worker–offender relationship.

Range of violent behaviours

To begin with it is helpful to clarify and define what is meant by violent offending: crimes that involve "the exercise of physical force so as to injure or damage persons or property" (Archer and Browne, 1989: 3). Prins (2005) goes on to identify the limitations of this definition, suggesting that violent offending can also be seen to include sexual assaults, such as rape, and non-contact offences, like harassment.

Second, it should be acknowledged that men commit the majority of violent offences. This gender difference, as the chapter considers later, for some offenders helps in an understanding of the function of violent acts for the perpetrator. Although women's convictions for violence are increasing, up by 14% between 1994 and 2003 (Home Office, 2004), as Batchelor (2005: 360) points out, "the overwhelming majority of female offending is non-violent ... while the number of women convicted of a violent crime is increasing, violence (particularly serious violence) is still an overwhelmingly male activity". This gender difference raises questions about the causes of violent behaviour that a practitioner should bear in mind. Are there, for example, features of men's and women's lives and circumstances that help to explain this difference?

Violent behaviour occurs in diverse circumstances and knowledge of circumstances can inform an understanding of the behaviour. Henderson (1986) found men's violence clustering around four distinct situations:

- alongside another crime;
- within the family;
- in a public place;
- in institutions.

These were not exclusive categories, with many offenders in the study being violent in more than one situation, suggesting that using violence for some offenders is a stable behavioural response in a range of circumstances. Women's violent offending may also be influenced by circumstances; many women are primary carers, which may affect the context and triggers for their behaviour and the most likely victims.

Violent behaviour occurs for a variety of reasons; the motivation for the offending and the rewards associated with it will vary. Rutter et al (1998) suggest that violent offending can be divided into two broad categories. The first category is violence that is a means to an end rather than the end in itself, in other words, violence that is used to achieve other goals:

• instrumental aggression, for example, a planned robbery;
• sadistic violence, where violence is intrinsically rewarding and being used to meet other psychological needs of the offender.

The second category is violence that is linked to emotional arousal:

• angry violence, a response to perceived provocation, or negative feelings towards the victim, impulsive and unplanned;
• expressive violence, a result of boredom and frustration where violent damage is a by-product, not necessarily intended, for example, aggravated car thefts.

These categories are not mutually exclusive. There are overlaps and connections. A planned robbery might have an element of sadistic reward within it. An individual might plan and use violence in the course of a robbery, but then become emotionally aroused during incidents, adding an element of anger to their motivation. Violent offenders may have an angry response associated with their violence, but may be primarily using the violence to achieve their goals, for example, to exercise control over others.

Activities and reflection 9.1
• Think about each of Rutter et al's (1998) motivations for violence: instrumental, sadistic, angry, expressive.
• Do you know of an offender whose behaviour exemplifies any of these categories?
• If so, what evidence are you drawing on to decide that their behaviour falls into a particular category?
• Is there any overlap between categories for this offender?

Violent behaviour often occurs in association with other difficulties, notably substance abuse and mental disorder. In Chapter Seven there is a discussion of the links between getting drunk and anti-social and aggressive behaviour. Alcohol and violent behaviour are also specifically addressed later in this chapter, and the association with potentially seriously harmful behaviour must be borne in mind. Chapter Six considers links between violent behaviour and mental disorder since "there does seem to be an association between some forms of schizophrenia (notably the paranoid varieties) and violence" (Prins, 2005:341). The co-occurrence of substance misuse, mental disorder and a pattern of violent behaviour in an individual is likely to mean that that individual displays a concerning level of social disorganisation. They are an important constellation of risk factors for harmful behaviour by that person.

Violent behaviour has links with social structures, with belief systems and with differences in power between groups or individuals. For example, hate crime comprises violent and abusive behaviours, which are targeted at particular vulnerable victims, rooted in patterns of oppression within society and in abusive and discriminatory patterns of beliefs (Hall, 2005; Mason, 2005). While hate crime is not exclusive to male offenders, there can be associations with particular beliefs about what it means to be male in these patterns of violence, including violence directed at the gay community (Stonewall, 2003). Later in the chapter domestic violence and racially motivated violence will be considered further.

Aggressive and abusive behaviour takes many forms, and is not confined to overt acts of physical aggression. Threats and harassment could be included, for example. Novaco and Welsh (1989) discuss the following behavioural manifestations of anger:

- Physical aggression – overt behaviour intended to produce harm or damage, and directed at either the provoking person or at a substitute target.
- Verbal aggression – including threatening statements intended to produce distress in a target person.
- Passive aggression – including coldness and neglect, again intended to produce distress in the target person.

Aggression that stops short of physical violence is likely to have more significant impact where the victims are vulnerable and/or where the aggressor is in a position of power. Examples of behaviours where victims may be particularly vulnerable may include: racially motivated aggression, domestic violence, homophobic aggression and violence, aggression towards elderly victims, or towards those with mental or physical handicaps. These latter patterns of aggression may overlap with domestic violence, or may involve violence within an institutional setting.

Activities and reflection 9.2

- Identify an example of violent behaviour you are familiar with or have read about recently in the newspaper.
- List the characteristics of the perpetrator and victim, including age, gender, 'race', culture, sexuality, health.
- Are there any issues of particular victim vulnerability? are there any identifiable differences in power? If so, how did they affect the violent behaviour itself and how might they have affected the experience of the victim?

Understanding the individual

The range of violent behaviours and the complexity of the associated motivations and causes of those behaviours have implications for the assessment of violent offenders and subsequent interventions. To respond effectively to the level of risk they pose it is important to have an accurate sense of the detail of an individual's past and present violent and aggressive behaviour and of the circumstances in which that behaviour occurs.

Violent behaviour does not simply emerge in adult life. Looking across the lifespan of an offender, the risk factors for violent behaviour seem to be very similar to the factors that cause delinquency more generally (Farrington, 1995). The violent offender is more likely to have exhibited hyperactive and impulsive behaviour from an early age; the problems caused by this behaviour are made worse by family poverty and poor parenting practices. The offender is more likely to have experienced difficulties at school. These difficulties, often caused by poor and aggressive behaviour and sometimes linked to low intelligence are likely to result in low school attainment and truancy, and this, in turn, may be supported by family, and later on by peers, who are themselves criminal and anti-social.

In addition, a violent family of origin is linked to aggressive behaviour, but many individuals who witness violence in their childhood do not themselves become perpetrators of violence. It is important therefore to understand how patterns of violent behaviour are supported and maintained in the present.

While an outsider might perceive violent behaviour as counterproductive and finally destructive to the perpetrator, as well as to the victims, from the individual offender's viewpoint it may be rewarding and reinforced. This reinforcement may be by the outside world, for example, by acts of violence increasing power and control over others, as well as by the individual's own thought processes and emotions.

A range of elements including motivations, contexts and patterns of behaviour all need to be considered in assessing risk. In order to do so, it is important to understand how a number of variables come together in particular individuals and circumstances. The following model (Figure 9.1), which is based on the work of Novaco and Welsh (1989) and adapted by McMurran (2002a), helps a process of focused information gathering and analysis.

A simple example using the model would be a young man with an established pattern of violent offending who is in a pool hall. Another young man knocks into him, disturbing his shot. This initial trigger or external event culminates in behaviour, a wounding offence, when the first young man hits the other with his pool cue, causing serious head injuries. The perpetrator will describe the incident later in largely emotional terms, having 'just lost it' or 'seeing red', an admitted over-reaction to a provocation, but simply a result of that provocation. The reality is, of course, much more complex and this model can help the practitioner think through the processes involved for this offender and others in more detail.

A perpetrator's immediate thoughts and beliefs about the world will affect how they see the initial trigger, their level of emotional reaction

Figure 9.1: Analysing violent behaviour

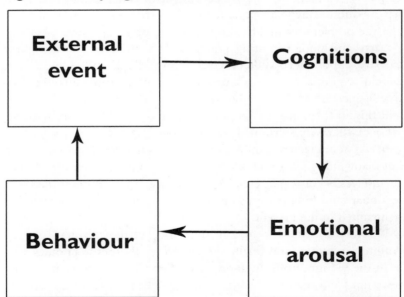

and how they understand and interpret that reaction. These thoughts and feelings will inform behavioural choices, which will then, in turn, have an effect on the external world, as well as on the internal world of the offender. All of this makes a violent response not just more likely on this occasion, but something that the individual finds rewarding in a range of different circumstances.

It will be helpful to take each of the components of the model in turn.

Cognitions

One of the key components is an understanding of the ways in which violent offenders perceive and make sense of events in the external world. Novaco and Welsh (1989) suggest a number of processes common in the cognitions of violent individuals:

- Violent individuals have a way of making sense of the world which is more likely to see the behaviour of others as hostile in intent. In other words 'they did it on purpose'. This may be a long-standing way of approaching the world; it can be seen, for instance, at an early stage, in the behaviour of children with conduct disorders (Graham, 1998).
- Violent offenders, like many other offenders, may have difficulties in their ability to apply problem-solving skills to social difficulties, and consider fewer of the consequences of their behaviour.
- Violent offenders will tend to see their own behaviour as a result of the circumstances in which they find themselves, but will explain other people's behaviour as a result of their personality, or who they are. This kind of thinking means that the other person can be blamed, but the offender sees themself as blameless, being led by circumstances.
- Violent offenders tend to think that others share their views more than is actually the case, and because of this they are less likely to understand other people's points of view, or to take different perspectives.
- Violent offenders tend to hold to their initial judgement even when they are faced with evidence to the contrary.

In assessing the offender with the pool cue it would be important, in asking them to talk about the detail of the incident, to establish examples of these problematic patterns of thinking.

As well as habits of thinking, many violent offenders will also have beliefs in the acceptability of violence. This belief in the legitimacy of violence has been linked to self-identity and with concepts of masculinity. As Bush (1995) points out, violent offenders will have a range of attitudes and beliefs that justify and sustain their violence, and make it seem normal and necessary.

Emotional arousal

Zamble and Quinsey (1997) looked at the self-reports of a large group of recidivists who commented on the factors prevalent at the time of a repeated offence. The robbers and property offenders said that the need for money was what led to their offending, while the most cited reason for assault was loss of emotional control, especially anger. For offenders who committed an assault there emerged chains of events, starting with an interpersonal conflict that the offender was unable to cope with or solve. Such conflicts lead to a degree of emotional instability that, in turn, makes a difference to how the offender perceives the actions of others, making them more likely to be seen as hostile. The study suggests that those who committed assault were intrinsically more likely to act impulsively, so that the violent assault did not involve planning or premeditation.

Behaviour

The state of arousal might trigger off actions – such as clenching a fist – that, in turn, support angry feelings. In addition, the offenders' perceptions of the situation and their difficulties in thinking through alternatives, will limit the behavioural choices they can make. Violent offenders will often also have some difficulty with the repertoire of behavioural skills they can draw on; they may, for example, lack skills in appropriately assertive behaviour, or lack negotiation skills. Because of this their response to the initial trigger is much more likely to be an aggressive one.

External world

The model is then completed by recognising the interaction between the behavioural choices of the offender and their environment. The external world provides the context for, and triggers to, violent behaviour, which is, in turn, often rewarded by some of the consequences of that behaviour. While violent behaviour may set up eventual negative outcomes, such as being arrested, the immediate consequences for the offender might be the approval of peers, the removal of what was perceived as a hostile threat, or a gain in control, all of which would be potentially rewarding. Violent behaviour also sets up internally rewarding patterns of thinking. It reinforces the offender's perceptions of others as hostile and confirms their understanding of the world.

The model can be very helpful, therefore, if used to think through an individual incident of violent behaviour. Such incidents do not occur in isolation, however, and the model also suggests that violent acts are part of a set of behaviours, linked to well-established patterns of thinking and feeling.

Offenders may have experienced difficult and rejecting upbringings and may have learnt to use violence and aggression to hold others at a distance. Novaco and Jarvis (2002) discuss the ways in which violence helps to minimise exposure to threat and defends vulnerability. Violent behaviours may set up self-fulfilling prophecies, where, because of their behaviour, the offender is more likely to get hostile responses from others. They will affect who wants to spend time with an individual offender, with the violent offender more likely to be with others who find that behaviour acceptable and reinforce its importance. Faced with a number of conflicts and a high degree of associated instability, violent offenders may reach a point where even an apparently trivial incident will be enough to trigger a violent response (Zamble and Quinsey, 1997).

Violent behaviour may have wider external causes, including social and economic pressures that may contribute to the conflicts the offender experiences. In order to work with offenders it is necessary to have an appreciation of these wider influences but also to concentrate on those factors that are most closely associated with the violent behaviour in the present.

What all of these processes culminate in is a pattern of thinking, feeling and behaving that is often powerfully rewarded, in that it is part of a way of understanding and reacting to the world that has its own unhelpful logic, that 'makes sense' to the offender.

Alcohol and violent offending

An important refinement of the model (Figure 9.1) is the notion of the disinhibition of internal control that needs to take place before feelings of anger are translated into violent acts. Individuals have some inhibitions against violent behaviour and while these are likely to be much weaker in a violent offender they still exist. In order to act violently those inhibitions have to be overcome perhaps by the presence of peers condoning the behaviour. The offender might also be under the influence of alcohol or drugs. The 1998/99 Youth Lifestyles survey (Harrington, 2000) found alcohol to be associated with violent offending (although not other offending) for males aged 22 to 30 years old. The 2000 British Crime Survey (Kershaw et al, 2000) found that in 40% of violent crimes victims perceived the offender to be under the influence of alcohol. Violent offences most commonly occur outside pubs and clubs where young people, and more particularly young men, are gathered together and drinking, often to the point of drunkenness. Violence is more likely because of large numbers of young men gathered together, but this effect is heightened by the involvement of alcohol. "Alcohol intoxication makes aggressive people violent in certain circumstances and the repeated co-occurrence of drinking and violence increases the likelihood that drinking will precipitate violence in the future" (McMurran, 2002a: 228).

There are well-established links between substance abuse and domestic violence. The British Crime Survey of 2000 indicated that 44% of domestic violence incidents occurred when the perpetrators had been drinking (Budd, 2003). Gilchrist et al (2003) suggest that 48% of their sample of domestic violence perpetrators were alcohol dependent. Finney (2004) found evidence that alcohol abuse played a particularly important role in escalating existing conflict.

This does not imply a simple causal relationship between alcohol or other substance abuse and violence, or that intoxication should be allowed to be an excuse for violent behaviour. The co-occurrence of substance abuse and violent and aggressive acts is significant, however, and needs to form part of an assessment and potentially of the resulting intervention.

Practice tool 9.1

When conducting an assessment interview with an offender who has been violent, Figure 9.1 and the following questions can be used to explore important areas.

External world:

- What are the immediate triggers for an incident?
- How often do similar triggers arise in the offender's life? Did they seek out circumstances in which a violent response was more likely?
- Apart from specific triggers what other kinds of pressures towards violence might be present in the offender's world?

Cognitions:

- What immediate thoughts did this offender have before and during the incident?
- What beliefs about others and about the acceptability of violence might this offender hold?
- What do they think now about what they did and about its effects on others?
- Is there anything about their relationship to the victim or the characteristics of that victim that affects the offender's perceptions and beliefs?

Emotional response:

- What was the offender's emotional response to the original trigger?
- How did their thoughts and beliefs affect that emotional response and how do they affect the way the offender makes sense of their own feelings?
- How is that affected by previous experience?

Behaviour:

- What gaps in skills might this offender have that make a violent response more likely to be chosen?
- How might this particular violent act have been rewarded in the short term?

Disinhibitors:

- Was the offender under the influence of alcohol or drugs and did this influence the behaviour?
- Did the offender use substances to give them the courage to act violently?

Women and violent offending

As has already been mentioned many of the victims of violent behaviour are young men; women are, however, also significant among the victims of violence, particularly in the context of intimate relationships. There is evidence that survivors of domestic violence are also likely to have significant problems of drug and/or alcohol abuse. Humphreys et al (2006) in a one-week screening of women in six domestic violence refuges found that between 33% and 86% of the total number of service users had experiences of problematic substance misuse. This suggests one of the themes running through a consideration of women as violent offenders, which is the link between their violence and their experiences as victims. Barnett and Fagan (1993, cited in Humphreys et al, 2006) found that women were more likely than men to drink after an assault and that 66% of the survivors interviewed reported using drugs or alcohol after the domestic violence had begun, to "dull the physical and emotional pain". Finney (2004) reports that 'offender only' drinking is common in intimate partner violence but 'victim only' drinking is rare. She suggests that many women develop alcohol problems following experiences of victimisation.

The issues surrounding the comparatively low levels of offending by women as opposed to men, and the way in which their behaviour is understood and responded to, are discussed in Chapter Three. Women's violence has been a difficult subject in a feminist literature (see Fitzroy, 2001) that has wanted to maintain a focus on the issue of men's violence towards women. The fear is that attention to women's use of violence could jeopardise progress that has been made, making it easier to blame women for the harm that is done to them.

Women's experience of violence, both as victim and as perpetrator, is a gendered experience, in other words an experience influenced by the fact that they are women living in a particular set of social and power relationships. Women's violence, at times, will be a direct response to domestic abuse and if this is the case then the provocation and pressure that led to their actions should be recognised and taken into account. There is, however, a danger that too narrow a focus on women as victims might distract from an understanding of women as active agents who make choices about their own behaviour. Women, like violent men, can be aggressive in a number of settings and for some women this can be a significant and stable element of their behaviour. Violent offending in women also has close links with substance misuse, as found by Batchelor (2005). The findings of this study suggest that "young women imprisoned for violent offences can be *both* victims of crime *and* agents who resist victim status" (Batchelor, 2005: 371).

Practitioners should inform their assessments of women's violent behaviour, with an understanding of the complexity of individual women's stories and of the precise circumstances surrounding the behaviour.

The model in Figure 9.1 can also be used to gather information about and analyse women's violent offences, but needs to be used in a way that takes account of women's gendered experiences.

Activities and reflection 9.3

Go back to Activities and reflection box 9.1. Whatever the gender of the offender you considered, go through your answers and think about how those responses were affected by the gender of the offender you were considering.

Domestic violence

While violent behaviour commonly occurs in social settings outside the home, violence in intimate relationships within the home is also significant. The Home Office definition of domestic violence is "any violence between current or former partners in an intimate relationship, wherever and whenever the violence occurs; the violence may include physical, sexual, emotional or financial abuse" (Walby and Allen, 2004: 18).

Reports on findings from the British Crime Survey 1996 (Mirrlees-Black, 1999) and from the British Crime Survey 2001 (Walby and Allen, 2004) cover physical assaults and frightening threats committed by current and former partners, against men and women aged 16 to 59. The most recent of those reports finds that one in four women and 17% of men had been subject to non-sexual domestic abuse, threat or force. The report goes on to point out that more detailed examination of the findings suggests important differences between the sexes, with women being much more likely to experience frightening threats. A minority of victims, almost all women, experienced many repeat attacks and several forms of violence. The findings as the report suggests are "consistent with the understanding of domestic violence as a pattern of coercive control" (Walby and Allen, 2004: 44). The Criminal Statistics for England and Wales (Home Office, 2003) show that nearly half of women who are murdered are killed by their partners, while only 5% of men who are murdered are killed by partners. In considering domestic violence this chapter will therefore concentrate on male perpetrators.

Increasingly, the assessment of perpetrators of domestic violence will involve an assessment of their suitability for a domestic violence programme, involving an additional, more specific assessment. The Probation and Prison Services currently use the Spousal Risk Assessment Guide (SARA) (Kropp et al, 1995) for assessment of the perpetrators of domestic violence. This aid to "structured professional judgement" (Kropp et al, 1995: 5) includes information about criminal history, psychosocial adjustment and spousal assault history as well as a consideration of the current offence. This approach asks assessors to consider attitudes that support violent behaviour, including minimisation and denial.

An examination of risk factors for domestic violence is revealing in what it suggests about the motivations for this behaviour and the patterns of thoughts, feelings, behaviour and circumstances leading to such violence.

Walby and Myhill (2001) review a range of research, identifying a number of risk factors for domestic violence:

- Domestic violence is more common where the *relative power between the partners is unequal* with greater male power and, sometimes, but not exclusively, economic dependence of the woman. Such family structures may, of course, also be linked to particular attitudes towards women which themselves are supportive of domestic violence.
- The period following *separation* is the most dangerous. This may be because the offender wants control at the point of separation, when their ability to exercise power has been weakened.
- A number of indicators of *economic disadvantage* are linked to a greater incidence of domestic violence. Poverty, social exclusion and financial stress are all significant. Mirrlees–Black (1999) found that households in financial difficulties were two or three times more at risk of domestic violence. Perhaps this is influenced by the processes suggested earlier in this chapter by Zamble and Quinsey (1997); the offender may face a number of interpersonal conflicts they are unable to cope with, they become increasingly emotionally unstable and reach a point where even an apparently trivial incident will be enough to trigger a violent response. Domestic violence is less common in professional households than in the least skilled households. However, it is essential to recognise that it occurs across the class spectrum.
- *Women who are unemployed and women who experience poverty* are at greater risk, perhaps because of their relative dependence, and because of their lack of access to formal and informal support networks, and to choices about their own lives. *Pregnancy* and the early months after the birth appear to increase risk but whether this is a causal relationship or, simply, that this correlates with other factors such as age is unclear. Similarly, *ill health and disability* in women are correlated but again cause and effect are less clear. Both physical and mental health difficulties may be the result of the violence rather than the cause of it. These difficulties

might, however, also serve to increase an individual woman's vulnerability.

- The risk of domestic violence decreases steadily with *age*, in common with other forms of criminality. Practitioners need, however, to avoid falling into the trap of thinking that domestic violence never occurs in older age groups, but need to be alert to its greater prevalence among young people, who may of course also be more likely to experience poverty and social exclusion.

- *A violent family of origin* is linked to domestic violence, and may be explained in part as part of a process of learning particular patterns of behaviour and attitudes towards women. It may also be linked to a subculture that reinforces those attitudes and behaviours and to a more generally anti-social personality. It should not be seen as an excuse for the violence. Silverman and Williamson (1997, cited in Walby and Myhill, 2001) found that associating with abusive men and holding beliefs that violence against women was acceptable was more important than a violent family of origin. In Chapter Seven there is a discussion about shared beliefs rooted in ideas of masculinity that might affect both drinking and violence.

If an assessment of domestic violence does not take into account abusive beliefs, their context and the element of coercive control, it will fail to suggest interventions that properly understand the perspectives of victims and that seek to protect their interests. This is also true when assessing racially motivated offending.

Racially motivated offending

There are links between racially motivated, homophobic violence and domestic violence in that they all include what Stanko (2000) calls 'targeted violence', where victims are in some kind of relational disadvantage to the perpetrator.

To consider racially motivated offending in more detail, it is first of all necessary to define its parameters more accurately. The Macpherson report (1999: 47.12) offered the following definition which has been widely adopted: "A racist incident is any incident which is perceived to be racist by the victim or any other person".

This definition has the advantage of simplicity and does not depend on the view of police officers to define whether a particular incident is, or is not, racially motivated. It does include not only direct physical violence. Sibbitt's (1997) study covered a range of acts including:

- verbal abuse;
- threats;
- vandalism and theft;
- assaults, direct and indirect.

The definition also incorporates offences where the victims are White, but where those individuals perceive the incident to be racist. A key concept in defining racially motivated offending is an understanding that the actions of the perpetrators are at least influenced by prejudices about the victim, not as an individual person, but as a member of a broader racial group (Kay and Gast, 1999). This does not exclude the racist behaviour of individuals from minority communities. It, however, is important to recognise that:

- The chance of being a White victim of a racially motivated incident is lower than that of being a Black or Asian victim (Salisbury and Upson, 2004). The experience and perceptions of White victims are often different from those of Black victims and racially motivated incidents comprise a greater proportion of the total offences committed against minority ethnic communities – the British Crime Survey (2000) suggests 15% as opposed to the 1% of offences against White victims.
- While Black or Minority Ethnic offenders who offend violently against members of other groups may be motivated by feelings of prejudice and by distorted perceptions, their minority position in a society where institutional racism and other forms of discrimination exist may influence their thinking and motivations.
- Patterns of victimisation will change over time and vary in different locations. The distribution of racially motivated offending in England and Wales is uneven, with high levels of racial incidents in large metropolitan areas where there are significant Black populations, but also high rates in areas where the population of Black people is small (Mynard and Read, 1997). Geographical mapping of racially motivated incidents suggests that attacks tend to cluster in areas where Black people form a small minority of the population, but appear to be challenging the territorial preferences of Whites (Brimicombe et al, 2001).
- The impact of racially motivated behaviour will be different for different communities. Research and police figures from Community Safety Units (Keilinger and Stanko, 2002) suggest that the majority of racial incidents happen in ordinary everyday situations, and that many of the incidents involve 'low level' crime

such as damage to property, thefts, threats and verbal abuse. That is not to suggest that such offences are unimportant. The impact on the victim can be very significant and these behaviours together contribute to a climate within an area that increases the likelihood of abusive behaviour and itself impacts on the well-being of Black and Minority Ethnic residents.

As with domestic violence, an understanding of the attitudes and beliefs of perpetrators is important, as is an understanding of the context in which they emerge and are sustained. Sibbitt (1997) found that perpetrators tended to reflect the perceptions of ethnic minorities shared by the wider communities to which they belong, and see this as legitimising their actions. Their communities in turn may reinforce their attitudes and behaviours. Ray et al (2002) interviewed offenders, and Sibbitt (1997) held discussions with residents of neighbourhoods experiencing high rates of racist offences; both found common themes. Sibbitt describes perpetrator communities, where racism is endemic.

The themes identified included:

- predominantly White areas with few resources and high levels of unemployment and violence, where there is entrenched local racism and high levels of adult criminality and criminal networks;
- areas where there are few affordable youth facilities and only passive engagement alongside a violent youth subculture;
- the most highly victimised communities are also amongst the most deprived.

Ray et al (2002) found offenders to be predominantly young and male. Sibbitt (1997) found that the perpetrators of racial harassment and violence are of all ages, of both genders and often act together, as groups of friends or in families. Some perpetrators are involved in other sorts of violence or in crime more generally.

Very few of Ray et al's interviewees revealed knowledge of right-wing parties, or gave a political justification for their behaviour. More typically, they would minimise the racist element of their offending, while being quite open about the violent behaviour itself. They tended to see themselves as the real victims who have been overlooked and devalued. The victims (usually South Asian) of their offences were often in a commercial relationship with the offenders, as shopkeepers, or taxi drivers, for example. They were seen as being advantaged and obtaining rewards they had not worked for, by overcharging and taking advantage of the local population. The offences themselves were rarely premeditated and often exacerbated by drink.

The patterns of thinking of these offenders reflect the cognitive distortions common in violent offending and discussed earlier in this chapter. They see themselves as blameless for their lack of economic and social success, but their Asian victims as personally responsible for the prices they charge. The offenders often hold on rigidly to their distorted racist beliefs about the relative affluence of their victims, in the face of evidence to the contrary. It is important to be aware of both the thought processes, such as rigidity and poor moral reasoning, and specific examples of that thinking, which are influenced by racism.

Bush (1995) suggests a simple model (Figure 9.2) of 'victim blame' thinking that fits violent offenders generally but which is very applicable to racist offending.

The offenders described in the Ray et al (2002) study see themselves as powerless and excluded. They blame others for their position and, objectively, in some respects, they are right to identify inequalities in society as contributing to their experiences. They go further, however, in wrongly identifying specific communities as part of the cause of their difficulties. This limits their ability to feel empathy for their victims and enables them to justify their use of violence. This victim blame thinking is fuelled in young men who are socially excluded and who have a limited sense of their own identity. This may make them resentful of the stronger group identities they see in minority communities, fuelling a compensatory belief in a hierarchy of social groupings, with White

Figure 9.2: Victim blame thinking

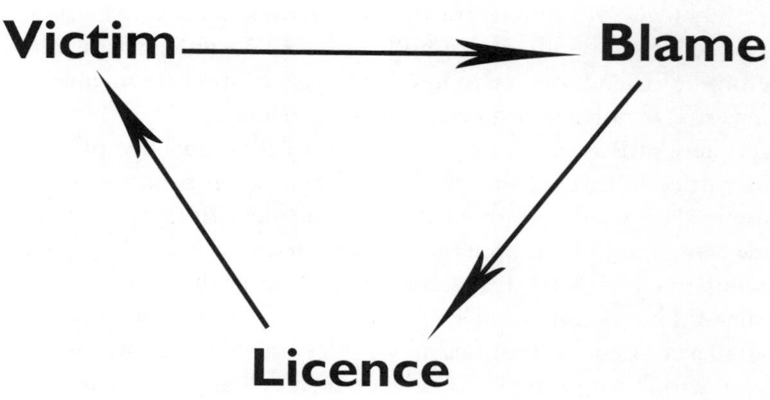

Source: Bush (1995). © John Wiley & Sons Ltd. Reproduced with permission.

British at the top. Racially motivated offenders will seek to avoid the stigmatising label of racist by explaining away their actions. They do this by further victim blaming which, in turn, gives them the licence or justification they need to act violently. The consequences of their actions tend to add to their feelings of victimisation, as they are drawn into the criminal justice system and as their behaviour contributes to the process of neighbourhood decline. Both personally, and in terms of the local community, the cycle continues and is reinforced.

These circumstances and patterns of thinking are, of course, common amongst offenders more generally. Racially motivated offenders are often generalists who engage in other patterns of offending. Racist attitudes are common amongst offenders more generally. In a sense, an offender charged with a racially motivated offence will have put into practice views held more widely. It is also likely that there are racist offenders under supervision whose racism influences some of their offending behaviour, but where this element of their offending has been overlooked. Racist beliefs are also likely to change, as the world around the offender changes and as different groups are perceived as threats. They may be affected as patterns of immigration change and as the media coverage of different groups alters. Many racially motivated offenders who commit other offences will also exhibit other patterns of unhelpful thoughts. They may, for example, share attitudes towards women that again support a sense of superiority between groups.

Racist hostility therefore often interacts with an underlying sense of resentment, of victimhood, a readiness to use violence to solve problems and with problematic relationships between communities. Racial harassment is functional for the offenders concerned, distracting them from problems they feel incompetent to deal with, including lack of identity and insecurity about the future.

Activities and reflection 9.4

You have just read a detailed application of 'victim blame' to racially motivated offending. Now apply it to a specific but different example. Identify:

- Specific beliefs that tend to blame victims.
- Specific justifications linked to those beliefs.

Within this general picture it is important to acknowledge that there are different levels of risk amongst violent offenders, both in terms of the likelihood of incidents occurring and in terms of the level of serious harm they pose to others. It is important to recognise that racist attitudes, however unpleasant they may be, do not necessarily imply that an individual offender poses a heightened risk of harm to others. To make a judgement about the extent to which they do pose such a heightened risk, an assessment would need to consider the nature of the attitudes and whether they have been translated into hostile behaviours. The risks individuals pose may also change over time, as the offenders, their circumstances and relationships with victims alter.

Intervening with violent offenders

A careful assessment of risk of reconviction and, in particular, of serious harm to others (Kemshall, 2001; Kemshall et al, 2006) should inform a risk management plan. This plan should identify any steps that need to be taken to protect potential victims and to work with others.

Work with violent offenders needs to consider the external control of their behaviour; the measures that are taken to limit their opportunities to offend and to protect victims. These might include curfews, conditions on licences and, in some cases, surveillance and monitoring. The most seriously harmful offenders will be managed through MAPPA (Kemshall et al, 2005). It is important, however, that these external controls on behaviour are based on an accurate assessment of risk factors, so that they are appropriately targeted to address them.

This chapter will focus on the other element of the successful management of risk from violent offenders, the treatment approaches that may help them to change and more effectively reduce and manage their own risk. Where there is a significant potential for serious harm, naive interventions, based on insufficiently detailed assessments, must be avoided.

Returning to the pool cue wielding offender and Figure 9.1, interventions could include:

- Educating the individual about anger, stress and aggression, helping them to self-monitor the frequency and intensity of anger and become more aware of triggers to aggressive behaviour.
- Helping them to manage their emotions more effectively through, for example, relaxation or 'time out'.
- Changing cognitions by addressing abusive beliefs and by helping to alter what they pay attention to and how they understand others' behaviour, facilitating the use of self-instructions to guide their own behaviour.

- Helping them, through modelling and practice, to increase their repertoire of positive behavioural skills, such as communication and appropriate assertiveness.

The level and extent of intervention must, however, be carefully judged. Polaschek and Reynolds (2000) suggest that low-intensity programmes, focusing only on anger management, are unlikely to reduce violent risk in those with an extensive and varied history of violence. Instead, interventions need to be based on a careful assessment that is clear about the extent of the problem and about what is sustaining the violent behaviour. Novaco and Welsh (1989) talk about levels of intervention:

- Anger management: a psycho-educational approach that imparts information about anger, and ways of controlling it, such as changing perceptions and relaxation. This approach requires less disclosure from the individual and is less threatening.
- Anger treatment: targets an enduring change in thinking and the acquisition of arousal reduction, and behavioural coping skills, combined with self-monitoring. This requires offenders to engage at a more personal level and to disclose and work with difficult emotions.

In addition, the practitioner needs to take into account the nature and function of the violent behaviour and any links to power and control. Specialist provision is needed for domestic violence and racially motivated violence where abusive beliefs, the exercise of control and targeted violence are central themes in the behaviour. Given the close links between substance misuse, and most especially alcohol misuse, and violent offending, work to address this will also often need to be integrated. Finally, specialist provision will be needed for women who offend violently, balancing a realistic appreciation of risk and an understanding of women as active agents, with an awareness of women's circumstances and in particular the impact of abuse.

While increasingly in England and Wales violent offenders may be dealt with via structured accredited programmes, the work of those programmes will need to be supported and maintained by others working with the offender. This requires a body of staff within prisons and outside, confident in dealing with sometimes difficult issues. The existence of such staff cannot be taken for granted. Ray et al (2002) found that some probation officers were nervous about broaching the subject of racial motivation. Sibbitt (1997) found that many probation officers were glad that racist attitudes remained hidden, as they were fearful of working with these issues if they were openly expressed.

Activities and reflection 9.5

- What work with violent offenders do you currently engage in or are you aware of in your agency?
- How does it fit with Novaco and Welsh's (1989) models of anger management and anger treatment?
- Are there aspects of violent behaviour that you are reluctant to discuss with offenders; if so, why, and in what circumstances?
- What might you do to overcome this?

A good deal of attention has begun to be paid to effective work with the perpetrators of domestic violence. Mullender and Burton (2001) draw on literature reviews and on the mapping of current perpetrator programmes to examine current practice in this area. This includes programmes run in the voluntary sector as well as those run by probation areas. They suggest that there is a greater acceptance that domestic violence is a crime and that the perpetrators should be held responsible for their criminal behaviour. They reinforce the point that perpetrators must not be allowed to shift the focus from their offending to their status as victim, by blaming their partner or other issues.

They found that most group work programmes for the perpetrators of domestic violence are based on a combined approach (Pence and Paymar, 1993):

- a cognitive behavioural approach, which views their violence as learnt behaviour; and
- a gender attitude component, which seeks to alter belief systems about the right to control women in intimate relationships.

Similar principles would also need to underpin interventions with racially motivated offenders where, again, practitioners need to use a cognitive behavioural approach, alongside addressing racist belief structures. A similar approach seems likely to be most appropriate for violent homophobic offences.

Interventions with domestic violence perpetrators need to avoid collusion with a minimisation of responsibility for their actions. Offenders will try to persuade workers, as they persuade themselves, that their violence was an understandably angry response to provocation, or that it only happened because they had been drinking. They will confuse association with cause and use this to minimise their responsibility. While alcohol misuse and emotional arousal, understood by the offender as anger, are associated with acts of domestic violence they should not be seen as causal. Similar considerations have already been raised in the context of racially motivated offending and the justifying thinking of the offenders.

Work with violent offenders therefore needs to be focused depending on the particular form of that behaviour, the circumstances in which it occurs and the motivations for the behaviour. The inspection (HMIP, 2006) into the actions of Damien Hanson, following his involvement in a murder while on parole licence, identified a failure to understand the instrumental nature of his motivation and, instead, assumptions being made about loss of control. Such mistakes in assessment may lead to inappropriate interventions, failing to address the real risk factors, or assuming that the offender is more motivated to manage their own behaviour than they are.

Engaging the violent offender

Engagement of the offender in the process of change is important for violent offenders, just as it is important for other groups of offenders discussed in this book. There are particular issues in achieving this, both because of the impact of the offending behaviour and attitudes on workers, and because of the resistance to change of many of these offenders. As earlier sections of this chapter make clear, violent behaviour appears functional for many individuals and is embedded in powerfully self-reinforcing patterns of thinking and behaviour, in the individual and often in the social groups to which they belong.

It is often, therefore, not easy behaviour to change, and interventions should challenge the logic underlying the behaviour and the justifications for it. Attention should always be paid to the victim of violent behaviour, both in terms of managing any risk, but also in reducing victim blaming. In addition, many violent offenders will need help to develop their ability to problem solve and to respond to difficulties without aggression. All of this needs to be delivered in a way that provides clear incentives for the offender to manage their own behaviour; MacLean (2000) stresses that there needs to be something in it for them. This has to be delivered within an approach that makes clear the disapproval of the behaviour, while still promoting a positive relationship with the offender. This requires close attention to the detail of the working relationship and the importance of avoiding collusion.

Key skills and qualities – avoiding potential pitfalls in managing risk

- Many forms of violent offending, including domestic violence and racially motivated offending, include elements of power and control and of dehumanising and the attempted destruction of their victim's sense of self. An overemphasis on responsivity in terms of ensuring engagement, without a proper balance in terms of an understanding of risk, might lead to false engagement, where an offender is apparently complying, while in truth they are simply becoming better at concealing their behaviour, or changing the nature of their abuse.

- Workers also need to be aware of their own potential to be manipulated by offenders and be very alert to attempts to pull them into collusion. Racist and abusive comments, when they occur, must be challenged, but in a way that does not prevent the offender from disclosing their real attitudes, so that they can be worked with. This is significant for all staff and of particular significance for men working with domestic violence perpetrators and for White staff working with racist offenders.

- There is always the potential for professional avoidance. Some violent offenders are threatening to staff, so individual workers need to be alert to the possibility of their decision making being influenced by fear. Another form of professional avoidance can happen when practitioners are lacking in confidence in their own ability to handle difficult issues, compounded by an unwillingness to seek help and admit when they are finding something difficult.

- Active and confident engagement may be particularly challenging in working with offenders whose offences and attitudes and beliefs are offensive. It may be even more challenging if some of those attitudes have resonance for an individual worker, who finds their own racism, or sexism, triggered by the statements of the offender.

- Many violent offenders are likely to have a lot to lose by recognising their problem, so that securing their full engagement is often difficult and they may show considerable resistance. The proper use of sanctions and enforcement is significant to ensure at least initial attendance and to maintain safety for victims as work progresses. Practitioners should maintain a clear understanding of their own responsibilities in managing risk.

It is therefore important that practitioners put into practice key understandings in relation to the management of risk of serious harm. An example would be the principle of *defensible decision making* (Carson, 1996; Kemshall, 1998a, 1998b; Kemshall et al, 2006) which includes the following components:

- Decisions grounded in the evidence and assessed using reliable risk assessment tools and based on all relevant information verified and evaluated.
- Attention paid to recording and accounting for decision making and communicating with relevant others, seeking missing information.
- Staying within agency policies and procedures maintaining contact with the offender, commensurate with the level of risk of harm.
- Matching risk management interventions to risk factors and responding to escalating risk, deteriorating behaviour and non-compliance.

Key skills and qualities – actively engaging the offender

This defensible practice needs to operate alongside work aimed at actively engaging the participation of the offender and indeed can contribute positively to the offender's ability to understand and respond to the process.

If interventions are to make a difference by promoting self-risk management, it is important to recognise the origins and maintenance of violent behaviour for many offenders. Violent behaviour can emerge from situations of loss and damage, and the function of the behaviour can include protecting the offender's vulnerability. Work with the most serious young violent offenders needs to consider the origins of that behaviour in trauma and abuse, as well as the factors promoting violent reactions in the present (see Boswell, 2000).

Geese Theatre (Baim et al, 2002) work extensively with violent offenders, using drama. They involve the offenders in work that requires significant personal disclosure and risk-taking. They discuss the qualities needed both in workers and the methods used, in order to promote participation and work effectively with resistance. Good practice with violent behaviour, in some senses, is simply a reminder of key skills and qualities workers should have in all work with offenders. *Pro-social modelling* (Trotter, 1999; Cherry, 2005) provides another way of thinking about some of those skills. Another significant way of thinking about good practice derives from an understanding of motivation and the skills of *motivational interviewing* (Miller and Rollnick, 2002).

Practice tool 9.2

The following checklist can be used to check that you are providing engagement without collusion:

- The ability to communicate empathy and a belief in the possibility of change.
- Clarity about role and about authority.
- A willingness to act on that authority when necessary.
- Modelling consistently pro-social behaviours and clearly communicating disapproval of antisocial behaviours.
- Giving consistent feedback based on those pro-social behaviours.
- Avoiding confrontation, recognising ambivalence.
- Helping the offender to shift their decisional balance in the direction of change.
- Providing offenders with opportunities to acquire the skills they need to bring about and sustain change.
- Actively reinforcing positive change in order to build self-efficacy.
- Remembering the victim and the centrality of public protection.

Conclusion

Offenders are more than the worst things they have done. This chapter has talked a great deal about the links between victimisation, perceived and real, and violent behaviour. Practitioners should aim to help offenders to use their own experiences of victimisation to build empathy with others (Baim et al, 2002) instead of to justify abuse. They should help offenders to develop the skills and self-belief they need to be able to deal with problems pro-socially, instead of using violence to achieve their ends.

Violent behaviour is diverse and it would be impossible to produce one simple approach equally applicable to all. Cognitive behavioural models do, however, provide frameworks to structure understandings and they can be helpful, providing attention is paid to the detail of each individual's behaviour and circumstances and to the implications for the risk that they may pose to others. This combination of structure and an understanding of risk applied to individuals implies another challenge to effective working relationships with such offenders. Practitioners must be able to develop empathy without collusion and help offenders to develop their own abilities to change their behaviours and reduce the risk that they pose.

TEN

Property offenders

Introduction

> Well it just happened; I didn't plan to do it or anything
> ...Taz dared me to nick it by putting it under my hoodie
> ... He was really laughing and I wasn't going to let him see
> I was scared so I took them ...

These statements are very typical of what offenders say when asked to
account for an offence. They frequently see offending as spontaneous
events which happen without reason. However, while acquisitive
crime, like most offending, has elements of impulsiveness, it is rarely
an isolated act:

> Most criminologists would agree that crimes are rarely
> random events, that there are patterns of victimisation and
> also offending that is often the result of rational decision-
> making that reflects offenders' perceptions and attitudes
> towards risks and rewards. (Kapardis and Krambia-Kapardis,
> 2004: 190)

If practitioners accept too readily the offender's account of the theft
or burglary as having 'just happened' and move too quickly to tackling
the criminogenic (offending-related) needs of the offender then this is
a missed opportunity. The opportunity missed is that of exploring in
depth the factors or processes that have led to the offence occurring and
thus being more precise in terms of understanding how to intervene to
reduce the risk of reoffending. Offenders are less likely to be challenged
about their offending behaviour and therefore more likely to see
themselves as passive individuals caught up in events which are beyond
their control, rather than people who have some choices in life.

The purpose of this chapter is to explore what is known about
property offending and to help practitioners develop an understanding
of how to work with it most effectively. Practitioners need to build
up their skills and confidence in using searching questions, in order to
have a better understanding of why offending occurs and how best to

tackle it. Without this exploration of the decision-making processes underlying much offending, the practitioner is less likely to be aware of when the offender is being drawn into more serious crime.

The chapter begins by considering property crime and risk before exploring a number of theories about property crime, such as routine activities and rational choice, in order to build an understanding about why it happens in the way that it does. The chapter moves on to look particularly at burglary and theft and, briefly, at car crime, before looking at recent developments in tackling acquisitive crime through crime prevention, group work and more targeted approaches. The final section of the chapter is devoted to translating how this understanding about acquisitive crime informs face-to-face work with offenders, particularly though the different roles of:

- generic practitioners, for example holding cases which are regarded to be low to medium risk offenders;
- specialist practitioners working in a multi-agency scheme with persistent/high volume offenders;
- practitioners involved in broader responses to crime control particularly through crime prevention and community safety.

This final section stresses the importance of assessment informing the intervention but also reinforces the practitioner's key role as supporter/ motivator during the process of change.

This chapter does not cover robbery or aggravated burglary, that is, offending that includes violence. Violent offending is covered in depth in Chapter Nine of this book.

Property crime and risk

Property offenders are often at high risk of reoffending but frequently do not pose a high risk of harm. As a result of this practitioners may find they are trying to work with them as part of a large caseload of similarly designated lower risk offenders.

By contrast to working with high risk offenders (who may be seen as professionally more challenging and therefore more 'exciting'), dealing with a large volume of lower risk offenders may be perceived as less demanding and dull. There may be real danger, when faced with large numbers of superficially similar cases ('Oh no, not another shoplifter or car thief!') that the practitioner makes assumptions about the offender's motivation and responds with less curiosity and interest. This is likely to reduce responsivity and effectiveness.

Throughout this book, the importance of 'attending to the detail' has been stressed as part of understanding the offender in front of you. This is particularly applicable to 'apparently' lower risk offenders. Crime reports, all too frequently, reveal that offenders previously considered to be lower/medium risk have become involved in much more serious and damaging crimes (see, for example, the account of the murder of Mary-Ann Leneghan by six men four of whom were under probation supervision for much less serious offences at the time of the murder [Payne, 2006]). While recognising that not all offending can be predicted or prevented, practitioners need to be alert to changing levels of risk of harm and reoffending (see Chapter Two of this book) and to be able to ask penetrating questions of the offender about their current activities. Through this process of challenge the practitioner is most likely to be able to make 'defensible decisions' (see Chapter Nine) in terms of their actions and interventions.

What is property crime?

Property offences constitute the largest proportion of illegal acts. Crime statistics suggest that theft and burglary make up 75% of all recorded crime. If all other crime against property, for example, criminal damage and fraud, is also included the figure rises to 90% (McGuire, 2000).

For the purposes of this chapter 'property crime' has been considered in its broadest sense and encompasses all illegal acts targeted at property, or with property as their focus, and covers a wide range of motivating factors that influence offenders.

In 1983 in response to the British Crime Survey it was estimated that "the average household could expect a burglary every 40 years" (Hough and Mayhew, 1983: 15). Mawby (2001) acknowledges that this statistic is not as reassuring as it first appears as no such average person exists. In reality, there are considerable variations in risk due to differences in area, household characteristics, design and planning features and lifestyle.

However, the fear of crime has continued to play a significant part in our sense of well-being as a society more generally. Fear of crime is only weakly related to being a victim of crime, such that, although young men are most at risk of being victims, it is the elderly who have the greatest fear of crime, not only in terms of personal consequences but also fearing the breakdown of society. This may be in part a response to media accounts of crime (James and Raine, 1998). There is a danger that practitioners underestimate the impact that relatively minor thefts and burglary have on victims. In an analysis of the 1998

British Crime Survey, Budd (1999) reported that 87% of victims of burglary felt affected emotionally, although violence and threatening behaviour towards the victim had occurred in only 11% of incidents. An appreciation of the relationship between fear of crime and general well-being in society helps lead to an understanding of the value of broader responses to crime control, which go beyond treatment and rehabilitation of offenders into prevention and deterrence of criminal acts wherever possible.

Property offending can flow from acquisitiveness and economic motivations (for example, theft, burglary, fraud and drug trafficking), and/or direct or displaced, expressive or instrumental, aggression (for example, criminal damage and robbery), or other emotional needs (for example, some cases of arson and 'joyriding').

Theories about property offending

Theoretical explanations for property offending have tended to fall into two main 'camps'. The first explains the offending in terms of the individual's predisposition to crime, for example, as a result of such factors as disrupted schooling and poverty. Approaches tend to be sociological in nature and emphasise the 'who' and 'why' questions when seeking to explain crime (see Farrington, 1995; Mawby, 2001). The second 'camp' encompasses approaches that suggest that the motivation to offend is to some extent determined by situational factors and that "individuals actually choose to commit crime as a result of rational decision making" (Bennett and Wright, 1984: 1).

These two schools of thought are not mutually exclusive, although, as McGuire (2004) comments:

> There is at present no adequately connective model of the relationship between rational choice theories (Clarke and Felson, 1993) and other concepts within criminology that are derivatives of the general idea of low self-control (Gottfredson and Hirschi, 1990). However it appears most likely that what we depict as the 'causal chain' leading to a given offence is marked along the route by fluctuations between some moments of impulse or absent-minded thoughtlessness and others of conscious deliberation. (McGuire, 2004: 338)

However, when taken together, these approaches provide the assessor with an understanding of the complexity of interrelated facts that go together to create the motivation to offend. It encourages thinking beyond 'who' and 'why' to ask 'what' and 'how' when assessing any criminal act. Bennett and Wright (1984: 17) cite the highly influential work of Clarke (1980), who "did not rule out the influence of a person's past history on the decision to offend but saw its causal significance as conditional upon immediate situational variables and present life circumstances". It is important to see the offender not as a passive casualty of previous life experiences, but as someone who can make choices in response to those events and also current life chances.

It will be helpful to the reader to explore the following key theoretical approaches in more detail:

- criminal career;
- routine activities theory;
- rational choice theory.

Criminal career

The notion of a criminal career is an important theme in this book and suggests the importance of onset, persistence and protective factors during upbringing (Farrington, 1997) which are highly influential in predicting subsequent involvement in anti-social behaviour and crime. Chapter Four contains a more detailed exploration of this concept. Farrington (1997) suggests that offenders fall into two broad categories either 'life-course persistent' (offending starts earlier and continues into adulthood) or 'adolescent limited' (offending starts and finishes during the teenage years). Frequently, both types of offender become involved in property offending.

Routine activities theory

This approach suggests the following equation: 'Likely offender + suitable target – capable guardian = offence' (Cohen and Felson, 1979). This theory pays less attention to who constitutes a 'likely offender' but is more interested in the opportunities that the 'suitable target – capable guardian' present. Routine activities theory promotes the importance of understanding the habitual activities of both offenders and victims and has been highly influential in crime prevention approaches (explored later in this chapter). Examination of particular crimes may reveal patterns of behaviour which illustrate the opportunities open to the individual to offend within other routines of daily life, for example, theft from a newsagent on the usual route to the job centre. Thus the increased burglary rate in the US during the 1960s and 1970s can be explained by the changes in lifestyle of the time with more homes (suitable targets) empty during the day (without a guardian), because of more single households and more women in work (Cohen and Felson, 1979).

Rational choice perspective

Clarke and Cornish (1986: 9) suggest that:

> ... crime is purposive behaviour designed to meet the offender's commonplace needs for such things as money, status, sex, and excitement and that meeting these needs involves the making of (sometimes quite rudimentary) decisions and choices, constrained as these are by the limits of time and ability and the availability of relevant information.

Clarke (1997: 10) suggests that it is important to distinguish between *criminal involvement* and *criminal events* as two distinct decisional processes. *Criminal involvement* is the process of becoming involved in particular forms of crime (this links with the idea of onset, persistence and desistance from crime) and encourages the identification of factors within the offender's life as a whole that promote or discourage criminal activity. A *criminal event* is the decision process involved in the commission of a specific crime, and is dependent on different types of information and is altogether a shorter process, focusing specifically on the immediate circumstances of a particular offence.

It may be helpful, for any practitioner working closely with an offender, in order to make an assessment, to see the difference between these two decisional processes, thus making a distinction between a more generalised understanding of the situation and influences upon an offender and the specific decision making that occurred in the commission of a particular offence. This is referred to elsewhere in this book as the 'journey to the offence' and is explored in Chapter Three. The model (see Figure 3.1) emphasises the importance of breaking down the steps to the offence by exploring with the offender their perception of the factors which contributed to their offending.

The offender's motivation is not constant or irrepressible. They may be seeking to derive money, goods or excitement. The decision may be precipitated by others or the presentation of an opportunity. It may be triggered by an expressive need, for example, for excitement or to take risks. Alcohol may operate as a disinhibitor or to give the offender courage. Rarely will there be just one determining factor or motivator; more likely there will be an original motivator and then intervening influences on the final decision (Bennett and Wright, 1984). Overall, the offender is reconciling conflicting opportunities, pressures and temptations and it is through careful exploration of this process that the practitioner and offender will come to understand the detail of their offending.

Rational choice theory is supported by many studies (Mawby, 2001; Kapardis and Krambia-Kapardis, 2004) which involve interviews with offenders of various types of offending and provide considerable information about motives, methods and target choices. It has enabled much more detailed research to be undertaken into the structural and situational opportunities for property crime, strengthening understanding about why, when and how it happens in order to try to reduce the risk of it happening again.

What do we know about burglary and theft?

- Burglary is defined as "illegal entry to homes and other premises, such as garages, offices, shops ... it is an incident where someone enters a property without permission to steal something" (Mawby, 2001: 4).
- Although domestic burglary has fallen in recent years, in contrast with the rapid rise in the 1980s and early 1990s, it is still a high volume crime. The British Crime Survey estimated 1.28 million burglaries in 1999, accounting for one in 10 of crimes measured by the survey. Property stolen was worth £680 million (Budd, 2001).
- Prior to the 1968 Theft Act, burglary used to be defined as 'breaking and entering', that is, there needed to be the use of physical force to enter. Now physical force does not need to occur and entering through an open door or window without permission or by trickery constitutes a burglary.
- 'Theft' is a generic term used to describe all crimes in which a person appropriates property of another with the intention of permanently depriving them of it (1968 Theft Act). Theft is generally a much more opportunistic offence, whereas burglary involves more planning and premeditation.
- Being a victim of crime is not randomly distributed. The development of the concepts of *hot spots* and *repeat victims* (places or people who suffer a series of crimes within a relatively short

period of time) has enabled crime prevention efforts to be targeted at the points where they are likely to yield greatest benefit (Everson and Pease, 2001).

- Single parent households, students, unemployed people, privately rented or council property dwellers are more often victims of burglary (Mawby, 2001).

- *Repeat victimisation* occus where there is a high risk of being burgled again within 6 to 8 weeks of the original offence (Everson and Pease, 2001). "The first offence against a target educates an offender in ways that boost the risk of repeat victimisation by making it easier, more attractive or more profitable to the same perpetrator" (Everson and Pease, 2001: 202).

- There has been been development of the concept of *hot products* (Clarke, 1999), that is, those items most likely to be stolen. The ultimate hot product is cash which (unless the notes are marked) is difficult to identify as stolen. It is lightweight and immediately ready for use.

- *Hot products* in a burglary are cash, jewellery and consumer 'electricals'; hot products for shoplifting depend to a certain extent on the store but usually include magazines, tobacco products, CDs and beauty and fashion items. These are not always the most valuable but are often the least protected.

- Except for cash, most products have a life cycle in terms of burglary and theft such that patterns in the type of property stolen will change in response to social pressures. For example, since 1998 theft of computers and mobile phones has increased while theft of video players and car radios has decreased.

- There is a widespread assumption that drug use is a primary motive behind acquisitive crime (not necessarily causal but the exact relationship is unclear). Allen (2005) suggests that shoplifting usually precedes induction into drug use, but acknowledges that regular use of heavy drugs (such as heroin and crack cocaine) more readily links with street crime, particularly robbery, in order to obtain cash.

- Distinction is usually made when sentencing between burglary of 'homes' and of other places, for example garages, shops and so on, to reflect the significance of the emotional impact on victims (Mawby, 2001).

- Burglary tends to be a local enterprise. Mawby (2001: 71) found 85% of offences being committed within 5 miles of the offender's home. Targeted properties were often these identified during other life experiences: job centre, school, pub, near traffic lights.

- Burglary targets did not always offer 'the richest pickings' but were seen as attractive because of ease of access and the absence of alarms, what Mawby (2001: 75) calls "limited rationality" in terms of offender thinking.

What about the offenders themselves?

- *Individual profile* – relatively little research has focused on the offenders themselves and they are not necessarily seen as a distinct group. Burglars, particularly, often also commit other offences too (Mawby, 2001).
- *Age* – 16- to 25-year-olds are the most prominent group of offenders being 14 times more likely to commit property offences than 36- to 60-year-old age groups (Rutter et al, 1998).
- *Gender* – men are one and a half times more likely to commit property offences than women, although acquisitive crime has been found to account for over 50 per cent of women's offending (Rutter et al, 1998).
- *Role of co-offending* – there is considerable debate about the role of co-offending in acquisitive crime. Felson (2003: 49) suggests that half to two thirds of all crime occurs through co-offending. Co-offending may be seen as going beyond "cooperating together to simultaneously commit a criminal act" (Felson, 2003: 15) but also includes the cooperation that goes on before, and after, an offence takes place.
- *Impact of co-offending*
  - It reinforces criminal impulses and encourages risky behaviour.
  - It allows exchange of information about potential crime targets, methods and departure routes.
  - It provides direct assistance, for example, 'lookout' and disposal of stolen goods.
  - Co-offenders usually meet through routine activities and "offender convergence settings" (Felson, 2003: 58), for example, fast food outlets, school gates, street corners and drug sale points.

> ### Activities and reflection 10.1
>
> - Think about a property offender you have recently been in contact with. How might you use some of these ideas to ask more searching questions about their offending?
> - Are there aspects of their offence that you did not ask about but could have done? For example, 'where did you meet your co-defendants'?
> - Readers not currently in contact with offenders may wish to think about the following question: 'in the light of these ideas what might you do differently to avoid becoming a victim of property crime?'

Some ideas about car crime

- Police in England and Wales recorded 1.1 million car thefts between 1998 and 2001. Although the trend suggests that car theft is declining, it still constitutes about six per cent of all recorded crime (Levesley et al, 2004).
- *Car theft* – there are different types of vehicle offending (Clarke and Harris, 1992):
  - thefts for temporary use (taking and driving away a vehicle without the owner's consent sometimes referred to as TWOC or TDA); for the purpose of getting home; 'joyriding';
  - theft from the vehicle, for example, radios, wheels, seats;
  - theft of the vehicle which is taken for permanent retention.
- Cars are frequently targeted to meet these specific needs, such that 'joyriders' may seek cars with performance and acceleration, and the 'car stripper' looks for popular cars with a ready resale market for parts. Those seeking permanent retention will also select cars that can readily be resold but usually cars of greater value and therefore greater profit.
- *Individual profile – gender:* car crime is overwhelmingly a male activity. In an analysis of TDA offenders in Belfast from 1930 to 1939 almost 100 per cent were male (O'Connell, 2006). Although women now feature more visibly in the motoring statistics, they remain significantly in the minority. In England and Wales in 2004, 97 per cent of those convicted of dangerous driving and 96 per cent of people convicted of unauthorised vehicle taking (TDA) or theft of a vehicle were male.
- *Age:* 66% of those convicted of theft of a vehicle or TDA were under 21 (Home Office National Statistics, 2004).
- The mandatory fitting of electronic immobilisers since 1995 has been an effective method of reducing theft of newer vehicles. However, there is an emerging trend of keys being used to steal

cars, the keys being obtained either through burglary (37%) or through the owners leaving them in the ignition (18%) (Levesley et al, 2004).

Recent developments aimed at tackling acquisitive crime

During the past 20 years there has been a broadening of response to crime control. Although treatment and rehabilitation remain important elements in any crime-reduction strategy, prevention and deterrence have been the growth areas in terms of research and development.

Offender-centred strategies (such as treatment and rehabilitation) rely on catching and sentencing offenders but the detection rates for acquisitive crime have been getting worse; for example, in 1981, for every 1,000 burglaries committed 27 resulted in convictions, but by 1995 this had been reduced to six per 1,000 (Mawby, 2001: 174).

Walklate (2005: 160) suggests that it is possible to see four identifiably different strategies deployed to tackle crime. These strategies are not mutually exclusive, tend to be problem focused and often exist side by side:

- *Offender centred* – use of prison to incapacitate, programmes, diversion, reparation.
- *Victim centred* – for example, crime prevention leaflets giving victim avoidance advice.
- *Environment centred* – focus is on the offence rather than the offender and usually involves target hardening, for example, 'chip and PIN' technology with credit cards, CCTV. (See Pawson and Tilley, 1994: 301 for a discussion about the different 'mechanisms' through which CCTV may lead to a reduction in car crimes.)
- *Community centred* – for example, neighbourhood watch and multi-agency cooperation.

Most crime prevention strategies tend to focus on visible crime rather than less visible offences such as domestic violence, child abuse and crimes in business such as insider trading and fraud (Hughes, 1998; Walklate, 2005). Thus crime prevention strategies tend to be very partial in terms of overall crime reduction.

In view of the likely roles and interest of the criminal justice practitioner, this chapter will focus specifically on the following recent developments and their implications in practice:

- situational crime prevention
- group work approaches
- targeted work at prolific (and priority) offenders.

Situational crime prevention

The appeal of the situational crime prevention approach lies not in its theoretical purity but that it is offers the potential of a 'technical fix' (Hughes, 1998). Thus the pragmatic approach to preventing crime is to modify the environment and to increase the likelihood of detection. As (Clarke, 1999: V) notes, "crime is not spread evenly across all places, people or times and to be effective preventative measures must be directed to where crime is most concentrated".

Clarke (1997: 15) offers a list of 16 techniques of situational crime prevention that are currently available and which have been shown to work. He divides these techniques into four groups: those which make it harder for the offender to commit the crime, for example, 'chip and PIN' technology on credit cards; those which increase the risk of being detected or caught, for example, electronic merchandise tags in shops; those which reduce the rewards of crime, for example, property marking; and those that increase the shame and guilt of crime, for example, roadside speed monitors that give immediate feedback when limits are exceeded.

Hughes (1998: 66) suggests that "situational techniques have resulted in tangible crime reduction success" (see Pease, 1997). Not only are some techniques relatively easy and straightforward to implement but they also offer scope for evaluation to demonstrate they work. Hughes (1998) cites the example of the installation of CCTV cameras in 1975 in a number of London underground stations where theft was rife. After 12 months a reduction of 27 per cent for thefts could be shown in those stations. It is worth noting that CCTV is increasingly being relied on to support all stages of the crime management process, not only to deter offending, but also to support detection, such as in the case of missing children and to provide evidence for the court process.

Criticism of the situational crime prevention approach centres on the limitations of its focus. It cannot tackle all types of crime, for example, business crime or crimes within the home. It also places heavy responsibility on the general public to avoid becoming targets for crime, such that victims may feel that they have taken insufficient care of themselves or their property (Garland, 2001; Walklate, 2005) when reporting crime.

Attempts to "design out crime" (Hughes, 1998: 69) also have

implications in terms of how we live our lives. It encroaches on civil liberties, encourages social segregation and restricts the use of public space. Lastly, but perhaps most importantly, it distracts the focus of government policy away from the social conditions that often give rise to crime. By suggesting that offenders can 'choose' whether or not to commit crime, it underplays the importance of issues like poor education, poverty and unemployment in creating the conditions when offending is most likely to result. Thus situational crime prevention needs to be accompanied by social crime prevention measures.

Group work approaches

The Probation Service and the Home Office have in recent years introduced a series of pathfinder programmes across England and Wales. These are mainly cognitive behavioural group work programmes and seek to change the thinking patterns (beliefs and values) that support offending behaviour. They include generic offending behaviour programmes such as Enhanced Thinking Skills and Think First. There are also a number of offence-specific programmes for addressing domestic violence, sex offending, substance misuse and violence. Although most offenders participate in these cognitive behaviour programmes as part of a group, some Probation Service areas offer a generic offending behaviour programme which can be delivered to an offender on a one-to-one basis. This is for offenders whose personal circumstances or problems and characteristics make it difficult to attend or learn in a group.

Adult car offenders are accommodated in the generic offender group work programmes along with offenders convicted of burglary, theft and criminal damage. The aim of such programmes is to "help individuals acquire, develop and apply a series of social problem solving and associated skills that will enable them to manage difficulties in their lives and to avoid future offending" (Home Office, 2000a: 3).

These accredited programmes are subject to extensive and ongoing evaluations which have produced mixed results. Gorman et al (2006: 16) suggests that:

> ... there remains a notable absence of hard evidence as to the success of these programmes in terms of discouraging participants from offending ... The initial promise of research into a pre-accredited cognitive skills programme, which revealed 2 year reconviction rates for treatment groups that

were 14% lower than for matched comparison groups has
not been echoed by subsequent research findings.

Merrington and Stanley (2004: 9) suggest that it is not simply a case
of identifying "what works and what doesn't". They emphasise that
each research study provides many learning points which contribute
to a greater understanding about what works, with whom and under
what circumstances. However, as Gorman et al (2006: 17) note,
"explicit Home Office links between performance and funding and
the continuing threat of financial penalties if targets are not met"
is likely to have led to offenders being allocated inappropriately to
programmes to meet area targets rather than to meet offender need.
This, in turn, makes it harder to judge with any confidence the efficacy
of an intervention.

The problem-solving focus of the programmes requires that the tutors
make explicit the connections between the skills being explored and
practised in any session with the original offending behaviour. The
generic nature of the programme means that the group may be made
up of individuals who vary greatly in terms of age, life experience
and offending histories. This makes it harder for the tutors to link the
exercises so readily with offending behaviour. Anecdotal feedback from
treatment managers suggests that some tutors would prefer offence-
specific groups, even when using the same programme materials,
in order to enable them to make better linkages with the original
offending. Another problem identified is that of offender motivation.
Most areas rely on report writers identifying whether the offender is
suitable to be placed on a programme. Area targets can result in pressure
on assessors to ensure that offenders go into groups wherever possible.
This can result in tutors struggling with groups which contain a number
of unmotivated offenders who are less ready to change, thus making it
harder for groups to be effective.

These are clearly important issues for all practitioners, especially
those in a case management role who may be referring an offender to
a group or supporting an offender while on a programme, particularly
in terms of developing and sustaining motivation. This will be returned
to later in the chapter.

Targeted work at prolific offenders

The last major development area that this section covers is that of
targeted work at prolific offenders. Sometimes these offenders may be
identified as persistent, priority or prolific; whatever the terminology,

they are the small number of anti-social offenders who are responsible for a disproportionate amount of crime. Exact percentages vary from study to study but generally the statistics are startling. In West and Farrington's (1977) Cambridge study of 400 delinquent families, 6 per cent of the sample of males accounted for half of all convictions. Home Office figures from 2001 (Dawson, 2005) identify that "10% of all active offenders are responsible for half of all crime".

The developing philosophy in crime reduction strategies of targeting efforts in ways that are likely to be most productive has led to the creation of specific schemes which target persistent offenders. These schemes aim to identify and work with the most 'troublesome', who are usually seen to start earlier, and offend at a more frequent rate. Dawson (2005: 2) suggests that the characteristics of a persistent offender are as follows:

- overwhelmingly male (95%);
- White (88%);
- demonstrated through assessment to have higher levels of criminological needs than usual offenders;
- in the age range 17 to 40 (84%);
- predominantly involved in acquisitive crime, but versatile in nature, generally committing lots of different types of crime;
- often start younger (consistent with Farrington's ([1997] concept of early onset and 'life-persistent' offenders).

These initiatives usually involve close collaboration between the police, the Probation Service, YOTs and other partnership agencies, especially through crime and disorder partnerships.

The emphasis is on high levels of police monitoring and surveillance, intensive supervision arrangements, and data sharing between agencies (Worrall and Walton, 2000). Those with drug problems are given a 'fast track' into treatment. Offenders can go onto these schemes immediately on release from prison. Although the schemes have yet to be fully evaluated (Dawson, 2005), initial indications are that these schemes can be successful in reducing recorded crime. The attraction of the improved interagency partnership is that it allows for a more comprehensive view of the offender and a rapid response, by all concerned, if the offender gets back into prolific offending or the risk of harm the offender poses is seen to rise.

How can the practitioner use these ideas on property crime to inform face-to-face work with offenders?

As in all the chapters of this book, emphasis has been placed on the key practitioner tasks of *assessment* and *intervention*. How the practitioner intervenes depends to a certain extent on the role the practitioner currently occupies, for example, as a generic or specialist offender manager or in crime prevention. The differing implications for practitioners will be flagged up under the intervention section.

Assessment

The practitioner is likely to be assisted in the assessment process by risk assessment tools and the interview is likely to have generated a great deal of information. The assessor needs to analyse that information in order to answer the fundamental question as to 'Why did this offender commit this offence?'. The assessor and the offender need to develop a clear understanding of the 'journey to the offence' (see Chapter Three for a diagram and explanation of this concept) and the significant factors for that offender in terms of their particular motivation to offend, for example, the influence of peers, the need to buy drugs, or the lack of legitimate opportunities to earn money.

Practice tool 10.1

Using the 'journey to the offence' model (Figure 3.1), but applying it to property offending, the assessor may be helped in their analysis of the offence by answering the following questions.

'Situational press':

- What problem did this offence solve?
- Did drink or drugs affect the offender's thinking?
- What influence did the offender's peers have?

Emotional provocation:

- What was the offender's emotional state before, during and after the offence?

Opportunity:

- What made the offender choose this particular target?
- What preparations did they make in order to commit this offence?
- What previous knowledge, experience and contacts did the offender have which enabled them to commit this offence?
- What alternatives did they consider?
- What did they do with the stolen property?

Cost–benefit perception:

- What fears/concerns did the offender have to overcome in order to commit this offence?
- What did the offender gain or hope to gain?
- What was their attitude towards the victim?
- Consequences versus benefits – what tipped the balance?

As explained in Chapter Three, it is the way that these factors interact and are played out that culminates in the offence which is the end of this particular journey. Applying this model to property offending seems to generate more questions to answer about 'opportunity' and 'cost–benefit perception'. However, this fits with current theoretical explanations for property offending explored in the earlier sections of this chapter.

It is important that the practitioner focuses on the particular details of the offending behaviour and avoids making assumptions. By understanding the individual motivation to offend and the 'payback' that offending gives them, the assessor is likely to be more realistic in any plans to target the problem behaviour. Frequently, prior to a court appearance, an offender will profess unrealistic statements as to their determination to stop offending.

It is therefore useful to explore their motivation to change and aspects that may inhibit engagement (see Chapter Seven for a more detailed exploration of these issues), so that any subsequent supervision arrangements are as realistic as possible. This is particularly relevant in terms of referral to group work programmes, in the light of comments made earlier in this chapter about the difficulties of working in group settings with ill-prepared, unmotivated offenders.

Once equipped with a clear assessment of the offender's specific decision-making processes and motivation it is then possible to move into intervention.

Intervention

Exactly how the practitioner intervenes with an offender depends to a certain extent on the roles and responsibilities currently held by the practitioner in relation to the offender. Thus for some offenders who are due to attend an accredited programme, the role of case/offender manager may be a slightly more limited one, knowing that considerable energy and time will be devoted within the group to helping the offender develop problem solving and self-management skills. This role will be returned to later.

However, it is important to look at intervening with all those offenders who, for whatever reason (perhaps they are outside the targeting matrix of the specific programme or are unable to learn in a group), will not be attending an accredited programme. The practitioner needs to recognise the importance of challenging the offending behaviour and not moving too quickly to deal with many of the other problems that offenders present with, for example, poor accommodation. This is not to dismiss the importance of these issues but to recognise that practitioners can become embroiled in providing practical assistance while allowing their offending activities to remain largely unchallenged. Exactly how to intervene depends on what came from the process of assessment. For example, with an offender who has been involved in stealing from commercial warehouses with friends after drinking and who shows little awareness of the victims or their losses, it would be appropriate to select exercises which help the offender to develop victim awareness and empathy. It would also be useful to explore with the offender how they are using alcohol as a disinhibitor and to devise approaches that explore and counter the influence and impact of anti-social friends and alcohol.

Much of the desistance literature (see Cusson and Pinsonneault, 1986) stresses the importance of the decisional balance in the process of 'giving up' crime. Cusson and Pinsonneault (1986) carried out research with 17 ex-robbers in Canada and from this they argue that while criminals may offend over a long period they do not remain unchanged psychologically by the process. They suggest that an offender's criminal drive is worn down by the accumulation of punishments, by 'doing time' in prison and remembering the experience of 'getting caught' or when offences have gone wrong. Their analysis is primarily speculative but it does encourage practitioners to explore this 'decisional balance' with an offender, weighing up the costs of continuing offending against the potential of re-establishing links with society and severing contact with co-offenders. The role of the worker is to reinforce and strengthen the offender's resolve and to look at issues of temptation and pressure, for example, money worries.

A key element in the practitioner's role is that of promoting and sustaining motivation, irrespective of whether undertaking offence-focused work on a one-to-one basis, or when acting as a 'supporter' while an offender attends an accredited programme or a partnership agency for particular assistance, debt management for example. It is vital that the practitioner, if acting as an offender or case manager, sees their role as a much more critical one, particularly as 'supporter/motivator' rather than simply as 'broker' and/or 'enforcer'.

Effective practice developments have sometimes overemphasised the importance of getting the right technical components in supervision and have undervalued the importance of the worker–offender relationship. Particularly when working with large numbers of lower to medium risk offenders, practitioners need to avoid workload management approaches which routinise and devalue face-to-face contact with offenders. Holt (2002) suggests that to support offender change, the worker–offender relationship needs to be characterised by the following:

- *consistency* in terms of setting boundaries and expectations;
- *continuity* in providing a constant point of reference and steering the individual through what may be a potentially complex and confusing range of interventions;
- *consolidation* by monitoring progress and reinforcing change;
- *commitment* throughout the whole process of change, however difficult that might be.

As Holt (2002: 18) notes, "these issues have critical importance, not only in preventing a fragmented experience of supervision for the offender, but also in providing opportunities for consolidation of the changes into pro-social lifestyles".

Activities and reflection 10.2: Thinking about your relationships

Think about your worker–offender relationship with a particular property offender:

- To what extent does it reflect Holt's four 'C's; consistency, continuity, collaboration and commitment?

- Can you think of things that you have said or done which show you have motivated and supported the offender during the process of trying to change?
- What feedback have you sought about how the offender experienced your work with them?
- Does this alert you to any areas you need to develop?

Practitioners involved in specialist roles

For practitioners involved in specialist projects, working with prolific offenders, the issue of offender motivation is paramount. In some ways the task is more sharply in focus because in coming on to a scheme an offender is likely to have been reminded that any lapse into reoffending will be quickly detected and they will be arrested and/or returned to prison. However, the offender's dynamic risk factors are likely to be more entrenched and thus more difficult to overcome. It is particularly important that the practitioner puts energy and commitment into working collaboratively with other key agencies and it would be useful to look at the guidance given in Chapter Six in terms of working effectively in partnership with others.

For those practitioners involved in crime prevention roles, the focus will be markedly different. It is helpful if the practitioner is able to take the offender perspective into discussions about crime reduction thus ensuring that social crime prevention measures sit alongside situational crime prevention schemes when combating local anti-social behaviour issues.

Conclusion

This chapter has sought to explore the whole issue of property crime, particularly burglary, theft and vehicle crime. Such offenders continue to be the mainstay of many caseloads and for many practitioners the work may seem more routine and less professionally challenging. Offenders often present accounts of this type of offending which imply its random and unpredictable nature. Research included in this chapter shows that much can be learnt about how and when acquisitive crime occurs and charts the successful development of much situational crime prevention.

Theories about criminal career, rational choice and routine activities stress the importance of exploring with the offender the risk factors that have led to their criminal involvement, but also the decision-making process that results in specific incidents of offending. It emphasises the importance of exploring the detail of their offending if subsequent interventions are to be targeted appropriately.

Practitioners need to feel confident and competent in the practice of challenging offending behaviour. They also need to recognise the importance of their role in motivating and supporting offenders through the process of change. Workload management schemes undervalue the role of the practitioner as a key player in the process of encouraging offenders' desistance from crime. Practitioners need to be technically equipped to challenge offending behaviour but they need to bring their power and influence to bear through the worker–offender relationship if change is to be sustained.

Part Five
Conclusions

ELEVEN

Evaluating and ending well

Introduction – evaluation then and now

One of the authors, remembering their early years as a newly qualified probation officer in the 1980s, recounts that on their 'patch' there were many Asian boys, aged 14 to 15, getting into offending. Supervising them as a White female seemed remote and unhelpful so they felt a group work approach might be more effective. After finding an Asian male social worker to co-work the group, approval was sought from local managers. They asked how much it would cost, decided the budget could afford it and left the author and co-worker to get on and plan the programme.

With hindsight it seems astonishing that no questions were asked about whether the proposed approach could be shown to work or how it was to be evaluated. The group appears to have been successful, attendance remained high throughout the 10 evenings and the boys participated enthusiastically. The author cannot be any more certain than this because they did not evaluate the programme. Looking back, although professionally exciting and creative for the workers involved, there was little protection for group members in terms of tried and tested methods of intervention. A great deal was learnt from the experience but this learning was not shared beyond immediate colleagues and it did not contribute to the development of practice more widely. This was a missed opportunity.

In contrast, the principle of evaluation is now largely accepted as an essential component of evidence-based practice. Practitioners will need to be evaluating their own work with individual offenders and may find themselves contributing to the development and evaluation of new initiatives. However, evaluating the impact of work with offenders is complex and practitioners may, at times, wonder how they can realistically contribute to this process. This chapter is very much an introduction to evaluation with a view to encouraging the practitioner to feel more confident about evaluating their own practice with offenders and also to read and make use of published research. It begins by exploring the historic lack of evaluation of work with offenders before outlining the benefits to the offender, particularly in terms of 'ending well', but also for the practitioner and service delivery as a whole. It then examines terminology and techniques of evaluation, particularly the practice of single case design. The emphasis throughout is on the practitioner perspective and the contribution evaluation and reflective practice can make to improving risk management and responsivity. Practice driven by the relentless pursuit of targets can dull the inquiring mind unless counterbalanced by the practitioner reflecting on what those results do, or do not, mean in terms of impact on offenders.

What is meant by evaluation?

Evaluation is the "systematic collection of information about a programme or intervention in order to assess and improve its effectiveness. Evaluation can emphasise developmental aspects, design quality, process, outcomes or value for money" (Merrington and Hine, 2001: 9-1). In this statement 'programme' has a broad meaning and includes both group work and individual interventions. Evaluation is not an end in itself but is a purposeful process which provides a way of thinking about and assessing whether your values and priorities, aims and objectives have been met, with a view to improving effectiveness.

The contribution of evaluation to evidence-based practice

As the opening example illustrates, historically, criminal justice agencies have lacked a research culture and as a consequence they devoted very limited resources into researching the effectiveness of different interventions. Partly this was due to uncertainty as to how effectiveness should be measured (Burnett, 1996) but also the difficulties of establishing causative links between interventions and their impact on reoffending. Prior to the 1990s there appears to have been a disregard of the need to obtain proof of supervision effectiveness, and sentencing courts seemed largely unconcerned by the absence of evidence of results (Nutley and Davis, 1999).

Professional training devoted very little time to equipping the practitioner to be research-minded during the 1970s and 1980s. Despite, or maybe because of, this, practitioners continued to work optimistically with offenders, primarily buoyed by their own experiences of success and failure with individual offenders. Most felt they were too busy 'doing the work' to be involved in something as time consuming as evaluation which could more readily be done by academics or those in specialist roles. Research into impact seemed particularly difficult because of the long history of practitioners adopting an individualised approach to service delivery. How could anyone evaluate what had worked and why?

With hindsight, the reluctance to engage with these questions seems astonishing and naive but the impact of Martinson's (1974) research suggesting 'nothing worked' should not be underestimated. Although Martinson's research design was subsequently identified as flawed, there remained scepticism amongst policy makers about the contribution of research findings to policy developments. As Nutley and Davies (1999: 51) note, "Policy-making at Home Office level has not always been guided by evidence of what works ... much criminal justice policy has had more of a political and ideological flavour".

The knowledge drawn from meta-analyses in North America (Vennard et al, 1997) that there were interventions which could be shown to be effective in bringing down reconviction rates with offenders was subsequently seen as critical both in terms of justifying expenditure on offender services but also in revaluing the contribution research could make to practice development. Meta-analysis involves the "aggregation and side-by-side analysis of large numbers of experimental studies" (reporting different outcome measures, based on different subjects and even varying in the rigour of experimental design) (McGuire, 2000: 97). This statistically based method enables reviewers to combine findings from different experiments into an all-encompassing statistical analysis. These meta-analyses enabled the development of the 'What Works' principles, which have subsequently been adopted and promoted nationwide (Chapman and Hough, 1998). The need for criminal justice agencies to improve and demonstrate effectiveness does mean that obtaining evidence through the process of evaluation is critical to proving effect but is also the mechanism by which the knowledge base of practice is extended (see Harper and Chitty, 2004, for a review of the evidence base for offending behaviour programmes in England and Wales).

McGuire (2000) stresses that a great deal of research is still needed, particularly because much of the research base for effective practice developments has been drawn from America and Canada which have different populations to those in Europe. There is also less knowledge of effectiveness with women, different ethnic groups and people with particular criminogenic factors such that many practical questions remain unanswered. Evaluation therefore has much to contribute to developing work with offenders (Harper and Chitty, 2004).

Difficulties of evaluation in criminal justice

As Nutley and Davies (1999: 49) identify, "there is no agreed 'gold standard' for the evaluation of criminal justice interventions". In the medical world there is a long tradition of random allocation to experimental and control groups as the means of evaluation, whereas in the criminal justice sector experimentation is often seen as unethical and impractical.

There is also the question as to what is a good measure of effectiveness of interventions. Official reconviction rates over a two-year period have come to be regarded as the international standard for assessing the impact of interventions. This is problematic for a number of reasons. First, reconviction rates may not be an accurate measure of reoffending, given that only 3 per cent of offending results in reconviction (Barclay, 1991). Also two years may be regarded as too long for many policy makers and practitioners to wait for results. Furthermore, reconviction rates may be insufficiently sensitive to pick up a reduction in the risk (frequency and seriousness) of reoffending as a beneficial impact from intervention (see Merrington, 2006).

Ascertaining that change has occurred is a relatively easy process but it is more difficult to assess cause and effect relationships because of the problem of isolating other influences (Pawson and Tilley, 1994). How far should evaluators cast their net in terms of possible contributing factors? For example, when evaluating a group work programme, pre-group and post-group work is rarely included in the process of evaluation because of the time and expense involved, but these components may be significant in terms of effect of the programme and also on risk of reoffending.

This example illustrates the real tension that exists in the pursuit of evidence of effectiveness. On the one hand, there needs to be sufficient competence in the evaluation, otherwise "inappropriate conclusions may be drawn from inadequately conceived, badly implemented and carelessly assessed projects" (Parry and Raine, 2004: 66). On the other, evaluation may be seen as so complex and difficult it remains in the province of expert researchers and outside the remit of practitioners. The effect of this is that "managers and practitioners are not encouraged to develop research skills and are disempowered by the process of evaluation which makes them research subjects" (Oulton, 2003: 154) or data collectors at best. Arguably power, control and ownership of the process need to be actively shared with the practitioner because of the beneficial effects they have on the development of practice.

Why evaluate?

What are the benefits for the offender?

Much of the focus so far in this chapter has placed the offender as a research subject rather than an active participant. However, there can be significant benefits of involving the offender in the process of evaluation. Supervision planning involves the setting of SMART objectives or goals. This acronym emphasises the importance of objectives being specific, measurable, achievable, realistic and time-limited. If done carefully and with sufficient involvement of the offender, the goals should give guidance as to the changes they can anticipate as the objective is achieved.

Risk assessment tools guide the practitioner through the process of objective setting but there is a real danger that if it becomes too time pressured the offender is unlikely to participate fully. Giving time to evaluation and the careful exploration of progress provides the opportunity for the practitioner and the offender to celebrate milestones, however small, and to consolidate change. It also aids reassessment, planning and improving responsivity for any subsequent period of supervision. If the objective has not been achieved the practitioner needs to explore with the offender why the goals were not achieved. Were they too vague or unrealistic? Could they be revised to make them more helpful and achievable? Does the intervention need to be delivered differently to improve responsivity?

Much time and effort is put into assessment at the beginning of supervision but it is also important to make use of the ending of a supervisory relationship to reinforce a sense of progression and to encourage the offender to experience a greater feeling of control and optimism over aspects of their life in the future. Some offenders may experience the ending of supervision as an indication that the practitioner is losing interest in them. It is therefore helpful if this ending is 'reframed' through the process of review and evaluation to enable the offender to see this 'ending' as a natural progression into independence.

Hedderman (2004b) makes the bold suggestion that practice should move away from:

> ... evaluating the impact of discrete programmes to offender-focused evaluations. Initially this will need to focus on the period of supervision to completion but ultimately for repeat offenders it would be desirable to link up progress during one sentence with progress on previous ones so that

we move away from crude and unrealistic expectations that one shot of programme x will do the job and instead appreciate that some changes happen incrementally over a number of sentences and because of the interactive contribution of a number of different interventions. (Hedderman, 2004b: 38)

This would be facilitated by practitioners accumulating and reviewing previous assessments of repeat offenders and ensuring that these inform subsequent supervision plans. It is important that the practitioner looks for evidence of what has not worked with a particular offender as well as what has been effective in the past. This avoids the offender being put through the same repeat experiences and also wasting time and resources. Hedderman's (2004b) argument that for some offenders the process of rehabilitation occurs over a number of sentences is an important reminder to practitioners that not all change can be achieved through a 'quick fix' and that a subsequent period of supervision should not be viewed automatically as proof of failure in the past. In terms of the motivational theories explored in Chapter Seven, lapse can be part of the process of change if lessons are learnt from the experience. The practitioner needs to remain alert to the evidence presented by the offender to make judgements about progress or deterioration and its resultant implications in terms of risk assessment and public protection.

What does evaluation bring to the practitioner's own development and wider service delivery?

There is a real sense that routinised processing of offenders can deaden the sensitivity of the practitioner, particularly to issues of risk and responsivity. The practitioner needs to seek out feedback on their own performance. This helps them to reflect on the impact of their interventions (are they delivering services in ways which encourage responsivity?) and promotes the fine-tuning of skills. It also provides the opportunity to extend the knowledge base about particular types of offender, offences and potential responses to both.

Practice on evaluation should be encouraged to develop at all levels in the organisation and not as an activity which is separate from service delivery and done by experts away from the field. Practitioners and teams need to be searching out the evidence or effect of their interventions as part of practice development.

It is possible to see this as similar to driving a journey to somewhere new and unfamiliar. Before setting off the driver can consult a road map to identify the route to be taken and estimate the approximate time it will take. If the journey is an important one and likely to be repeated on many occasions it will be useful for the driver, after they have made the journey a number of times, to reflect on their progress. Are there particular parts of the route that are problematic? Are the problems temporary, for example, because of roadworks, or are they rooted in the poor design of a junction? By going back to the map it may be possible to identify how the particular hold-up can be avoided and the journey made more easily. So it is with work with offenders. The practitioner may be able to identify aspects or techniques which hindered or promoted change and affected the impact of the intervention. If this evaluative and reflective approach is adopted and the results subsequently shared with others it can promote the development of expertise and good practice within teams.

Doing evaluation

Much of day-to-day practice offers the scope and potential for evaluation to be undertaken and practitioners need to recognise that it need not be overly complex or costly. Indeed, as Merrington and Hine (2001: 3-1) note, "the systematic recording of ordinary practice can be a useful evaluation method" particularly when a standardised procedure is applied to a number of cases. The data collected can be compared for different subgroups and the evaluator may be able to identify potentially different responses from those groups. The practitioner is not in a position to prove a hypothesis but may identify an issue that requires further investigation.

Before embarking on evaluation it is vital that the practitioner gives appropriate attention to issues of quality and purpose. The following Practice tool will help this.

Practice tool 11.1: Preparing for evaluation

To clarify thinking on evaluation the practitioner will be helped by writing down the answers to the following questions:

* What is this evaluation for?
* What question am I seeking to evaluate?
* What use would be made of any results and (if appropriate) how would I disseminate them?

- What resources would be involved (time, money, access, equipment) and are these available?
- Is this question answerable?
- Does the question justify the resources?
- Are the chosen methods appropriate to answer the question?

This checklist remains appropriate whether the practitioner plans for a small-scale piece of evaluation, for example, to detect change with a particular offender, or a much larger research study. Obviously, the more ambitious the evaluation in terms of influence and effect, the more rigorous the research methodology will need to be (see Spencer et al, 2003: Appendix 13). The practitioner also needs to investigate what is already known about this subject area: are there previous evaluations available locally or nationally to avoid 'reinventing the wheel'?

There are also a number of ethical considerations. For example, if the practitioner hopes to use the results beyond the case itself then this requires permission from the subjects involved. It is also important to ensure that individuals who participate are not damaged or distressed by involvement in the evaluation process.

It may be helpful to share evaluation plans with colleagues, particularly where there is shared management of cases or processes to ensure that data are recorded accurately. They may also want to discuss the results of any evaluation and its potential for practice development.

Activities and reflection 11.1

Please think about the following questions:

- To what extent do you evaluate progress with offenders?
- When you undertake supervision planning and objective setting with offenders, do you include sufficient detail so that you know what evidence to look for in terms of results?
- How can you build in the use of feedback from offenders to develop your own practice?

Glossary of terms

Spencer et al (2003) have developed a framework which will guide assessments of quality of qualitative research evaluations. This framework includes discussion about objectivity and bias and explores in depth concepts like validity and reliability which will be particularly of use to those wishing to pursue evaluation more deeply (see Spencer et al, 2003: 58–82). For the novice evaluator, the following list will provide a basic understanding of some of the more frequently used technical terms in evaluation (drawn from Merrington and Hine, 2001) although it is far from exhaustive. It will encourage practitioner confidence to embark on evaluation but also to read and make use of findings from research studies more generally:

- *Outcome evaluation* – a type of evaluation which focuses on whether a programme or activity achieves its objectives.
- *Process evaluation* – a type of evaluation which focuses on how well the programme or activity was carried out.
- *Psychometrics or psychometric testing* – the application of measurement to psychological concepts such as attitudes.
- *Quantitative research* – relates to facts and figures. For example, 63 per cent of offenders on a programme reported a reduction of more than 25 per cent in alcohol intake.
- *Qualitative research* – provides reasons, explanations or opinions about an issue. For example, an offender believed his reduction in drinking had improved his ability to gain and keep a job.
- *Reliability* – a measure has reliability if it consistently gives the same results under the same conditions.
- *Triangulation* – answering the same research question by using different methods, which enables cross-checking and greater confidence in results.
- *Validity* – a measure has research validity if it measures what it is intended to measure.

Different types or methods of evaluation

Single case design

Although single case evaluation has been around since the early 1980s it is only recently that it has been seen as a useful technique for demonstrating progress with individual cases (Kazi, 1998). It is based on the principle of the practitioner "measuring the subject's target problem (that is, the object of intervention) repeatedly over time using an appropriate indicator of progress which is as reliable as possible" (Kazi, 1998: 187). The technique is particularly useful for showing that progress has been achieved, although it may not be able to provide any explanation as to why the change has occurred. Single case evaluation can be integrated into daily practice relatively simply, particularly with the development of more formal design and delivery of interventions. It can allow full participation of the offender in evaluation and can be incorporated into routine contact. In order to determine the offender's progress the practitioner will need to select a number of outcome measures appropriate to the target problem:

- *Diaries of behaviour occurrence and other self-report mechanisms* – an example of this would be a *drink diary* recording either daily or weekly consumption in terms of quantity or money spent. Another example is using a *Risk Swamp*; this is a measure of the offender's perception of how likely they are to reoffend. The risk swamp is shaped like a target of circles decreasing in size to the 'bull's eye' in the middle. The offender is asked to indicate where on the target they would rate their own risk of reoffending, ranging from low risk outside the target to very high risk in the centre of the bull's eye. The offender is encouraged to complete the risk swamp at the beginning and at the end of supervision (Marshall et al, 1991). The pitfall of self-report mechanisms is that they rely on honesty during completion and the offender may feel reluctant to reveal lapses in progress. It may be helpful to combine these techniques with other measures, for example, observation and third party feedback.
- *Attitudinal questionnaires and other rating scales* – practitioners can draw on a number of standardised measures to detect changes in attitude. These are readily available (see Fischer and Corcoran, 1994; Merrington and Hine, 2001) and offer high reliability for use before and after a programme of intervention.
- *Observations and other classificatory indicators* – the practitioner and other third parties may detect changes in behaviour, for example, obtaining or maintaining employment, or a reduction in positive drug test results.

Single case evaluation is a short-term tool which allows the study a level of detail that is often not possible in larger-scale surveys. It is particularly helpful to be able to draw on case studies to provide insights to more quantitative approaches (Merrington and Hine, 2001), although it does not help make comparisons with other cases. It is also a useful technique for the practitioner to build up data for the purposes of evaluating and refining their own practice skills.

Before and after studies

The practitioner/evaluator collects data shortly before and after the intervention takes place by using a questionnaire, interview or more formalised psychometric testing. Collecting data in this way, particularly if results are paired (that is, the pre-intervention response can be linked to their post-intervention response), allows comparisons to be made with other similar offenders. This method of evaluation would have been particularly useful for the group work programme outlined at the beginning of this chapter.

The collection of data close to the point of intervention makes tracking participants easier than in studies of a longer timescale, so response rates are better. Having gathered data from two points in time, the evaluator may be able to confirm that change has taken place but cannot say with any accuracy whether the change is due to the intervention or some other influence or if the change will be sustained over time.

Longitudinal studies

The evaluator assesses the impact of an intervention over a longer period of time, which may be months or years. This approach relies on being able to access participants over the time frame. The longer the study the higher the attrition (fall-out) rate; offenders frequently move or lose contact and those that remain may be unwilling to cooperate with what may be viewed as intrusive questions once formal contact has ceased.

One of the preferred methods of evaluating offender programmes is by quasi-experimental design with a carefully selected comparison group and a two-year reconviction study using recorded statistics, for example, Offenders Index or PNC (Police National Computer) data. Again this approach does not explain why something has or has not worked, so needs to be combined with more open exploratory studies which look at the dynamics of offending and intervening in detail (Merrington and Stanley, 2004; see also Pawson and Tilley, 1994).

Mixed method studies

In mixed method evaluation designs there is a combination of data collection approaches allowing for triangulation to occur between different sources of data and possibly between quantitative and qualitative material. By using different collection methods, for example, documentary analysis, questionnaires, interviews and observations, a more detailed understanding of processes and outcomes can be achieved (Freeth et al, 2005).

Action research studies

Evaluator and practitioners work in close collaboration to develop, deliver and evaluate a programme or method of intervention. The evaluator is likely to be less detached and more involved in reporting on change as it occurs. Through this process evaluators may support an individual or team through a series of action and research cycles adapting practice along the way. This dynamic method gives the evaluator a very central role. It is demanding and time consuming for the evaluator but does offer scope to provide rapid feedback on implementation issues particularly on complex new practice developments (Stringer, 1996).

Conclusion

It is vital that practitioners recognise that evaluation is an essential component of evidence-based practice helping to develop understanding about offenders and their situations. It is the mechanism by which certain ways of intervening are validated and subsequently refined. It offers the opportunity to confirm and consolidate changes made by an offender and the prospect of 'ending well'.

Evaluation and practice must not become separated, otherwise practice will ossify and lack responsiveness to changes in the rest of the criminal justice system. Much of the current knowledge base has been taken from North American research studies and practitioners have much to contribute through implementing innovative practice and to the further development of the knowledge base for working with offenders. This will enable criminal justice policy to be firmly built on evidence of effectiveness rather than being driven by ideological and political fashions.

TWELVE

Return to concepts

Introduction

This final chapter sums up the key ideas about risk, responsivity and diversity, spelling out the messages for practice along the way. It sets the reader a number of challenges to take forward in their own development and also in one-to-one work with offenders.

In *Part One, the book introduces the concepts of risk, responsivity and diversity, having briefly charted the changing nature of face-to-face work with offenders.* It notes the move away from faith-driven approaches and highly individualised practice towards a more organisationally accountable approach to service delivery and the development of the concept of evidence-based practice. Standardised approaches to case management pose the potential to blunt the practitioner's sensitivities to the detail of offender's lives and issues of risk and responsivity. Such a blunting of sensitivity can lead to ineffective and overly generalised interventions. It can also limit the ability of practice to provide interventions to which a diverse population of offenders can respond.

It is curious that in social work and most other areas of public service there has been significant development in terms of service user involvement, both in terms of valuing their perspective, but also using that input to shape and evaluate the delivery of services. Pycroft (2006) suggests that this has not happened so readily in criminal justice because service users in this sphere are more readily seen as being the courts, or victims, but not the offenders themselves. It is almost as if there is reluctance to accept the importance of listening to offenders, in case this tips the balance away from victims and the wider community. The voice of the offender is, however, an important source of information in developing understanding of offending behaviour and how to reduce it. This will be apparent to the reader in the detail of much of the research that has been drawn on in Parts Two to Five of this book.

In *Part Two*, the issue of working with offender groups who fall outside the majority, adult, White, male offenders, is explored. *These chapters, which focus on offenders from certain groups (women, young people and minority ethnic offenders), suggest that their diversity should be appreciated and that this will have implications in terms of how they are worked with.*

The emphasis throughout these chapters has been for the practitioner to be alert to the differences that lie between themselves and the offender and to avoid making assumptions that are more to do with the practitioner's own characteristics and experience than an understanding of the particular experiences of the offender and their situation. The practitioner is encouraged to reflect on their own current identity, recognising that identity is multifaceted, dynamic and highly significant in terms of how the practitioner views and is viewed by the world.

Activities and reflection 12.1

Look at Activities and reflection box 5.1, which encourages you to think about your own identity.

- Answer those questions if you have not already done so.
- Can you see any difference between your personal and your professional identities?
- In the light of your reflections about your identity, which of the groups/chapters included in this section pose most challenge to you as a practitioner?
- What is the nature of the challenge and how might you overcome it?
- How will you evaluate the changes you have made?

Many offenders have other significant problems which may or may not be linked to their offending. *Part Three* examines the issues of mental disorder, substance misuse and poor basic skills, because of their prevalence in offender populations. *These problems are important as potential risk factors for offending behaviour and also in terms of their impact on the offender's responsivity. The practitioner will need to adopt a holistic approach which recognises the offender, their offending and their wider problems but still pays appropriate attention to the detail of risk.* Problems like mental disorder and substance misuse can pose a huge challenge for the offender and the practitioner; there may be issues of balancing and sequencing interventions to avoid overwhelming levels of activity. It is also important to recognise the need to draw on other resources and expertise within the wider community, which may help promote integration and more extensive support mechanisms which are outside the criminal justice process.

Activities and reflection 12.2

Think about an offender you worked with who had experienced mental disorder or substance misuse or had problems with basic skills:

- Did you adopt an offence-focused or problem-solving approach?
- Were you able to achieve a balance in terms of the focus and sequencing of your interventions?
- To what extent did you encourage them to take personal responsibility for their offending or did you find yourself 'excusing them' because of their problems?
- What feedback did you obtain (and from whom: the offender themselves, their family, other agency workers) to help evaluate the effectiveness of your interventions?

Part Four tackles the issue of responding to offenders who illustrate different aspects of risk, in terms of the risk of reoffending and the degree of harm they may pose to others. Risk is a dynamic concept and practitioners need to be looking for evidence of changes. As in all the chapters, they are urged to pay careful attention to the detail of an individual's offending and to challenge accounts of events which seem implausible, or too readily absolve the offender from having responsibility. Working with high risk offenders can bring a whole mixture of emotions for the worker: professional excitement at 'dealing with serious crime' but also the possibility of fear, alarm and anxiety when faced with uncertain and unpredictable situations. At the other end of the spectrum, working with lower risk of harm but often high volume offenders, the challenge for the practitioner is to avoid workload management approaches which dehumanise contact with the offender and thereby undermine both an alertness to changing levels of risk, as well as the potential for change through the offender–worker relationship.

Activities and reflection 12.3

Think about an offender you have recently assessed:

- How easily did you get into the detail of their account of their offending?
- How did you challenge their account of events?
- How were you able to strike a balance between responsivity whilst avoiding collusion?
- What would you do differently next time?

The final two chapters (*Part Five*) of the book deal with the issues of evaluation and endings. All too frequently energy, thought and guidance are put into the beginnings of the supervisory relationship with very little comment made about the closure or completion of a period of contact. In part, this is often the result of pressure on the agency and the need to get on to the next piece of work. *However, taking time to evaluate is important to both the offender and the practitioner.* For the offender it is an opportunity to acknowledge progress and to give encouragement for them to go on to make further changes. For the practitioner, listening to the offender and hearing how they experienced services is a vital source of information to help evaluate practice. It also encourages the practitioner to think about their own development and ways to improve face-to-face work with offenders.

Activities and reflection 12.4

Select one of the Activities and reflection boxes in this chapter:

- Use it to identify a personal development objective for yourself.
- How will you achieve this objective?
- How will you know you have met this objective?
- What tools will you use to help you measure your progress? (You may find it helpful to refer back to methods of evaluation in Chapter Eleven to help in this process.)

Conclusion

In order to reduce offending risk and deliver responsive interventions, practitioners must assess accurately and deliver interventions based on those assessments. The detail contained within this book will help to develop this accuracy and the Practice tools will support assessment and interventions.

Equally significantly, however, the impact of this book will depend on its readers and the way in which they use the information it contains. Practitioners should seek to be the kind of individuals who can work confidently and competently with a diverse group of offenders. To achieve this they will need more than knowledge. They need to be self-reflective and willing to contribute to the development of that knowledge, through paying attention to detail and listening to the offenders with whom they work.

References

Adult Learning Inspectorate (ALI) (2004) *Basic Skills for Offenders in the Community*, London: ALI.

Ahmad, B. (1990) *Black Perspectives in Social Work*, Birmingham: Venture Press.

Allen, C. (2005) 'The Links between Heroin, Crack Cocaine and Crime: Where Does Street Crime Fit In?', *British Journal of Criminology*, vol 45, no 3, 355-72.

Allen, R. (2002) 'Offenders Suffering from Mental Health Problems', *Justice of the Peace*, vol 166, 400-1.

Andrews, D.A (1995) 'The psychology of criminal conduct and effective treatment', in J. McGuire (ed) *What Works: Reducing Offending*, Chichester: Wiley.

Andrews, D.A. (2001) Principles of effective correctional programs in L.L. Motuik and R.C. Serin (eds) *Compendium 2000 on Effective Correctional Programming*. Ottawa: Correctional Service Canada.

Andrews, D.A. and Bonta, J. (1994) *The Psychology of Criminal Conduct*, Cincinnati, OH: Anderson.

Andrews, D.A. and Bonta, J. (2003) *The Psychology of Criminal Conduct* (3rd edn), Cincinnati, OH: Anderson.

Andrews, D.A., Bonta, J. and Hoge, R.D. (1990) 'Classification for effective rehabilitation: rediscovering psychology', *Criminal Justice and Behaviour*, vol 17, 19-51.

Andrews, D.A., Zinger, I., Hoge, R.D., Bonta, J., Gendreau, P. and Cullen, F.T. (1990) 'Does Correctional Treatment Work? A Clinically Relevant and Psychologically Informed Meta-Analysis', *Criminology*, vol 28, no 3, 369-404.

Archer, J. and Browne, K.D. (1989) 'Concepts and Approaches to the Study of Aggression', in J. Archer and K.D. Browne (eds) *Human Aggression: Naturalistic Approaches*, London: Routledge, 3-20.

Atkinson, D. (2004) 'The What Works Debate: Keeping a Human Perspective', *Probation Journal*, vol 51, no 3, 248-52.

Audit Commission (1996) *Misspent Youth: Young People and Crime*, London: Audit Commission.

Audit Commission (1999) *Misspent Youth '99: The Challenge for Youth Justice*, London: Audit Commission.

Aust, R. and Smith, N. (2003) *Ethnicity and Drug Use: Key findings from the 2001/2002 British Crime Survey*, Home Office Findings 209, London: Home Office.

Baim, C., Brooke, S. and Mountford, A. (2002) *The Geese Theatre Handbook, Drama with Offenders and People at Risk*, Winchester: Waterside Press.

Baker, K. (2004) 'Is *Asset* really an asset?', in R. Burnett and C. Roberts (eds) *What Works in Probation and Youth Justice*, Cullompton: Willan.

Baker, K. (2007) 'Risk in Practice – Systems and Practitioner Judgment', in M. Blyth, K. Baker and E. Solomon (eds) *Young People and 'Risk'*, Bristol: The Policy Press.

Baker, K., Roberts, C., Jones, S. and Merrington, S. (2002) *Validity and Reliability of ASSET. Findings from the first two years of the use of ASSET*, Final Report to the Youth Justice Board of England and Wales, Youth Justice Board and the Probation Studies Unit, Centre for Criminological Research, University of Oxford.

Bandana, A, (1990) *Black Perspectives in Social Work*, Birmingham: Venture Press.

Bandura, A, (1997) *Self-Efficacy*, New York, NY: W.H. Freeman.

Barclay, G.C. (ed) (1991) *A digest of information on the Criminal Justice System*, London: Home Office Research and Statistics Department.

Barn, R. (2001) *Black Youth on the Margins – A Research Review*, York: Joseph Rowntree Foundation.

Barnett, O.W. and Fagan, R.W. (1993) 'Alcohol Abuse in Male Spouse Abusers and their Female Partners', *Journal of Family Violence*, vol 18, no 1, 1–25.

Barrow Cadbury Trust (2005) *Lost in Transition: A Report of the Barrow Cadbury Commission on Young Adults and the Criminal Justice System*, London: Barrow Cadbury.

Barton, A. (2004) 'Women and Community Punishment: The Probation Hostel as a Semi-Penal Institution for Female Offenders', *The Howard Journal*, vol 43, no 2, 149–63.

Basic Skills Agency (1997) *International Numeracy Survey: A comparison of the basic numeracy skills of adults 16-60 in seven countries*, London: ORB on behalf of the Basic Skills Agency.

Basic Skills Agency (BSA) (2000) *Effective Basic Skills for Adults*, London: BSA.

Basic Skills Agency (BSA) (2004) *Fast Track 20 Questions*, London: BSA.

Batchelor, S. (2005) '"Prove me the bam!": Victimisation and agency in the lives of young women who commit violent offences', *Probation Journal*, vol 52, no 4, 358–75.

Batchelor, S. and Burman, M. (2004) 'Working with Girls and Young Women', in G. McIvor (ed), *Women who Offend*, London: Jessica Kingsley, 266–87.

Bazemore, G. and Erbe, C. (2004) 'Reintegration and restorative justice: towards a theory and practice of informal social control and support', in S. Maruna and R. Immarigeon (eds) *After Crime and Punishment: Pathways to Offender Reintegration*, Cullompton: Willan.

Bean, P. (2004) *Drugs and Crime* (2nd edn), Cullompton: Willan.

Bebbington, P. (2005) 'What shall we do about the high rates of mental disorders in prisoners?' *Criminal Justice Matters*, no 61, 6-7.

Beech, A. and Mann, R. (2002) 'Recent Developments in the Successful Treatment of Sex Offenders', in J. McGuire (ed) *Offender Rehabilitation and Treatment*, Chichester: Wiley.

Bennett, T. (2000) *Drugs and Crime: The results of the second developmental stage of the NEW-ADAM programme*, Home Office Research Study No 205, London: Home Office.

Bennett, T. and Holloway, K. (2005) *Understanding Drugs, Alcohol and Crime*, London: McGraw-Hill/Open University Press.

Bennett, T. and Wright, R. (1984) *Burglars on Burglary*, Aldershot: Gower.

Bennett, T., Holloway, K. and Williams, T. (2001) *Drug Use and Offending: Summary results from the first year of the NEW-ADAM research programme*, London: Home Office.

Birgden, A. (2004) 'Therapeutic Jurisprudence and Responsivity: Finding the Will and the Way in Offender Rehabilitation', *Psychology, Crime and Law*, vol 10, no 3, 297-398.

Bhui, H.S. (1999) 'Race, Racism and Risk Assessment: Linking Theory to Practice with Mentally Disordered Offenders', *Probation Journal*, vol 46, no 3, 171-81.

Bhui, K. (1999) 'Cross Cultural Psychiatry and Probation Practice: A discourse on Issues, Context and Practice', *Probation Journal*, vol 46, no 2, 89-100.

Blackburn, R. (2000) 'Treatment or incapacitation? Implications of research on personality disorders for the management of dangerous offenders', *Legal and Criminological Psychology*, vol 5, 1-21.

Blackburn, R. (2004) '"What works" with mentally disordered offenders', *Psychology, Crime and Law*, vol 10, no 3, 297-308.

Blanchette, K. and Brown, L. (2006) *The Assessment and Treatment of Women Offenders: An Integrative Perspective*, Chichester: Wiley.

Bond, F. and Dryden, W. (eds) (2002) *Brief Cognitive Behaviour Therapy*, Chichester: Wiley.

Blyth, M., Baker, K. and Solomon, E. (eds) (2007) *Young People and 'Risk'*, Bristol: The Policy Press.

Bonta, J. and Andrews, D.A. (2003) 'A Commentary on Ward and Stewart's Model of Human Needs', *Psychology, Crime and Law*, vol 9, no 3, 215-18.

Boswell, G. (2000) *Violent Children and Adolescents: Asking the Reasons Why*, London: Whurr.

Bowen, E., Brown, L. and Gilchrist, E. (2002) 'Evaluating Probation Based Offender Programmes for Domestic Violence Perpetrators: A pro-feminist approach', *The Howard Journal*, vol 41, no 3, 221-36.

Bowers, L. (2001) *Dangerous and Severe Personality Disorder: Response and Role of the Psychiatric Team*, London: Routledge.

Bowling, B. and Phillips, C. (2002) *Racism, Crime and Justice*, London: Longman.

Bradley, H. (2003) *Fractured Identities: Changing Patterns of Inequality*, Cambridge: Polity Press.

Brennan, T., John, P. and Stoker, G. (2006) 'Active Citizenship and Effective Public Services and Programmes: How Can We Know What Really Works?', *Urban Studies*, vol 43, no 5/6, 993-1008.

Briggs, S., Gray, B. and Stephens, K. (2003) 'Offender Literacy and Attrition from the Enhanced Thinking Skills Programme', *Vista*, vol 8, no 2, 73-80.

Brimicombe, A.J., Ralphs, M.P., Sampson, A. and Yuen Tsui, H. (2001) 'An Analysis of the Role of Neighbourhood Composition in the Geographical Distribution of Racially Motivated Incidents', *British Journal of Criminology*, vol 41, no 2, 293-308.

Brown, I.A. (1997) 'Theoretical Model of the Behavioural Addictions – Applied to Offending', in J.E. Hodges, M. McMurran. and C.R. Hollin (eds) *Addicted to Crime?*, London: Wiley, 13-61.

Budd, T. (1999) *Burglary of Domestic Dwellings, Findings from the British Crime Survey*, Home Office Statistical Bulletin, Issue 4/99, London: Home Office.

Budd, T. (2001) *Burglary: Practice Messages from the British Crime Survey*, Briefing Note 5/01, London: Home Office.

Budd, T. (2002) 'Alcohol Crime and Offending', in *Alcoholis, The Newsletter of the Medical Council on Alcohol*, vol 21, no 3, 1-3.

Budd, T. (2003) *Alcohol-related assault: Findings from the British Crime Survey*, Online report 35/03, London: Home Office.

Burke, L., Mair, G. and Ragonese, E. (2006) 'An evaluation of service provision for short-term and remand prisoners with drug problems', *Probation Journal*, vol 53, no 2, 109-23.

Burman, M. (2004) 'Breaking the Mould: Patterns of Female Offending', in G. McIvor (ed), *Women who Offend*, London: Jessica Kingsley, 38-65.

Burnett, R. (1996) *Fitting supervision to offenders: Assessment and allocation decisions in the Probation Service*, Home Office Research Study No 153, London: Home Office.

Burnett, R. (2000) 'Understanding Criminal Careers Through a Series of In-Depth Interviews', in *Offender Programs Report*, vol 4, no 1, 1–16.

Burnett, R. and McNeill, F. (2005) 'The place of the officer–offender relationship in assisting offenders to desist from crime', *Probation Journal*, vol 52, no 3, 221–42.

Burnett, R. and Roberts, C. (eds) (2004) *What Works in Probation and Youth Justice*, Cullompton: Willan.

Bush, J. (1995) 'Teaching Self-Risk Management to Violent Offenders', in J. McGuire (ed) *What Works: Reducing Reoffending*, Chichester: Wiley.

Bynner, J. (2000) *Risks and outcomes of social exclusion insights from longitudinal data*, OECD, available at www.oecd.org/dataoecd/19/35/1855785.

Callahan, D., Kelly, G. and Wilkinson, B. (2004) *The Jigsaw Approach: A programme for young people*, unpublished.

Calverley, A., Cole, B., Kaur, G., Lewis, S., Raynor, R., Sandeghil, S., Smith, D., Vanstone, M and Wardak, A. (2004) *Black and Asian Offenders on Probation*, Home Office Research Study 277, London: Home Office.

Carlen, P. (1983) *Women's Imprisonment*, London: Routledge, Kegan and Paul.

Carlen, P. (ed) (2002) *Women and Punishment*, Cullompton: Willan.

Carson, D. (1996) 'Risking legal repercussions', in H. Kemshall and J. Pritchard (eds), *Good Practice in Risk Assessment and Risk Management*, London: Jessica Kingsley Publishers.

Chapman, T. and Hough, M. (1998) *A Guide to Effective Practice*, London: Home Office.

Cherry, S. (2005) *Transforming Behaviour: Pro-Social Modelling in Practice*, Cullompton: Willan.

Chigwada-Bailey, R. (1997) *Black Women's Experiences of Criminal Justice: Discourse on Disadvantage*. Winchester: Waterside Press.

Chigwada-Bailey, R. (2004) 'Black Women and the Criminal Justice System', in G. McIvor (ed) *Women who Offend*, London: Jessica Kingsley.

Chui, W.-H. (2003) 'What works in reducing offending: Principles and programmes', in W.-H. Chui and M. Nellis, (eds) *Moving Probation Forward: Evidence, Arguments and Practice*, London: Pearson.

Chui, W.-H. and Nellis, M. (eds) (2003) *Moving Probation Forward: Evidence, Arguments and Practice*, London: Pearson.

Clark, D. and Howden-Windell, J. (2000) *A Retrospective Study of Criminogenic Factors in the Female Prison Population,* unpublished report to the Home Office.

Clarke, R.V. (1980) 'Situational Crime Prevention: Theory and Practice', *British Journal of Criminology,* vol 20, no 2, 136-47.

Clarke, R.V. (1997) *Situational Crime Prevention: Successful Case Studies* (2nd edn), Albany, NY: Harrow and Heston.

Clarke, R.V. (1999) *Hot Products: Understanding, anticipating and reducing demand for stolen goods,* Police research series paper 112, London: Home Office.

Clarke, R.V. and Cornish, D.B. (eds) (1986) *The Reasoning Criminal: Rational Choice Perspectives on Offending,* New York, NY: Springer-Verlag.

Clarke, R.V. and Felson, M. (eds) (1993) *Routine Activity and Rational Choice. Advances in Criminological Theory,* vol 5, New Brunswick, NJ: Transactional Publishers.

Clarke, R.V. and Harris, P.M. (1992) 'A rational choice perspective on the targets of autotheft', *Criminal Behaviour and Mental Health,* vol 2, 25-42.

Cohen, L.E. and Felson, M. (1979) 'Social change and crime rate trends: a routine activity approach', *American Sociological Review,* vol 44, 588-608.

Coleman, J.S. (1990) *Foundations of Social Theory,* London: Belknap Press.

Connexions (2003) *Skills for Life: A Reader,* London: DfES.

Crewe, B. (2006) 'Prison Drug Dealing and the Ethnographic Lens', *The Howard Journal,* vol 45, no 4, 347-68.

Cusson, M. and Pinsonneault, P. (1986) 'The decision to give up crime', in R.V. Clarke and D.B. Cornish, (eds) *The Reasoning Criminal: Rational Choice Perspectives on Offending,* New York, NY: Springer-Verlag.

Davies, K., Lewis, J., Byatt, J., Purvis, E. and Cole, B. (2004) *An evaluation of the literacy demands of general offending behaviour programmes,* London: Home Office.

Davies, P. (2002) 'Women and Crime: doing it for the kids?', *Criminal Justice Matters,* no 50, 28-9.

Davis, G. and Vennard, J. (2006) 'Racism in Court: The Experience of Ethnic Minority Magistrates', *The Howard Journal,* vol 45, no 5, 485-501.

Dawson, P. (2005) *Early findings from the prolific and other priority offenders evaluation,* Home Office Development and Practice Report, available at www.homeoffice.gov.uk/rds (accessed 18 May 2006).

Day, A., Howells, K. and Rickwood, D. (2004) 'Current Trends in the Rehabilitation of Juvenile Offenders', in *Trends and Issues in Crime and Criminal Justice*, no 285, 1-6.

De Cou, K. (2002) 'A gender-wise prison: opportunities for, and limits to, reform', in Carlen, P. (ed) *Women and Punishment*, Cullompton: Willan.

Department for Education and Skills (DfES) (2004) *The Offender's Learning Journey*, available at www.dfes.gov.uk/offenderlearning/uploads/documents/adult_OLJ_VO.5a.doc (accessed 9 March 2007).

Department of Health (1996) *An audit pack for monitoring the Care Programme Approach: Background and explanatory notes*, London: HMSO.

Department of Health (2005) *Delivering race equality in mental health care: An action plan for reform inside and outside services and the Government's response to the independent inquiry into the death of David Bennett*, London: Department of Health.

Desai, P. (1998) *Spaces of Identity, Cultures of Conflict: The Development of New British Asian identities*, PhD dissertation, Goldsmiths College, University of London.

Dickens, C. (1838) *Oliver Twist*, London: Chapman and Hall.

Di Clemente, C. and Velasquez, M.M. (2002) 'Motivational Interviewing and the Stages of Change', in W. Miller and S. Rollnick (eds) *Motivational Interviewing* (2nd edn), New York, NY: The Guilford Press, 201-16.

Dominelli, L. (2006) 'Dangerous Constructions: Black Offenders in the Criminal Justice System', in K. Gorman, M. Gregory, M. Hayles and N. Parton, *Constructive Work with Offenders*, London: Jessica Kingsley, 123-40.

Dowden, C. and Andrews, D.A. (1999) 'What works for female offenders: A meta-analytic review', *Crime and Delinquency*, vol 45, no 4, 438-52.

Drake, R. and Wallach, M. (2000) 'Dual diagnosis: 15 years of progress', *Psychiatric Services*, vol 51, no 9, 1126-9.

Durrance, P. and Williams, P. (2003) 'Broadening the Agenda Around What Works for Black and Asian Offenders', *Probation Journal*, vol 50, no 3, 211-24.

Durrance, P. Hignell, C. Merowe, L. and Asamoah, A. (2001) *The Greenwich and Lewisham Self Development and Educational Attainment Group*, London: Inner London Probation Service.

Eadie,T. and Canton, R. (2002) 'Practising in a context of ambivalence: the challenge for youth justice workers', *Youth Justice*, vol 2, no 1, 14-26.

East, K. and Campbell, S. (2000) *Aspects of Crime:Young Offenders 1999*, London: Home Office.

Engineer, R., Philips, A., Thompson, J. and Nicholls, J. (2003) *Drunk and Disorderly: A qualitative study of binge drinking among 18 to 24 year olds*, Home Office Research Study No 262, London: Home Office.

European Offender Employment Forum (undated), available at www. eoef.org/ (accessed 4 October 2006).

Everson, S. and Pease, K. (2001) 'Crime against the same person and place: detection opportunity and offender targeting', in G. Farrell and K. Pease (eds) *Repeat Victimisation*, Crime Prevention Studies, vol 12, New York, NY: Criminal Justice Press, 199-220.

Farrall, S. (2002) *Rethinking What Works with Offenders: Probation, social context and desistance from crime*, Cullompton: Willan.

Farrall, S. (2004) 'Social capital and offender reintegration: making probation desistance focused', in S. Maruna and R. Immarigeon (eds), *After Crime and Punishment*, Cullompton: Willan.

Farrant, F. (2006) 'Knowledge production and the punishment ethic: The demise of the probation service', *Probation Journal*, vol 53, no 4, 317-33.

Farrell, G. and Pease, K. (eds) *Repeat Victimisation*, Crime Prevention Studies, vol 12, New York, NY: Criminal Justice Press

Farrington, D. (1996) *Understanding and Preventing Youth Crime*, York: Joseph Rowntree Foundation.

Farrington, D. (1997) 'Human development and criminal careers', in M. McGuire, R. Morgan and R. Reiner (eds) *The Oxford Handbook of Criminology* (2nd edn), Oxford: Oxford University Press.

Farrington, D.P. (1995) 'The development of offending and antisocial behaviour from childhood: Key findings from the Cambridge study in delinquent development', *Journal of Child Psychology and Psychiatry*, vol 36, 929-64.

Farrington, D.P., Coid, J.W., Harnett, L.M., Jolliffe, D., Soteriou, N., Turner, R.E. and West, D.J. (2006) *Criminal Careers up to age 50 and life success up to age 48: New findings from the Cambridge Study in Delinquent Development* (2nd edn), Home Office Research Study 299, London: Home Office.

Farrow, K. (2004) 'Still committed after all these years? Morale in the modern-day probation service', *Probation Journal*, vol 51, no 3, 206-20.

Felson, M. (2003) 'The process of co-offending', in M.J. Smith and D.B. Cornish (eds) *Theory for Practice in Situational Crime Prevention*, Crime Prevention Studies, vol 16, New York, NY: Criminal Justice Press, 149-67.

Ferrell, J. and Websdale, N. (eds) (1999) *Make Trouble Cultural: Representations of Crime*, New York, NY: Aldine de Gruyter.

Finney, A. (2004) *Alcohol and Intimate Partner Violence: Key Findings from the Research*, Home Office Findings 216, London: Home Office.

Fionda, J. (2005) *Devils and Angels*, Oxford and Portland, OR: Hart Publishing.

Fischer, J. and Corcoran, K. (1994) *Measures for clinical practice: A source book*, vols 1-2, New York, NY: The Free Press.

Fitzroy, L. (2001) 'Violent Women: Questions for Feminist Theory, Practice and Policy', *Critical Policy*, vol 21, no 1, 7-34.

Fleck, D., Thompson, C. and Narroway, L. (2001), 'Implementation of the Problem Solving Skills Programme in a Medium Secure Unit', *Criminal Behaviour & Mental Health*, vol 11, no 4, 262-72.

Foster, J., Newburn, T. and Souhani, A. (2005) *Assessing the Impact of the Stephen Lawrence Inquiry*, London: Home Office.

Fox, A., Khan, L., Briggs, D., Rees-Jones, N., Thompson, Z. and Owens, J. (2005) *Through care and aftercare approaches and promising practice in service delivery for clients released from prison or leaving residential rehabilitation*, Home Office online report 01/05, London: Home Office.

Freeth, D., Reeves, S., Koppel, I., Hammick, M. and Barr, H. (2005) *Evaluating Interprofessional Education: A Self-Help Guide*, Occasional Paper No 5, Higher Education Academy, Health Sciences and Practice Network, London: City University.

Frosh, S., Phoenix, A. and Pattman, R. (2002) *Young Masculinities*, London: Palgrave.

Fryers, T., Brugha, T., Grounds, A. and Melzer, D. (1998) 'Severe mental illness in prisoners', *BMJ*, vol 317, 1025-6.

Fuller, C. and Taylor, P. (2003) *A Toolkit of Motivational Skills*, London: National Probation Directorate.

Galvani, S. (2004) 'Responsible disinhibition: Alcohol, men and violence to women', *Addiction, Theory and Research*, vol 12, no 4, 35-71.

Gardner, F. (2001) *Self-Harm: A Psychotherapeutic Approach*, Hove: Brunner-Routledge.

Garland, D. (2001) *The Culture of Control: Crime and Social Order in Contemporary Society*, Oxford: Oxford University Press.

Gelsthorpe, L. (ed) (1993) *Minority Ethnic Groups in the Criminal Justice System*, Cambridge: Cambridge Institute of Criminology.

Gelsthorpe, L. (2002) 'Feminism and Criminology', in M. McGuire, R. Morgan and R. Reiner (eds) *The Oxford Handbook of Criminology*, Oxford: Oxford University Press, 113–43.

Gelsthorpe, L. (2003) 'Theories of crime', in W.-H. Chui and M. Nellis (eds) *Moving Probation Forward: Evidence, Arguments and Practice*, London: Pearson, 19–34.

Gelsthorpe, L. (2004) 'Female Offending – A Theoretical Overview', in G. McIvor (ed) *Women who Offend*, London: Jessica Kingsley, 13–36.

Gendreau, P., Little, T. and Goggin, C. (1996) 'A meta-analysis of the predictors of adult offender recidivism: What Works!', *Criminology*, vol 34, no 4, 575–607.

Gilchrist, E., Johnson, R., Takriti, R., Weston, S., Beech, A. and Kebbell, M. (2003) *Domestic Violence Offenders: Characteristics and Offending Related Needs*, Home Office Findings 217, London: Home Office.

Gilligan, C. (1982) *In a different voice*, Harvard, MA: Harvard University Press.

Goldson, B. and Muncie, J. (eds) (2006) *Youth Crime and Justice*, London: Sage.

Goldstein, A.P. (1999) *The Prepare Curriculum: Teaching pro-social competencies*, Champaign, IL: Research Press.

Gorman, K., O'Byrne, P. and Parton, N. (2006) 'Constructive Work with Offenders: Setting the Scene', in K. Gorman, M. Gregory, M. Hayles and N. Parton (eds) *Constructive Work with Offenders*, London: Jessica Kingsley Publishers, 13–32.

Gorski, T. and Trundy, A. (2000) *Relapse Prevention Counselling Workbook: Practical Exercises for Managing High-Risk Situations*, Spring Hill, FL: Herald House/Independence Press.

Gottfredson, M. and Hirschi, T. (1990) *A General Theory of Crime*, Stanford, CA: Stanford University.

Goulden, C. and Shondhi, A. (2001) *At the margins: Drug use by vulnerable young people in the 1998/1999 Youth Lifestyles Survey*, Home Office Research Study No 228, London: Home Office.

Graham, P. (1998) *Cognitive Behavioural Therapy for Children and Families*, Cambridge: Cambridge University Press.

Hall, N. (2005) *Hate Crime*, Cullompton: Willan Publishing.

Halliday, J. (2000) *The Halliday Report – 'Making Punishments Work: A Review of the Sentencing Framework for England & Wales'*, London: Home Office.

Harper, G. and Chitty, C. (2004) *The Impact of Corrections on Re-offending: A Review of 'What Works'*, Home Office Research Study No 291, London: Home Office.

Harrington,V. (2000) *Underage drinking: Findings from the 1998/1999 Youth Lifestyles Survey*, Home Office Research Findings 125, London: Home Office.

Harris, P. (2005) *Drug Induced:Addiction and Treatment in Perspective*, Lyme Regis: Russell House Publishing.

Harris, P. (2006) 'What Community Supervision Officers Need to Know about Actuarial Risk Assessment and Clinical Judgement', *Federal Probation*, vol 69, no 2, 8-14.

Haslewood-Pocsik, I. and McMahon, G. (2004) 'Probation interventions to address basic skills and employment needs', in R. Burnett and C. Roberts (eds) *What Works in Probation and Youth Justice*, Cullompton: Willan.

Hassan, E. and Thiara, R. (2000) *Locked Out: Black Prisoners' Experiences of Rehabilitative Programmes*, Warwick: University of Warwick, Centre for Research in Ethnic Relations.

Hawton, K. and Fagg, J (1988) 'Suicide and other causes of death following attempted suicide' *British Journal of Psychiatry*, vol 152, 359-66.

Hedderman, C. (2004a) 'Why are more women being sentenced to custody?', in G. McIvor (ed), *Women who Offend*, London: Jessica Kingsley.

Hedderman, C. (2004b) 'What Works: the tensions between delivering and measuring "what works"', *Prison Service Journal*, no 154, 36-8.

Hedderman, C. (2004c) 'The "Criminogenic" Needs of Women Offenders', in G. McIvor (ed) *Women who Offend*, London, Jessica Kingsley.

Hedderman, C. and Dowds, L. (1997) *The Sentencing of Women*, Home Office Research and Statistics Directorate: Research Findings No. 58, London: Home Office.

Hedderman, C. and Gelsthorpe, L. (1997) *Understanding the Sentencing of Women*, London: Home Office.

Heidensohn, F. (2002) 'Gender and Crime', in M. McGuire, R. Morgan and R. Reiner (eds) *The Oxford Handbook of Criminology*, Oxford: Oxford University Press, 491-530.

Henderson, M. (1986) 'An Empirical Typology of Violent Incidents Reported by Prison Inmates with Convictions for Violence', *Aggressive Behaviour*, vol 12, no 1, 21-32.

Heneghan, M. (2000) *Race, Women and Treatment*, London: Drug Link.

Her Majesty's Inspector of Prisons (HMIP) (2005) *Women in Prison*, London: Home Office.

Her Majesty's Inspector of Prisons (HMIP) (2006a) *An Independent Review of a Serious Further Offence Case: Damien Hanson and Elliot White*, London: Home Office.

Her Majesty's Inspector of Prisons (HMIP) (2006b) *Half Full and Half Empty: An Inspection of the National Probation Service's substance misuse work with offenders*, London: Home Office.

Her Majesty's Inspector of Prisons (HMIP) (2006c) *Women in Prison*, London: Home Office, available at www.inspectorates.homeoffice. gov.uk/hmiprisons/thematic-reports1/womeninprison.pdf.

Hipwell, A., Loeber, R., Stouthamer-Loeber, M., Keenan, K., White, H. and Kroneman, L. (2002) 'Characteristics of girls with early onset disruptive and antisocial behaviour', *Criminal Behaviour and Mental Health*, vol 12, no 1, 99-118.

Hodgins, S. (1995) 'Assessing mental disorders in the criminal justice system: feasibility versus clinical accuracy', *International Journal of Law and Psychiatry*, vol 18, 15-28.

Hodgins, S. (2000) 'Offenders with major mental disorders', in C. Hollin (ed) *Handbook of Offender Assessment and Treatment*, Chichester: Wiley.

Hodgins, S. and Muller-Isberner, R. (2000) *Violence, Crime and Mentally Disordered Offenders: Concepts and Methods for Effective Treatment and Prevention*, Chichester: Wiley.

Hollin, C. (ed) (2001) *Handbook of Offender Assessment and Treatment*, Chichester: Wiley.

Hollin, C., Palmer, E., McGuire, J., Hounsome, J., Hatcher, R., Bilby, C. and Clark, C. (2004) *Pathfinder Programmes in the Probation Service: A Retrospective Analysis*, Home Office Online Report no 66/04, London: Home Office.

Hollin, C.R. and Palmer, E.J. (2005) *Criminogenic Factors Among Women Offenders*, London: Prison Service.

Holt, P. (2000) *Case Management: Context for Supervision. A Review of Research on Models of Case Management: Design Implications for Effective Practice*, Community and Criminal Justice Monograph 2, Leicester: De Montfort University.

Holt, P. (2002) 'Case Management Evaluation: Pathways to Progress', *Vista*, vol 7, no 1, 16-25.

Home Office (1989) *Children and Young Persons Act*, London: HMSO.

Home Office (1991) *Criminal Justice Act*, London: HMSO.

Home Office (1993) *Car Theft – The Offender's Perspective*, Research Study 130, London: HMSO.

Home Office (1994a) *Criminal Justice Act*, London: HMSO.

Home Office (1994b) *Reported and Unreported Racial Incidents in Prisons*, London: HMSO.

Home Office (1998a) *Crime and Disorder Act*, London: HMSO.

Home Office (1998b) *Research, Development and Statistics: A Guide to the Criminal Justice System in England and Wales*, London: HMSO.

Home Office (2000a) *Think First Programme Outline*, London: HMSO.

Home Office (2000b) *Multi-agency Guidance for Addressing Domestic Violence*, London: HMSO.

Home Office (2000c) *The Government's Strategy for Women Offenders*, London: HMSO.

Home Office (2002a) *OASys – Offender Assessment System*, London: HMSO.

Home Office (2002b) *Tackling Crack: A National Plan*. London: HMSO.

Home Office (2002c) *Probation Statistics in England and Wales*, London, HMSO.

Home Office (2003) *Statistics on Women and the Criminal Justice System*, London: HMSO.

Home Office (2004a) *Criminal Statistics, England and Wales*, London: HMSO.

Home Office (2004b) *Home Office Citizenship Survey: People, Families and Communities*, Research Study 289, London: Home Office.

Home Office (2005a) *Reducing Re-offending Through Skills and Employment*, London: HMSO.

Home Office (2005b) *Race and the Criminal Justice System: An overview to the complete statistics 2003-2004*, London: Home Office.

Home Office (2006) *OASys – Offender Assessment System Version 2 Revised*, London: National Offender Management Service.

Home Office and Department of Health (1992) *Review of Health and Social Services for Mentally Disordered Offenders and Others Requiring Similar Services*, London: HMSO.

Home Office and Department of Health (1999) *Managing Dangerous People with Severe Personality Disorders: Proposals for Policy Development*, London: HMSO.

Home Office National Statistics (2004) *Offences relating to motoring vehicles in England and Wales, Supplementary Tables*, London: Home Office, available at www.homeoffice.gov.uk (accessed 23 May 2006).

Hook, T.D. Cordoray, D.S., Hartmann, H., Hedges, L.V., Light, R.L., Louis T.A. and Mosteller, F. (eds) *Meta-analysis for explanation*, New York: Russell Sage Foundation.

Hopkins, M. and Sparrow, P. (2006) 'Sobering up: Arrest referral and brief intervention for alcohol users in the custody suite', *Criminology and Criminal Justice*, vol 6, no 4, 389-410.

Hough, M. (1996) *Drug Misuse and the Criminal Justice System: A Review of the Literature*, Drug Prevention Initiative paper 15, London: Home Office.

Hough, M. and Mayhew, P. (1983) *The British Crime Survey: First Report*, London: HMSO.

Houlders, A. (2005) 'Multidisciplinary aspects of the Care Plan Approach', in S. Wix and M. Humphreys (eds) *Multidisciplinary Working in Forensic Mental Health Care*, London: Elsevier Churchill Livingstone.

Howells, K. and Hollin, C.R. (eds) (1989) *Clinical Approaches to Violence*, Chichester: Wiley.

Hudson, B. (2002) 'Gender issues in penal policy and penal theory', in P. Carlen (ed) *Women and Punishment*, Cullompton: Willan, 21-46.

Hudson, B. and Bramhall, G. (2005) 'Assessing the "Other" constructions of "Asianness" in Risk Assessments by Probation Officers', *British Journal of Criminology*, vol 45, no 5, 721-40.

Hudson, W. (1993) 'Index of Self-Esteem', in J. Fischer and K. Corcoran *Measures for clinical practice: A source book*, vols 1-2, New York, NY: The Free Press.

Hughes, G. (1998) *Understanding Crime Prevention: Social control, risk and late modernity*, Buckingham: Open University Press.

Humphreys, C., Thiara, K. and Regan, L. (2006) 'Domestic violence and substance use: overlapping issues in separate services?', *The Domestic Abuse Quarterly*, Winter 2006, 21-3.

James, A. and Raine, J. (1998) *The New Politics of Criminal Justice*, London: Longmans.

Jarvis Probation Officers Manual (1996) Sheffield Hallam University and Association of Chief Officers of Probation.

Jean Piaget Archives Foundation (1989) *The Jean Piaget Bibliography*, Geneva: Jean Piaget Archives Foundation.

Jenkins, A. (1998) 'Invitations to responsibility', in W.L. Marshall, R. Jones, T. Ward and Y. Fernandez (eds) *Source Book of Treatment Programmes for Sexual Offenders*, New York, NY: Plenum Press, 163-89.

Kapardis, A. and Krambia-Kapardis, M. (2004) 'Enhancing fraud protection and detection by profiling offenders', *Criminal Behaviour and Mental Health*, vol 14, 189-201.

Kay, J. and Gast, L. (1999) *From Murmur to Murder – Working with Racially Motivated and Racist Offenders*, Midland Probation Training Consortium.

Kazi, M. (1998) 'Putting Single-case evaluation into practice', in J. Cheetham and M. Kazi (eds) *The working of social work*, London: Jessica Kingsley.

Keilinger, V. and Stanko, B. (2002) 'What can we Learn from People's Use of the Police?', *Criminal Justice Matters*, no 48, 4-5.

Keith, Mr Justice (2006) *Inquiry into the Death of Zahid Mubarak*, London: Home Office.

Kelly, G. and Wilkinson, B. (1996) *The Midland Region: An Audit on 'What Works' Training and Development*, Birmingham: West Midlands Probation Service.

Kelly, G. and Wilkinson, B. (2000) 'Research into Practice-working with children and young people who offend', *Criminal Justice Matters*, no 41, 28.

Kemshall, H. (1996) *Reviewing Risk: Implications for policy and practice in the Probation Service. A review of research on the assessment and management of risk and dangerousness*, London: Home Office, Research and Statistics Directorate.

Kemshall, H. (1997) *The Management and Assessment of Risk: Training Pack*, London: Home Office.

Kemshall, H. (1998a) *Risk in Probation Practice*, Aldershot: Ashgate.

Kemshall, H. (1998b) 'Defensible Decisions for Risk: Or It's the Doers Wot Get the Blame', *Probation Journal*, vol 45, no 2, 67-72.

Kemshall, H. (2001) *Risk Assessment and Management of Known Violent and Sexual Offenders: A review of current issue*, Police Research Series, 140, London: Home Office.

Kemshall, H. (2003) *Understanding risk in criminal justice*, Maidenhead: Open University Press.

Kemshall, H. (2004) 'Risk, Dangerousness and Female Offenders', in G. McIvor (ed) *Women who Offend*, London: Jessica Kingsley.

Kemshall, H. and Pritchard, J. (1996) *Good Practice in Risk Assessment and Risk Management*, London: Jessica Kingsley Publishers.

Kemshall, H. and Pritchard, J. (eds) (1997) *Good Practice in Risk Assessment and Risk Management*, vol 2, London: Jessica Kingsley Publishers.

Kemshall, H. and Wright, L. (1995) 'Service Delivery to Women Offenders: how can we get it right?', *Vista*, vol 1, no 2.

Kemshall, H., Boerk, T. and Fleming, J. (2006) *The Context of Risk Decisions: Does Social Capital make a Difference?*, Presentation to 'Pathways in and out of Crime: Resilience and Diversity', International Symposium, April 2006.

Kemshall, H., Holt, P., Bailey, R. and Boswell, G. (2004) 'Beyond Programmes: organisational and cultural issues in the implementation of What Works', in G. Mair (ed) *What Matters in Probation*, Cullompton: Willan.

Kemshall, H., Mackenzie, G., Miller, J. and Wilkinson, B. (2006) *Risk Guidance and Resource Pack*, (CD Rom) London: National Offender Management Service.

Kemshall, H., Mackenzie, G., Wood, J., Bailey, R. and Yates, J. (2005) *Strengthening Multi-Agency Public Protection Arrangements (MAPPAs)*, Home Office Development and Practice Report 45, London: Home Office.

Kendall, K. (2002) 'Time to think again about cognitive behavioural programmes', in P. Carlen (ed) *Women and Punishment: The Struggle for Justice*, Cullompton: Willan.

Kershaw, C., Budd, T., Kinshott, G., Mattinson, J., Mayhew, P. and Myhill, A. (2000) *The 2000 British Crime Survey*, Home Office Statistical Bulletin 18/00, London: Home Office.

Kolb, D.A. (1984) *Experiential learning: Experience as the source of learning and development*, Upper Saddle River, NJ: Prentice Hall.

Kohlberg, L. (1958) *The Development of Modes of Thinking and Choices in Years 10 to 16*, PhD dissertation, University of Chicago.

Kohlberg, L. (1973) *Collected papers on moral development and moral development*, Cambridge, MA: Harvard University, Center for Moral Education.

Kothari, G., Marsden, J. and Strang, J. (2002) 'Opportunities and Obstacles for Effective Treatment of Drug Misusers in the Criminal Justice System in England and Wales', *British Journal of Criminology*, vol 42, no 2, 412-32.

Kreitman, N. (ed) (1977) *Parasuicide*, London: Wiley.

Kropp, P., Whittemore, R., Hart, S.C., Webster, C.D. and Eaves, D. (1995) *Manual for the Spousal Assault Risk Assessment Guide* (2nd edn), Vancouver: British Columbia Institute on Family Violence.

Kushner, T. (2006) 'An Alien Problem? Criminality and Immigration', *Criminal Justice Matters*, no 65, 14-15.

KWP (2002) *Building on our Assets: Effective Assessment and Planning in Work with Young People who Offend*, London: Youth Justice Board.

Lea, J. (2000) 'The MacPherson Report and the Question of Institutional Racism', *The Howard Journal*, vol 39, no 3, 219-33.

Leach, T. (2003) '"Oh, my country, how I leave my country": Some reflections on a changing probation service', *Probation Journal*, vol 50, no 1, 20-9.

Leitner, M. (1993) *Drug Use and Drug Prevention: The Views of the General Public*, London: Home Office.

Levesley, T., Braun, G., Wilkinson, M. and Powell, C. (2004) *Emerging method of car theft – theft of keys*, Findings 239, London: Home Office Research Development and Statistical Directorate.

Lipton, D., Pearson, C. and Yee, D. (2002) 'The effectiveness of cognitive Behavioural Treatment Methods on Recidivism', in J. McGuire (ed) *Offender Rehabilitation and Treatment*, Chichester: Wiley, 79-112.

Lipsey, M. (1992) 'Juvenile Delinquency Treatment: A meta-analytic inquiry into the variability of effects', in T.D. Hook, D.S. Cordoray, H. Hartmann, L.V. Hedges, R.L. Light, T.A. Louis and F. Mosteller (eds), *Meta-analysis for explanation*, New York, NY: Russell Sage Foundation, 83-127.

Lloyd, C., Mair, G. and Hough, M. (1994) 'Reconviction rates: methodological errors', in Home Office, *Explaining Reconviction Rates: A Critical Analysis*, London: Home Office.

Lochner, L. and Moretti, E. (2003) *The Effect of Education on Crime: Evidence from Prison Inmates, Arrests and Self-Reports*, available at www.econ.berkeley.edu/~moretti/lm46.pdf (accessed 9 March 2007).

Lords Hansard (2006) 'Mental Health: Residential Services', Lords Hansard text for 27 February 2006, available at www.publications.parliament.uk/pa/ld/lords_hansard_by_date.htm (accessed 9 January 2007).

Lynch, J.E. (2005) 'Violence? Which violence?', *Criminal Justice Matters*, no 61, 12-13.

Lynch, J.E. and Skinner, S. (2004) 'Resettling Mentally Ill Offenders', *Criminal Justice Matters*, no 56, 26-7.

Lyon, J. (2002) 'Women who Offend', *The Magistrate*, London: Magistrate's Association.

Macey, M. (2001) 'Interpreting Islam: young Muslim men's involvement in criminal activity in Bradford', in B. Spalek (ed) *Islam, Crime and Criminal Justice*, Cullompton: Willan.

MacLean, Lord (2000) *Report of the committee on Serious Violent and Sexual Offenders*, Edinburgh: Scottish Executive.

Macpherson, W. (1999) *The Stephen Lawrence Inquiry: Report of an Inquiry by Sir William Macpherson of Cluny*, London: The Stationery Office.

Mair, G. (ed) (2004) *What Matter in Probation*, Cullompton: Willan.

Mair, G. and May, C. (1997) *Offenders on Probation*, Home Office Research Study No 167, London: Home Office.

Makkai, T. and Payne, J. (2005) 'Illicit drug use and offending histories: A study of male incarcerated offenders in Australia', *Probation Journal*, vol 52, no 2, 153-68.

Malloch, M. (2004) 'Not "fragrant" at all: criminal justice responses to "risky" women', *Critical Social Policy*, vol 24, no 3, 385–405.

Maruna, S. (2001) *Making Good: How Ex-Convicts Reform and Rebuild their Lives*, Washington, DC: American Psychological Association Books.

Maruna, S. and Immarigeon, R. (eds) (2004) *After Crime and Punishment*, Cullompton: Willan.

Marshall, K., Weaver, P. and Lowenstein, P. (1991) *Targets for Change*, Nottingham: Nottinghamshire Probation Service.

Marshall, W.L., Jones, R., Ward, T. and Fernandez, Y. (eds) (1998) *Source Book of Treatment Programmes for Sexual Offenders*, New York, NY: Plenum Press.

Martinson, R. (1974) 'What Works? Questions and answers about prison reform', *The Public Interest*, vol 35, 22–54.

Mason, G. (2005) 'Hate Crime and the Image of the Stranger', *British Journal of Criminology*, vol 45, no 6, 837–59.

Mavunga, P.K. (1993) 'Probation a Basically Racist service', in L. Gelsthorpe (ed) *Minority Ethnic Groups in the Criminal Justice System*, Cambridge: Cambridge Institute of Criminology.

Mawby, R.I. (2001) *Burglary*, Cullompton: Willan.

McCulloch, C. (2004) 'Through the eyes of a Missionary: Probation 100 Years on', *Vista*, vol 9, no 3.

McCulloch, T. (2006) 'Reviewing "What Works?": A Social Perspective', *British Journal of Community Justice*, vol 4, no 1, 1.

McGuire, J. (ed) (1995) *What Works: Reducing Reoffending*, Chichester: Wiley.

McGuire, J. (2000) *Cognitive Behavioural Approaches, An introduction to theory and research*, Liverpool University: HMIP.

McGuire, J. (2001) 'Property Offences', in C. Hollin (ed) *Offender Assessment and Treatment*, Chichester: Wiley.

McGuire, J. (ed) (2002a) *Offender Rehabilitation and Treatment*, Chichester: Wiley.

McGuire, J. (2002b) *Integrating Findings from Research Reviews in Offender Rehabilitation and Treatment Effective programmes and Policies to Reduce Re-offending*, Chichester: Wiley.

McGuire, J. (2004) 'Commentary: Promising answers, and the next generation of questions', *Psychology, Crime and Law*, vol 10, no 3, 335–45.

McGuire, M. and Raynor, P. (2006) 'How the resettlement of prisoners promotes desistance from crime: Or does it?', *Criminology and Criminal Justice*, vol 6, no 1, 19–38.

McGuire, M., Morgan, R. and Reiner, R. (eds) (2002) *The Oxford Handbook of Criminology* (3rd edn), Oxford: Oxford University Press.

McInerney, T. and Minne, C. (2004) 'Principles of treatment for mentally disordered offenders', *Criminal Behaviour and Mental Health*, vol 14, S43-S47.

McIvor, G (ed) (2004) *Women who Offend*, London: Jessica Kingsley.

McMahon, G. (2003), 'Basic Skills and Offenders in the Community', *Vista*, vol 8, no 3, 155-62.

McMahon, G., Hall, A., Hayward, G., Hudson, C., Roberts, C., Fernandez, R. and Burnett, R. (2004) *Basic Skills Programmes in the Probation Service: Evaluation of the Basic Skills Pathfinder*, Home Office Online Report 14/04, available at www.homeoffice.gov.uk/rds/pdfs04/rdsolr1404.pdf.

McMurran, M. (2002a) 'Alcohol, Aggression and Violence', in J. McGuire (ed) *Offender Rehabilitation and Treatment*, Chichester: Wiley, 221-41.

McMurran, M. (2002b) *Motivating Offenders to Change: A Guide to Enhancing Engagement in Therapy*, Chichester: Wiley.

McNeill, F. (2005) *A Desistance Paradigm for Offender Management*, Glasgow: University of Glasgow and Strathclyde.

McNeill, F. (2006) 'Community Supervisions: Context and Relationships Matter', in B. Goldson and J. Muncie, *Youth Crime and Justice*, London: Sage.

McNeill, F. and Batchelor, S. (2002) 'Chaos, Containment and Change', in *Youth Justice*, vol 2, no 1, 27-43.

McNeill, F. and Batchelor, S. (2004) *Persistent Offending by Young People: Developing Practice*, Issues in Community and Criminal Justice Monograph Number 3, London: NAPO.

McNeill, F., Batchelor, S., Burnett, R. and Knox, J. (2004) *21st Century Social Work, Reducing Offending: Key Practice Skills*, Glasgow: Glasgow School of Social Work.

McWilliams, W. (1983) 'The Mission to the English Police Courts 1876-1936', *The Howard Journal* vol 22, no 3, 129-47.

McWilliams, W. (1985) 'The Mission Transformed: Professionalisation of Probation Between the Wars', *The Howard Journal*, vol 24, no 4, 257-73.

McWilliams, W. (1986) 'The English Probation System and the Diagnostic Ideal', *The Howard Journal*, vol 25, no 4, 241-59.

McWilliams, W. (1987) 'Probation, Pragmatism and Policy', *The Howard Journal*, vol 26, no 2, 97-121.

Melrose, M. (2004) 'Fractured Transitions: Disadvantaged Young People, Drug Taking and Risk', *Probation Journal*, vol 51, no 4, 327–42.

Mental Health Alliance (2006) 'Mental Health Bill still not fit for the twenty-first century', available at www.mentalhealthalliance.org.uk/resources/press/prbillpublished.html (accessed 8 January 2007).

Merrington, S. (2004) 'Assessment Tools in Probation: their development and potential', in R. Burnett and C. Roberts (eds) *What Works in Probation and Youth Justice Developing Evidence-Based Practice*, Cullompton: Willan, 46–69.

Merrington, S. (2006) 'Is more better? The value and potential of intensive community supervision', *Probation Journal*, vol 53, no 4, 347–60.

Merrington, S. and Hine, J. (2001) *A Handbook for Evaluating Probation Work with Offenders*, London: HMIP, ACOP and NPRIE.

Merrington, S. and Stanley, S. (2004) 'What Works?: Revisiting the evidence in England and Wales', *Probation Journal*, vol 51, no 1, 7–20.

Merrington, S., Baker, K. and Wilkinson, B. (2003) 'Using Risk and Need Assessment Tools in Probation and Youth Justice', *Vista*, vol 8, no 1, 31–8.

Miller, W. and Rollnick, S. (2002) *Motivational interviewing preparing people for change* (2nd edn), New York, NY: The Guilford Press.

Mirrlees-Black, C. (1999), *Domestic Violence: Findings from a New British Crime Survey Self-Completion Questionnaire*, London: Home Office.

Modood, T. and Berthoud, R. (1997) *Ethnic Minorities in Britain: Diversity and Disadvantage*, London: Policy Studies Institute.

Moffitt, T.E. (1993) 'Adolescence-limited and life-course persistent antisocial behaviour: a developmental taxonomy', *Psychological Review*, vol 100, no 4, 674–701.

Moffitt, T.E. and Caspi, A. (2001) 'Childhood predictors differentiate life-course persistent and adolescence-limited antisocial pathways among males and females', *Development and Psychopathology*, vol 13, no 2, 335–75.

Moore, B. (1996) *Risk assessment – a practitioner's guide to predicting harmful behaviour*, London: Whiting & Birch.

Moore, R., Howard, P. and Burns, M. (2006) 'The Further Development of OASys', *Prison Service Journal*, no 167, 36–42.

Moorthy, V., Cahalin, K. and Howard, P. (2004) *Ethnicity and parole*, London: Home Office.

Morgan, M. and Patton, P. (2002) 'Gender-responsive programming in the justice system – Oregon's guidelines for effective programming for girls', *Federal Probation*, vol 66, no 2, 57–65.

Mott, J.R. (1992) *Probation, Prison and Parole*, Sussex: Temple House Books.

Motuik, L.L. and Serin, R.C. (eds) *Compendium 2000 on Effective Correctional Programming*, Ottawa: Correctional Service Canada.

Mullender, A. and Burton, S. (2001), 'Dealing with Perpetrators', in A. Mullender and S. Burton (eds) *What Works in Reducing Domestic violence*, London: Whiting & Birch.

Muncie, J. (2004) *Youth and Crime* (2nd edn), London: Sage.

Murji, K. (1999) 'Wild Life: Representations and Constructions of Yardies', in J. Ferrell and N. Websdale (eds) *Make Trouble Cultural: Representations of Crime*, New York, NY: Aldine de Gruyter, 25-46.

Murphy, M. (2004) *Developing Collaborative Relationships in Interagency Child Protection Work*, Lyme Regis: Russell House Publishing.

Mynard, W. and Read, T. (1997) *Policing Racially Motivated Incidents*, Police Research Group, Paper 84, London, Home Office.

Nacro (2005) *Findings of the 2004 survey of court diversion/Criminal Justice Mental Health Liaison Schemes for mentally disordered offenders in England and Wales*, Nacro, available at www.nacro.org.uk. accessed 3 October 2006.

Naffine, M. (ed) (1995) *Gender, Crime and Feminism*, Aldershot: Dartmouth.

National Institute of Health and Clinical Excellence (NICE) (2004) *Self-harm: Short term treatment and management, information for people who self harm, their advocates and carers and the public*, London: NICE, available at www.nice.org.uk (accessed 7 June 2006).

National Offender Management Service (NOMS) (2005) *Women's Offending Reduction Programme: Annual Review 2004-2005*, London: Home Office.

National Statistics Online (2006) available at www.statistics.gov.uk/CCI/nscl.asp?ID=5752 (accessed 6 March 2007).

Nellis, M. (1999) 'Towards the "field of corrections": Modernising the Probation service in the late 1990s', *Social Policy and Administration*, vol 33, no 3, 302-23.

Newburn, T. (2002) 'Young people, crime and youth justice', in M. McGuire, R. Morgan and R. Reiner (eds) *The Oxford Handbook of Criminology* (3rd edn), Oxford: Oxford University Press.

Newburn, T., Shiner, M. and Hayman, S. (2004) 'Race Crime and Injustice? Strip Search and the Treatment of Suspects in Custody,' *British Journal of Criminology*, vol 44, no 5, 677-94.

Newman, G., Clarke, R.V. and Shloham, S. (eds) (1997) *Rational Choice and Situational Crime Prevention: Theoretical Foundations*, New York, NY: Dartmouth Press.

Nolan, P. (2005) 'The historical context', in S. Wix and M. Humphreys (eds) *Multidisciplinary Working in Forensic Mental Health Care*, London: Elsevier Churchill Livingstone.

Novaco, R.W. and Jarvis, K. (2002) 'Brief Cognitive Behavioural Intervention for Anger', in F. Bond and W. Dryden (ed) *Brief Cognitive Behaviour Therapy*, Chichester: Wiley.

Novaco, R.W. and Welsh, W.N. (1989) 'Anger Disturbances: Cognitive Mediation and Clinical Prescriptions', in K. Howells and C.R. Hollin (eds) *Clinical Approaches to Violence*, Chichester: Wiley.

Nutley, S. and Davies, H.T. (1999) 'The Fall and Rise of Evidence in Criminal Justice', *Public Money and Management*, January–March, 47–54.

O'Beirne, M. (2004) *Religion in England and Wales: Findings from the 2001 Home Office Citizenship Survey*, Home Office Research Study No 274, London: Home Office.

O'Connell, S. (2006) 'From Toad of Toad Hall to the "Death Drivers" of Belfast, an Exploratory History of "Joyriding"', *British Journal of Criminology*, vol 46, no 3, 455–69.

Office of the Deputy Prime Minister (ODPM) (2005) *Transitions: Young Adults with Complex Needs*, available at www.socialexclusion.gov.uk/publications.asp?did=785 (accessed 9 March 2007).

O'Grady, J. (2004) 'Prison Psychiatry', *Criminal Behaviour and Mental Health*, no 14, S25–S30.

O'Hagan, K. (2001) *Cultural Competence in the Caring Professions*, London: Jessica Kingsley.

Organisation for Economic Cooperation and Development (OECD) (2007) *About Human and Social Capital*, available at www.oecd.org.

Osher, F. and Kofoed, L. (1998) 'Treatment of psychiatric and psychoactive substance abuse disorders', *Hospital and Community Psychiatry*, vol 40, 1025–30.

Oulton, J. (2003) 'Involving practitioners in evaluation', *Probation Journal*, vol 50, no 2, 154–8.

Paludi, M. (2002) *The Psychology of Women* (2nd edn), Englewood Cliffs, NJ: Prentice Hall.

Parry, T. and Raine, J. (2004) 'Assessing "what works" in criminal justice', *Vista*, vol 8, no 2, 66–72.

Parsons, S. (2002) *Basic Skills and Crime*, London: Basic Skills Agency.

Pawson, R. and Tilley, N. (1994) 'What works in evaluation research?', *British Journal of Criminology*, vol 34, no 3, 291–306.

Payne, S. (2006) 'Mary-Ann's killers were on probation', *Telegraph.co.uk*, available at www.telegraph.co.uk (accessed 20 June 2006).

Pease, K. (1997) 'Predicting the Future: The Roles of Routine Activity and Rational Choice Theory', in G. Newman, R.V. Clarke and S. Shloham (eds) *Rational Choice and Situational Crime Prevention: Theoretical Foundations*, New York, NY: Dartmouth Press.

Pence, E. and Paymar, M. (1993) *The Duluth Domestic Abuse Intervention Project*, Minnesota: Springer.

Persons, J.B. and Silbersatz, G. (1998) 'Are the results of randomised controlled trials useful to psychotherapists?', *Journal of Consulting and Clinical Psychology*, vol 66, 126–35.

Petersen, C., Maier, S. and Seligman, M. (1995) *Learned Helplessness: A Theory for the Age of Personal Control*, New York, NY: Oxford University Press.

Pickford, J. (2000) *Youth Justice: Theory and Practice*, London: Cavendish.

Plomin, R., DeFries, J.C., McLean, G.C. and Rutter, M. (1997) *Behavioural Genetics*, New York, NY: Freeman.

Polaschek, D. and Reynolds, N. (2001), 'Assessment and Treatment: Violent Offenders', in C. Hollin (ed) *Handbook of Offender Assessment and Treatment*, Chichester: Wiley.

Porporino, F. and Robinson, D. (1992) *Does Educating Adult Offenders Counteract Recidivism?*, Ottawa: Research and Statistics Branch of the Correctional Service of Canada.

Porporino, F.J. and Fabiano, E. (2005) 'Is There an Evidence Base Supportive of Women-Centered Programming in Corrections?', *Corrections Today*, no 28, 1–2.

Power, C. (2003) 'Irish Travellers: Ethnicity racism and pre-sentence reports', *Probation Journal*, vol 50, no 3, 252–66.

Priestley, P. and McGuire, J. (1978) *Social Skills and Problem-solving*, London: Tavistock.

Prins, H. (2005) 'Mental disorder and violent crime: A problematic relationship', *Probation Journal*, vol 52, no 4, 333–58.

Probation Circular 42/2005 (2005a) *Extension of Victim Contact Scheme to Victims of Mentally Disordered Offenders – The Domestic Violence, Crime and Victims Act 2004*, London: Home Office

Probation Circular 57/2005 (2005b) *The Effective Management of the Drug Rehabilitation Requirement (DRR) and the Alcohol Treatment Requirement (ATR)*, London: Home Office.

Prochaska, J.O. and DiClemente, C.C. (1983) 'Stages and process of self-change of smoking towards an integrative model of change', *Journal of Consulting and Clinical Psychology*, vol 51, 390–95.

Prochaska, J.O. and DiClemente, C.C. (1994) *The Transtheoretical Approach: Crossing the Traditional Boundaries of Therapy*, Homewood: Dow–Jones/Irwin.

Putnam, R. (1995) 'Bowling alone: America's declining social capital', *Journal of Democracy*, vol 6, 65–78.

Putnam, R. (2000) *Bowling Alone: The Collapse and Revival of American Community*, New York, NY: Simon and Schuster.

Pycroft, A. (2006) 'Too little, too late?', *Criminal Justice Matters*, no 64, 36–7.

Ramsey, M. (ed) (2003) *Prisoners Drug Use and Treatment: seven research studies*, Home Office Research Study No 267, London: Home Office.

Ray, L., Smith, D. and Wastell, E. (2002) 'Racist Violence and Probation Practice', *Probation Journal*, vol 49, no 1, 3–9.

Raynor, P. (2002) 'Community Penalties: Probation, Punishment, and "What Works"', in M. McGuire, R. Morgan and R. Reiner (eds) *The Oxford Handbook of Criminology* (3rd edn), Oxford: Oxford University Press, 1168–205.

Raynor, P. (2003) 'Evidence-based Probation and its Critics', *Probation Journal*, vol 50, no 4, 334–5.

Raynor, P. (2004) 'Opportunity, motivation and change: some findings from research on resettlement' in R. Burnett and C. Roberts (eds) *What Works in Probation and Youth Justice*, Cullompton: Willan.

Reith, M. (1997) 'Mental Health Inquiries: Implications for Probation Practice', *Probation Journal*, vol 44, no 2, 66–70.

Rex, S. (1997) *Desistance from Offending: Experiences of Probation*, Paper presented at the British Criminology Conference.

Rex, S. (1999) 'Desistance from offending: experiences of probation', *The Howard Journal*, vol 38, no 4, 366–83.

Rex, S. (2002) 'Re-inventing community penalties: the role of communication', in S. Rex and M. Tonry (eds), *Reform and Punishment: The Future of Sentencing*, Cullompton: Willan.

Rex, S. and Crosland, P. (1999) *Project on Pro-social Modelling and Legitimacy: Findings from Community Service*, Report to Cambridgeshire Probation Service, Cambridge: Institute of Criminology, University of Cambridge.

Rex, S. and Tonry, M. (eds) (2002) *Reform and Punishment: The Future of Sentencing*, Cullompton: Willan.

Richardson, A. and Budd, T. (2003) *Alcohol Crime and Disorder: A Study of Young Adults*, Home Office Research Study No 263, London: Home Office.

Risk Management Authority (RMA) (2006) *Risk Assessment Tools Evaluation Directory, Version 1*, Paisley: RMA.

Roberts, C. (1989) *Hereford and Worcester Probation Service Young Offender Project: first evaluation report*, Oxford: Department of Social and Administrative Studies.

Roberts, C. (2004) 'Offending Behaviour Programmes: emerging evidence and implications for practice', in R. Burnett and C. Roberts (eds) *What Works in Probation and Youth Justice*, Cullompton: Willan.

Roberts, C.H. (1995) 'Effective Practice and Service Delivery', in J. McGuire (ed) *What Works: Reducing Reoffending*, Chichester: Wiley.

Roberts, J. (2002) 'Women-centred: the West Mercia community-based programme for women offenders', in P. Carlen (ed) *Women and Punishment*, Cullompton: Willan, 110-24.

Robinson, G. and Raynor, P. (2006) 'The future of rehabilitation: What role for the probation service?', *Probation Journal*, vol 53, no 4, 334-46.

Rose, D.R. and Clear, T.R. (1996) 'Incarceration, Social Capital, and Crime: Implications for Social Disorganisation Theory', reprinted in *Criminology*, no 36, 441.

Rumgay, J. (1996) 'Women Offenders: Towards Needs-based Policy', *Vista*, vol 2, no 2, 104-15.

Rumgay, J. (2004a) 'Scripts for Safer Survival: Pathways out of Female Crime', *The Howard Journal*, vol 43, no 4, 405-19.

Rumgay, J. (2004b) 'Living with Paradox: Community Supervision of Women Offenders', in G. McIvor (ed), *Women who Offend*, London: Jessica Kingsley, 99-125.

Rutter, M., Giller, H. and Hagell, A. (1998) *Anti-Social Behaviour and Young People*, Cambridge: Cambridge University Press.

Ryan, P. (2003) 'Mental Health', *Research Matters*, October 2003–April 2004, 37-42, available at www.communitycare.co.uk (accessed 1 September 2004).

Sale, A. (2006) 'Paralysed Around Culture', *Community Care*, 16 March, no 1614, 28-9.

Salisbury, H. and Upson, A. (2004) *Ethnicity, Victimisation and Concern about Crime: Findings from the 2001/02 and 2002/03 British Crime Survey*, London: Home Office.

Sampson, R. and Laub, J. (1993) *Crime in the Making: Pathways and Turning Points through Life*, Cambridge, MA: Harvard University Press.

Sattar, G. (2001*) Rates and Causes of Death amongst Prisoners and Offenders under Community Supervision*, Home Office Research Study No 231, London: Home Office.

Scarman, Lord (1981) *The Brixton Disorders 10-12 April 1981*, London: HMSO.

Select Committee on Education and Skills (2005) *Seventh Report on Prison Education*, Parliamentary copyright, available at www.publications.parliament.uk/pa/cm200405/cmselect/cmeduski/cmeduski.htm (accessed 9 March 2007).

Sharp, D. and Atherton, S.R. (2006) 'Out on the Town. An evaluation of Brief Motivational Interventions to Address the Risk Associated with Problematic Alcohol Use', *International Journal of Offender Therapy and Comparative Criminology*, vol 50, no 5, 540-58.

Shaw, M. and Hannah-Moffat, K. (2004) 'How cognitive skills forgot about gender and diversity', in G. Mair (ed) *What Matters in Probation*, Cullompton: Willan.

Shoham, E. (2005) 'Gender, Traditionalism and Attitudes towards Domestic Violence Within a Closed Community,' *International Journal of Offender Therapy and Comparative Criminology*, vol 49, no 4, 427-29.

Shore, H. (2006) 'Artful Dodgers or Feral Youth?', *Prison Report*, no 69, 10.

Sibbitt, R. (1997) *The Perpetrators of Racial Harassment and Racial Violence*, Home Office Research Study No 176, London: Home Office.

Silver, E. and Miller, L.L. (2002), 'A Cautionary note on the Use of Actuarial Risk Assessment Tools for Social Control', *Crime and Delinquency*, vol 48, no 1, 138-61.

Silverman, J.G. and Williamson, G.M. (1997) 'Social context and entitlements involved in battering by heterosexual college males: Contributions of family and peers', *Violence and Victims*, vol 12, no 2, 147-64.

Singleton, N., Meltzer, H., Gatward, R., Coid, J. and Deasy, D. (1998) *Psychiatric Morbidity among Prisoners in England and Wales*, London: The Stationery Office.

Skeggs, B. (1997) *Formation of Class and Gender: Becoming Respectable*, London: Sage.

Smart, C. (1976) *Women, Crime and Criminology: A Feminist Critique*, London: Routledge, Kegan and Paul.

Smith, D. (2005) 'Probation and Social Work', *British Journal of Social Work*, vol 35, no 5, 621-37.

Smith, D. (2006) 'Youth Crime and Justice: Research, Evaluation and "Evidence"', in B. Goldson and J. Muncie, *Youth Crime and Justice*, London: Sage.

Smith, F., Hunt, E. and Brann, C. (2000) *Use of Rewards and Incentives in Work with Young People in Secure Accomodation*, London: YJB.

Smith, R. (2003) *Youth Justice: Ideas, Policy, Practice*, Cullompton: Willan.

Snider, L. (2003) 'Constituting the Punishable Woman', *British Journal of Criminology*, vol 43, no 2, 354–78.

Spalek, B. (ed.) (2002) *Islam, Crime and Criminal Justice*, Cullompton: Willan.

Spalek, B. (2006) *Crime Victims: Theory, policy and practice*, Basingstoke: Palgrave.

Spencer, A. (1999) *Working with Sex Offenders in Prisons and through Release to the Community: A Handbook*, London: Jessica Kingsley Publishers.

Spencer, L., Ritchie, J., Lewis, J. and Dillon, L. (2003) *Quality in qualitative evaluation: A framework for assessing research evidence*, London: National Centre for Social Research.

South, N., Akhtar, S., Nightingale, R. and Stewart, M. (2001)"*Idle Hands*", Drugs and Alcohol Findings', *Alcohol Concern*, (winter) issue 6, 24–29.

Squires, P. and Stephen, D.E. (2005) *Rougher Justice: Anti-social Behaviour and Young People*, Cullompton: Willan.

Stanko, B. (ed) (2000) *Reducing Domestic Violence: What Works?*, Policy and Reducing Crime Unit, Briefing Notes, London: Home Office.

Stewart, D., Gossop, M., Marsden, J. and Rolfe, A. (2000) 'Drug Misuse and Acquisitive Crime among clients recruited to the National Treatment Outcome Research Study', *Criminal Behaviour and Mental Health*, vol 10, 10–20.

Stephenson, M. and Brown, S. (2003) *Reader: Education, Training and Employment*, London: Youth Justice Board.

Stonewall (2003) *Profiles of Prejudice*, Citizenship 21, London: Stonewall.

Strachan, R. and Tallant, C. (1997) 'Improving judgement and appreciating biases in the risk assessment process', in H. Kemshall and J. Pritchard (eds) *Good Practice in Risk Assessment and Risk Management*, vol 2, London: Jessica Kingsley Publishers.

Stringer, E.T. (1996) *Action Research – A Handbook for Practitioners*, London: Sage.

Stutterford, T. (2005) 'What about me? Psychopathy and Anti-Social Personality Disorders', *The Times* (2), 1 July.

Taxman, F. (2006) 'Assessment with a Flair: Offender Accountability in Supervision Plans', *Federal Probation*, vol 70, no 2.

Taylor, C. and White, S. (2006) 'Knowledge and Reasoning in Social Work; Educating for Humane Judgement', *British Journal of Social Work*, vol 36, no 6, 937–54.

Taylor-Browne, J. (2001) *What Works in Reducing Domestic Violence*, London: Whiting & Birch.

T3 Associates (2002) *Acquisitive Programme for Women Programme*, unpublished draft, Pathway Programme for the National Probation Directorate.

Thomas, L. and Jones, M. (1998) *Women's Work: A Modular Programme of Intervention for Women Who Commit Offences*, LMT, Birmingham: West Midlands Probation Service.

Titterton, M. (2005) *Risk and Risk Taking in Health and Social Welfare*, London: Jessica Kingsley Publishers.

Tizzard, B. and Phoenix, A. (2002) *Black, White or Mixed Race?* (revised edn), London: Routledge.

Towl, G. (2005) 'Risk Assessment', *Vista*, vol 10, no 3, 134-7.

Trotter, C. (1993) *The Supervision of Offenders: What Works?*, Sydney: Victoria Office of Corrections.

Trotter, C. (1994) *The Effective Supervision of Offenders: A Training Manual*, Melbourne: Victoria Department of Justice.

Trotter, C. (1999) *Working With Involuntary Clients*, London: Sage.

Tuklo Orenda Associates (1999) *Making a Difference: A Positive and Practical Guide to Working with Black Offenders*, London: South West Probation Service.

Turner, T. and Colombo, A. (2005) 'Risky business: the problem with MAPPPs', *Criminal Justice Matters*, no 61, 34-5.

Underdown, A. (1998) *Strategies for Effective Offender Supervision*, Report of HMIP What Works project, London: Home Office.

United Nations Children's Fund (UNICEF) (2007) *Convention on the Rights of the Child*, available at www.unicef.org/crc/ (accessed 9 March 2007).

Utting, D. and Vennard, J. (2000) *What Works With Young Offenders in the Community?* London: Barnardo's.

Vennard, J., Sugg, D. and Hedderman, C (1997) *Changing Offenders Attitudes and Behaviour: What Works?*, Home Office Research Study No 171, London: Home Office.

Vige, M. (2005) 'Race and mental health treatment', *Criminal Justice Matters*, no 61, 28-31.

Waddington, P.A.J., Stenson, K. and Don, D. (2004) 'In Proportion: Race and Police Stop and Search', *British Journal of Criminology*, vol 44, no 6, 889-913.

Walby, S. and Allen, J. (2004) *Domestic Violence, Sexual Assault and Stalking: Findings from the British Crime Survey*, London: Home Office.

Walby, S. and Myhill, A. (2001) 'Assessing and Managing Risk', in J. Taylor-Browne (ed) *What Works in Reducing Domestic Violence*, London: Whiting & Birch.

Walklate, S. (2004) *Gender, Crime and Criminal Justice*, Cullompton: Willan.

Walklate, S. (2005) *Criminology: The Basics*, Oxford: Routledge.

Walmsley, R. (2001) *Mentoring for Women: A Review of the Literature*, London: Home Office: Offenders and Corrections Unit, draft report.

Ward, T. and Brown, M. (2004) 'The good lives model and conceptual issues in offender rehabilitation', *Psychology, Crime and Law*, vol 10, no 3, 243-57.

Ward, T., Vess, J., Collie, R. and Gannon, T. (2006) 'Risk management or goods promotion: The relationship between approach and avoidance goals in treatment for sex offenders' *Aggression and Violent Behaviour*, vol 11, no 44, 378-393.

Watkins, K.E., Burnam, A., Kung, F.Y. and Paddock, S. (2001) 'A national survey of care for persons with co-occurring mental and substance use disorders', *Psychiatric Services*, vol 52, 1062-8.

Weber, Z. (2004) 'Working towards culturally sensitive ethical practice in a multi cultural society', *Journal of Practice Teaching*, vol 5, no 3, 40-54.

West, D.J. (1982) *Delinquency: Its Roots, Careers and Prospects*, London: Heinemann.

West, D.J. and Farrington, D.P. (1975) *Who becomes delinquent? A second report of the Cambridge Study of Delinquent Development*, London: Heinemann.

West, D.J. and Farrington, D.P. (1977) *The Delinquent Way of Life*, London: Heinmann.

Whitehead, P. (1990) *Community Supervision for Offenders*, Aldershot: Avebury.

Whitehead, P. and Thompson, J. (2004) *Knowledge and the Probation Service*, Chichester: Wiley.

Wilkinson, B., Kelly, G. and Clare, R. (2002) *Building on our ASSETs: Effective Assessment and Planning in Work with Young People who Offend*, London: YJB.

Williamson, H. (2005), *Young Offenders and the Life Course: Reflections for Policy and Practice*, Presentation to 'Pathways in and out of Crime: Resilience and Diversity' Final Conference, available at www.pcrrd.group.shef.ac.uk/conferences/network_final_conference.htm (accessed 9 March 2007).

Wilson, D. (2004) '"Keeping Quiet" or "Going Nuts": Strategies Used by Young Black Men in Custody', *The Howard Journal*, vol 43, no 3, 317-30.

Winstone, J. and Pakes, F. (2005) *Community Justice: Issues for probation and criminal justice*, Cullompton: Willan.

Wix, S. and Hillis, G. (1998) unpublished training materials.

Wix, S. and Humphreys, M. (eds) (2005) *Multidisciplinary working in Forensic Mental Health Care*, London: Elsevier Churchill Livingstone.

World Health Organisation (WHO) (1999) *Pocket Guide to the ICD-10 Classification of Mental and Behavioural Disorders*, Geneva: Churchill Livingstone.

Worrall, A. and Hoy, C. (2005) *Punishment in the Community: Managing offenders, making choices*, Cullompton: Willan.

Worrall, A. and Walton, D. (2000) 'Prolific offender projects and the reduction of volume property crime: targeted policing and case management', *Vista*, vol 7, no 1, 34-7.

Youth Justice Board (YJB) (2003), *Reader on Assessment, Planning Interventions and Supervision*, London: ECOTEC.

Youth Justice Board (YJB) (2005) *Managing Risk in the Community*, London: ECOTEC.

Youth Justice Board (YJB) (2006) *Managing the Behaviour of Children and Young People in the Secure Estate*, London: YJB.

Zamble, E. and Quinsey, V.L. (1997) *The Criminal Recidivism Process*, Cambridge: Cambridge University Press.

Index

mental health 32, 41–4; *see also* mental
disorder
Mental Health Act (1983) 103, 112
mental health assessments 110
mental illness 103, 104, 107, 108,
111, 113, 117, 122; *see also* mental
disorder
mentoring 50, 51, 73
meta-analysis 25, 137, 219
migrants 81, 108
minimal approach 12
minimisation 178
minority ethnic groups 23, 25, 59,
77–97, 107–9, 180
mixed method studies 227–8
modelling 22, 71, 74, 95, 189, 190
monitoring 12, 20, 184, 207
moral development 68
motivation 14, 20, 22, 24, 27, 47, 72,
117, 125–6, 134, 140, 152, 167, 209,
211
motivational interviewing 59, 118, 134,
136, 190
multi-agency approach 47, 55, 70
Multi Agency Public Protection
Arrangements (MAPPA) 13, 20, 184
Multi-Agency Public Protection Panels
(MAPPP) 113
multi-agency teams 71
multidisciplinary working 114, 118
multi-modal interventions 21
Muslims 83, 87, 88

N

National Institute for Clinical
Excellence (NICE) 119
National Offender Management
Service (NOMS) 12, 13, 38, 45
National Standards 10
needs
assessment of 12
criminogenic 18, 193
employment 144
offence-related 48
of offenders 20, 23, 54, 55, 193
of women 43, 46
needs-focused service 70
negotiation skills 172
network of influences 69
NICE, *see* National Institute for Clinical
Excellence
night-time economy 132
NOMS, *see* National Offender
Management Service
non-judgemental approach 140, 141
non-offending opportunities 66
'Nothing Works' approach 9, 11

numeracy 143–5
numeracy programmes 143
numeracy skills 150

O

OASys risk assessment tool 17, 133
objective setting 224
oblivion seekers 127
observations 226
offence-focused approach 52, 70, 73,
147, 162, 231
offence-focused assessment 43, 45,49,
60
offence-focused goals 15
offence-focused programmes 52, 73,
151
offence-focused tools 27
offence-related needs 48
offender convergence settings 201
Offender Group Reconviction Score
(OGRS) 19
offender-centred goals 15
offender-centred strategies 203
offenders
adult 7
attitude of 70, 172
benefits of evaluation 221–2
changes in services to 7
chronic 66
employment needs 144
engagement with 14, 118, 140, 187–90
face-to-face work with 1, 2, 7–9,
13–16, 24, 67, 92, 151–5, 194,
208–12, 229, 232
history of work with 2, 8–10
influences on behaviour 16
labelling 24
listening to 229
matching interventions to 1
mentally disordered 3, 15, 133
minority ethnic 23, 25, 77–97
needs 20, 23, 193
prolific 206–7
racially motivated 82
rights of 19
strengths 20
understandings of 7
women 2, 31–52
young 2, 7, 27, 53–75
Offenders Index 227
offending
age and 57–9
basic skills and 143–62
by young people, *see* young offenders
context 11
individual pathology as cause 11
meaning of 69